# Shakespeare and Canada

## Essays on Production, Translation, and Adaptation

P.I.E.-Peter Lang

Bruxelles · Bern · Berlin · Frankfurt/M · New York · Oxford · Wien

# Dramaturgies

Texts, Cultures and Performances

Ric KNOWLES

# Shakespeare and Canada

## Essays on Production, Translation, and Adaptation

Dramaturgies
No.8

Research for this book was supported by a grant from the Social Sciences and Humanities Research Council of Canada.

© P.I.E.-Peter Lang S.A.,
PRESSES INTERUNIVERSITAIRES EUROPÉENNES
Brussels, 2004
1 avenue Maurice, 1050 Brussels, Belgium
info@peterlang.com; www.peterlang.net

Printed in Germany

ISSN 1376-3199
ISBN 90-5201-989-4
US ISBN 0-8204-6612-3
D/2004/5678/01
*CIP available from the British Library, GB
and the Library of Congress, USA.*

Bibliographic information published by "Die Deutsche Bibliothek"

"Die Deutsche Bibliothek" lists this publication in the "Deutsche Nationalbibliografie";
detailed bibliographic data is available in the Internet at <http://dnb.ddb.de>.

# Contents

# Acknowledgments

There are many debts to record in publishing a book of this kind, some of which are visible in footnotes and works cited, and some of which will necessarily go unrecorded as unconscious or forgotten influences. But among those many debts are some that must be stated explicitly at the outset.

The Introduction to the volume was first delivered as an oral presentation as part of the visiting speakers series at McGill University, in November 2002, and at Mount Allison University in February, 2003, when I was Visiting Professor of Canadian Studies there. I am grateful to Denis Salter and Karen Bamford, respectively, for inviting me to try out my ideas in those genial contexts, and to all those who gave me valuable feedback on those occasions.

Chapter One was first presented at a seminar session at the Shakespeare Association of America at Albuquerque, New Mexico in the Spring of 1994, where it benefited from the always valuable feedback of my colleagues there. It was first published in *Theatre Journal* 47 (1995).

Chapter Two resulted from a *Shakespeare Quarterly* commission to review the 1993 season at the Stratford Festival, and was first published as an "Issues" essay in volume 45.2 in the Summer of 1994.

For Chapter Three I owe more specific debts: to Marco Micone for sending me a copy of his translation, to France Ouellet and Le Théâtre du Nouveau Monde for access to the archival videotapes and press clippings for the production, and to Hélène Beauchamp for her contributions to my thinking through of the problematics of translation, for her hospitality and company, and for her always lively and challenging conversation. The essay was first presented to the World Congress of the International Shakespeare Association in Los Angeles in April 1996, and first published in *Essays in Theatre/Études théâtrales* 16 (1997), when it was improved significantly by the editorial wisdom of Harry Lane.

Chapter Four was the result of an invitation from Denis Salter, Michael Bristol, and Catherine Graham to present at the "Shakespeare and Theatrical Modernism" conference in Montreal in October 1997, where I also received invaluable feedback from Hugh Grady, Martin Van Dijk, and Dennis Kennedy, and benefited from a presentation by

Martine Beaulne. Harry Lane read and provided useful comments at different stages in the development of the essay, and Susan Bennett and the anonymous readers for *Theatre Journal* provided yet more useful feedback while the essay was prepared for its first publication in 1998 in volume 50 of that publication.

An early version of Chapter Five was first presented at the "Shakespeare in Canada" seminar of the Shakespeare Association of America, convened by Diana Brydon and Irena Makaryk in Cleveland in March, 1998. It benefited greatly from that seminar discussion, and in particular by comments by Skip Shand, Brydon, and Makaryk. It was first published in *Theatre Survey* 39 in 1998, with the helpful contributions of editors Gary Jay Williams and W.B. Worthen.

Finally, Chapter Six was written at the request of Diana Brydon and Irena Makaryk for inclusion in their collection, *Shakespeare in Canada: A World Elsewhere?*, published in 2002 by the University of Toronto Press, and it was greatly improved by their keen editorial eyes.

All of my work has benefited directly and indirectly from my colleagues in the Association for Canadian Theatre Research, the Shakespeare Association of America, the Association for Theatre in Higher Education, the International Federation for Theatre Research, and the American Society for Theatre Research. My particular and most important debts here are to Barbara Hodgdon, Harry Lane, Skip Shand, Bill Worthen, and, for the foundation on which it all stands, Sandy Leggatt. The immediate impetus for the volume came from Marc Maufort, to whom I am very grateful for ongoing support of my work, and the most immediate assistance in preparing the manuscript for publication came from my research assistant at the University of Guelph, Dave Hudson.

Most importantly of all, for her wisdom, insight, support, and companionship, I am deeply indebted, here and elsewhere, to Christine Bold, to whom this volume is dedicated.

\*\*\*

Research for this volume was conducted with the support of the Social Sciences and Humanities Research Council of Canada, for which I am very grateful.

Ric Knowles

# Shakespeare and Canada

Much work has been done on the topic of "Shakespeare in Canada" in recent years, including many accounts of productions of the plays across English Canada and in Québec, popular histories of theatre companies such as, pre-eminently, Ontario's Stratford Festival, essays that locate Canadian Shakespeares in a postcolonial context, and analyses and histories of theatre criticism that typically use Shakespeare as a touchstone or point of departure. In fact, as I write, much work has appeared on Shakespeare in Canada in recent months. The Summer 2002 issue of *Canadian Theatre Review* (Fischlin and Knowles) was devoted to *Adapting Shakespeare in Canada*, guest co-edited by Daniel Fischlin, the leader of a research team at the University of Guelph that is compiling an extensive data base on Canadian adaptations of Shakespeare. And in December of 2002 the University of Toronto Press launched a massive, 490-page collection of essays edited by Diana Brydon and Irena R. Makaryk entitled *Shakespeare in Canada: A World Elsewhere?*

The *CTR* volume includes articles on such things as Shakespearean "raves," "Dancing with Shakespeare," and Shakespeare on the net (with the delightful title, "Virtually Canadian"); on a production in Montreal in which an actor with cerebral palsy rehearses the role of Richard III, Shakespeare's "disabled" king; on the ubiquitous Shakespeare festivals across the country, from the Victoria Shakespeare Festival on Vancouver Island to Shakespeare by the Sea in St. John's, Newfoundland; on adapting Shakespeare to a prairie landscape; on an all-woman, Amazonian *Midsummer Night's Dream*; and on "the spectre of a straight Shakespeare." It also includes a document section with a checklist of 161 Canadian dramatic adaptations of Shakespeare, together with a Shakespeare pageant written by Sister Mary Agnes of St. Mary's Academy, Winnipeg, in 1915. The script featured is *Elsinore*, Robert Lepage's internationally acclaimed one-man *Hamlet*.

The University of Toronto Press *Shakespeare in Canada* volume includes, in Irena Makaryk's introduction, a good thumbnail history of Shakespearean performance in Canada, followed by a collection of essays under several categories: "Institutionalizing Shakespeare" (at

Industrial exhibitions, at the Canadian Broadcasting Corporation, at the Stratford Festival, and in social clubs, but, curiously, not in the educational system); "Shakespeare on Stage" (at the Stratford Festival, at Toronto's Necessary Angel Theatre, in Newfoundland, and, in an essay called "'Le Remaking' of Le Grand Will," in Québec); "Critical Debates and Traditions" (on Canada's most distinguished Shakespearean, Northrop Frye, on Shakespeare's characteristically Canadian "negative capability" in *Cymbeline*, on University actors meeting Shakespearean "universality," and – in an essay with the best title in the book, "Canadian Bacon" – on Canada's version of the authorship controversy); and finally "Reimagining Shakespeare" (on adaptations of Shakespeare in different places and periods, in theory and in practice.) The book concludes with an afterword "relocating Shakespeare, redefining Canada," by co-editor Diana Brydon, and an appendix offering "Research opportunities in Canadian Shakespeare," which are legion.

Most of this work assumes that both "Shakespeare" and "Canada" can be at least provisionally understood to be stable entities. I want here, however, to shift from "Shakespeare in Canada" to "Shakespeare *and* Canada." That is, I want to consider the two terms of my title as both shifting and mutually constitutive. For most scholars and theatrical practitioners of the period up to and including the Massey Commission Report in 1951, which laid the groundwork for arts funding in Canada, and the founding of the Stratford Festival in 1953, both "Shakespeare" (as Bard) and "Canada" (as Nation) were understood relatively clearly and simply, an understanding that I, as a white male Ontarion of Anglo-Scottish descent, inherited and took for granted. The first term, "Shakespeare," was a representative of British high culture, an agent of either cultural improvement or imperialist nationalism and class dominance, depending on your point of view. The latter, "Canada," was still very much understood to be the "Dominion of Canada," a former British colony, and a stalwart member of the British Commonwealth.

In my first chapter, below, I cite Denis Salter's argument in his essay, "The Idea of a National Theatre," that Canadians in this period "could only assume," in their own search for a national theatre, "that culture and nationalism were inseparable issues," that they "had the tendency to think of theatre as an instrument for the dissemination of high culture, which often meant Shakespeare." Indeed, he argues that "by a not unreasonable stretch of the imagination, Shakespeare could be regarded as a Canadian playwright" (1991: 78). Not surprisingly, then, Arnold Edinborough could describe the founding in 1953 of a small summer festival in rural Ontario dedicated to Shakespeare as an event "as momentous for Canada as the founding of the Old Vic was for England, or the Abbey Theatre for Dublin," this in spite of it being dedicated to an English playwright, run by an Englishman, and featuring English stars (Edinborough 1954: 50). Herbert Whittaker ten years later, was similarly able to describe that festival's production of *King Lear*, mounted in celebration of Shakespeare's 400th birthday, as a Canadian national coming of age (Whittaker, 1985: 104-107).

At the middle of the $20^{th}$ century, then, Shakespeare helped, perhaps belatedly, to constitute Canada as a Nation state, while Canada in turn constituted Shakespeare as its National Bard, its sign of high cultural maturity and value, and its great Canadian Playwright. Edinborough and Whittaker, of course, shared a number of assumptions about both Shakespeare and Canada that might not have been shared by (say) a young Cree boy from Brochet, Manitoba, an outport Newfoundlander, a francophone Lebanese-Canadian living in Montreal, or a Cantonese-Canadian woman in Vancouver – each of these phrases characterizes a prominent Canadian playwright – to and on behalf of whom *King Lear* at Stratford may have spoken less clearly, or even seemed less Canadian.

I want here to pick up the story from that point, and to ground the essays on "Shakespeare and Canada" that follow in my own, autobiographical position as a 50-something settler/invader subject as critic. This involves limiting the time frame to my own life, the period since the mid-century Massey Commission and the founding of Stratford. It also involves revisiting some familiar turf, including an alternative narrative to that of Edinborough and Whittaker, of the so-called "coming of age" of Canadian drama and theatre, which in this version was seen to have happened in the late 1960s and early 1970s – emerging "from the colonial twilight," as Alan Richardson and Don Rubin wrote in the lead-off article to a 1981 issue of *Canadian Theatre Review,* at the same moment as my own self-consciously "rebellious" generation of playwrights, critics, and audiences came of age. This now-dominant historiographic narrative of national theatrical maturation often articulates a supposed breaking *free* of what it considers to be the pernicious influence of the mother country, her Bard, and his theatrical outpost in Southwestern Ontario, as work from small, nationalist, alternative theatres swam "Up the Mainstream" (to use the title of Denis Johnston's history of Toronto theatre in the period) to spawn a new national dramaturgy. For many students of Canadian theatre history the clearest crystallization of *this* nationalist narrative came with that first issue of *Canadian Theatre Review* in 1974, which launched both the journal and the contemporary scholarly discipline of Canadian Theatre Studies through an attack on the Stratford Festival and its appointment of Robin Phillips, yet another British Artistic Director, to the top position at an organization that still occasionally billed itself as The Stratford National Theatre of Canada: "no other country in the world has a foreigner running its 'national' theatre," wrote the editors (Rubin, Mezei, and Stuart, 1974: 5). The issue included an interview with Phillips that confronted him on the ground of his nationality, followed by a parodic interview with the Canadian director John Juliani on his supposed appointment as artistic director of "the Strazione National Theatre of Italy" (Juliani, 1974: 65). Both interviews made reference to Juliani's notoriously petulant hurling down of a rubber glove as he challenged Phillips, who thought he had been hired to run a *Shakespeare* festival rather than a National Theatre, to a duel. "Why the rubber glove?" asked Phillips. "I wonder what disease he thinks he's going to catch?" (Phillips, 1974: 64).

But perhaps more important is the other bit of familiar ground I'm revisiting, the patch on which the white, male, settler/invader critic stands *as* postcolonial subject, a stance which now, with the obviousness of current common sense, seems much more privileged than it did to some of us in the middle of a 1970s Canadian nationalist movement (ironically sparked and spearheaded by American draft resisters such as Rubin), for whom the British were "our" (cultural), and the Americans "our" (economic), colonizers and oppressors. At the same time, however, for many 1970s Canadian nationalists, "liberated" women were often the entirely exploitable theatrical emblems of "our own" longed for liberation; minoritized cultures *within* Canada were largely invisible, and never the central subjects of the shows or the criticism; and First Nations peoples, except in a few historical plays by white writers about noble savages, and a few social action plays about downtrodden "Indians" (indistinguishable from downtrodden Ukrainians and others), were not a consideration at all. *This* nationalist narrative, then, was fundamentally a construction of *counter*hegemonies (as opposed to antihegemonic critiques) that were, like all hegemonies, productive of their own exclusions. As Amanda Hale asked in the wake of the "alternative theatre movement" of the 1970s, "after the revolution, where are the women" (1987: 81)? And as many theatre artists not of British or French descent also asked, where is the "difference" in a multiculturalism that directs their grant applications, not to the arts councils, like those of their colleagues of British or French descent, but to multiculturalism Canada – their cultural identities reduced to static "ethnicities" in contradistinction to the nation's two founding, growing, and institutionalized "cultures.

Canadian theatre has itself become more "diverse" since the mid-1970s, and the discourses of Canadian theatre criticism have to some small extent (though not yet in the newspapers) displaced the dominant positioning of the culturally authoritative settler/invader critic (or more recent British immigrant). I have no wish to return the white male settler-invader to the centre of the discourse – indeed, I'd like to see the critical fraternity (*sic*) and the academy more fully address its failures to hire outside of the traditional cultural profile (especially in Theatre Studies, and most especially in Shakespeare). I do wonder, however, if it is worth reconsidering the position of the settler-invader subject as critic, and together with it some of the binaries that are attendant upon a postcolonialism that has often excluded Canada and other settler/invader colonies, apart from their indigenous peoples, from consideration within postcolonial critique. My project is simply to (re)discover a productive place to stand for the Euro-Canadian critic, among other, equally important subject positions.

Although it is true that Canadians of British or French descent, having participated in and/or benefited from the colonial project, can no longer unproblematically position themselves in a simple relationship of oppressed colonials to imperial centres, Canada is nevertheless a peculiar hothouse of complex colonial relations: displaced settlers to colonizing England or France; displaced First Nations peoples to colonizing Europeans and other immigrants; defeated French to colonizing English; and various complex historical and contemporary layers of Irish, Scottish, Italian, Ukrainian and other Western and Eastern European, Asian, African, Caribbean, South American, and other immigrants to both the "founding cultures" and variously to one another in colonizing relationships having to do with period of immigration, visibility, skin colour, and accent – all of which shift in curious ways their relationships to both Canada and Shakespeare.

Similarly, the internally dominant settler-invader subject position may also usefully be understood as more complex than the binary of neo-imperialist inheritor of the benefits of plunder, invasion, and genocide, on the one hand, and guilt-ridden liberal apologist on the other. In short, there may be a place for a more nuanced scholarship, some of which might emerge from a reconceived, ideally collaborative, middle position.

One of the strands of postcolonial scholarship that has been most productive and influential in the last decade has derived from Homi Bhabha, the genealogy of whose work includes foundational writings on the psychology of colonialism by Frantz Fanon and Octave Mannoni – the latter, in a 1956 book named, in the English translation, after characters from Shakespeare's *The Tempest, Prospero and Caliban: The Psychology of Colonization* (the original French title was *La Psychologie de la colonisation, tout court*). That book concerned, among other things, colonization and co-dependency. Mannoni's position was that Prospero's (the colonialist's) urge to dominate stems from his minority position, which results in a sense of inferiority and a compensatory desire to exert authority, while Caliban's (the colonized's) willingness to be dominated stems from a need for security and discipline. Fanon, on the other hand, in a position echoed in Aimé Césaire's seminal postcolonial adaptation of *The Tempest*, argued that Mannoni had not felt himself into the "subjective experience" of either colonizer or colonized, which resulted in his failure to understand the European colonizer's feeling, not of inferiority, but of superiority.

In a series of articles, interviews, and books in the early 1990s that can be understood to have grown out of Fanon and Mannoni's debate, Bhabha grounds his own oppositional politics in a diverse and fragmented range of subversive formations that begin with the assertion that the colonizer and colonized are not discrete categories. For Bhabha it is the unruly circulation of colonial constructions of self and other which work to subvert colonial authority. Bhabha's concept of hybridity, for example, operates as a subversive strategy because it entails the colonized contesting colonial authority through seizing the given symbols of that authority, symbols which have, in Canada as elsewhere, included Shakespeare. Bhabha's charting of a psychologically grounded postcolonialism depends upon an understanding of the destabilizing anxieties that mimetic and hybrid formations produce for the colonizer. But Bhabha's work nevertheless remains grounded in the "Prospero and Caliban" binary that he inherited from Mannoni, and focuses on the *destabilization* of the position of an entrenched, colonialist Prospero as produced by the subversive mimicry of a clearly colonized Caliban, who has learned Prospero's language, and knows how to curse. Bhabha's complex psychoanalysis of colonialism largely omits consideration of a different kind of third position, one which might be considered to embody, externalize, or symbolize the complicating psychological positionings of which he writes. This third space is that of the settler/invader, the inheritor, and perhaps reluctant agent of colonization, who is both implicated in and subjected to the inequities and injustices of the imperial project. And this third position might be considered, at least provisionally, to be that of neither Prospero nor Caliban, but of Miranda, who has been the notable subject of a number of ground-breaking essays by the Canadian postcolonialist and feminist (and co-editor of the University of Toronto Press *Shakespeare in Canada* volume), Diana Brydon.

I have threatened an autobiographical narrative as the grounding of my own position as critic, and I want to continue that account with *The Tempest*, which is generally known among postcolonialists as Shakespeare's "new world play." Its sources derive in large part from various contemporary accounts of travel to the new world, and its action and structure are generally understood to mimic and bolster the colonial project. But Miranda's "Oh brave new world, that has such people in it" – among the plays' best known lines – is her comment, speaking as an (almost) second-generation settler/invader, not about the new world, but the old one – or, more accurately, speaking about debased representatives of old world culture on a temporary sojourn in the colonies. As someone who went on a school excursion when I was about Miranda's impressionable age to see the descendants of Alonso, Antonio, Sebastian, *et al* – sojourning and expatriate Europeans performing at the Stratford Festival – and as someone who, like her, was awestruck by (like her) the splendor of the costumes, the splendor of the language, and the authenticity of the accents – I have some sympathy for Miranda. It was new to me, too.

But not really. Like Miranda's, my past had been filled with stories of the world inhabited by these strange, brave, and beauteous creatures, and as for Miranda, my first encounter with them in the flesh was a moment of both recognition and wonder. In the context of contesting narratives of Canadian theatre history in a perennial process of maturation, with Canadian "identity" at stake and always found lacking, and in the context of an education that taught me that the role of playing was and is to hold the mirror up to nature, it may not be too much to suggest that for me, as for Miranda, those moments of wonder functioned as the late playing out of a Lacanian mirror stage. The mirror stage is perhaps best known through feminist critiques as a Bad Thing (or necessary evil), one that involves: recognition of the self as other (what, they ask, does it mean to say oxymoronically, "that's me"?); the beginning of self-alienation and the messiness of the "lack" that is desire; the disruption of the imaginary unity and coherence of the pre-symbolic, essentially female, semiotic chora; entry into the symbolic order and the repressive Law of the Father; and so on. And it is true that, for Lacan, the image in the mirror is always that of ego *Ideal*, a perfection that the child cannot hope to achieve or experience. For the postcolonial subject or, indeed, the postcolonial nation, this might be read as recognition through the image of Antonio and Sebastian, Shakespeare, or England, of the self as an always inadequate (and underdressed) approximation of the imperial ideal (and the proper accent). It might also be read as a rupturing of the unity of a romanticized semiotic chora that Canadian cultural criticism for many years identified as Nature, the (also feminized) landscape, or the North – a rupture accompanied by entry into a symbolic order that was civilized, urban, modernist, and elsewhere.

Another way of articulating this move from the natural, chaotic, and feminized chora of the land to the masculine symbolic order of cities and arts centres is to see it as a move from myth to history. It is not accidental that the great structuralist perpetrator of myth-criticism, Northrop Frye, was Canadian, in that, for Canadians, as Janice Kulyk Keefer has remarked, history happens elsewhere (Keefer 1986: 289).

Myth and literature, on the other hand, are inclusive, autonomous, anagogic, and non-alienating. As archetypes based on the seasons, the natural world, and the Bible, they are available to us as Canadians in a way that history is not. Entry into the symbolic order, in terms that Frye as both structuralist and biblical scholar might have used, could be understood as an archetypal neo-Aristotelean "reversal" (as he calls comparable structural principles in religion, politics, and literature in *The Myth of Deliverance* 13) – a kind of biblical Fall. The ongoing Oedipal crisis that the mirror stage initiates in the psychoanalytic narrative might equally for Frye have been understood as a series of periodic sojourns in a "green world" of the imagination that precede reassertions of "Oedipus" (to use Deleuze and Guattari's omnibus word) – a return, anagogically refreshed, to civilization and history.

But it is important in characterizing the mirror stage as a necessary evil to notice that Lacan does describe the child, at that point incapable of fully controlling his own limbs (like the colonial dummy on the lap of "your imperial ventriloquist" in Canadian Rick Salutin's play, *1837* [Salutin and Theatre Passe Muraille 231]), recognizing himself in the mirror with delight and wonder – delight and wonder not unlike Miranda's wonder at *her* brave new world – or mine at mine, on my high-school trip to the Stratford Festival: the child, according to Lacan, waves his (*sic*) limbs "in a flutter of jubilant activity" at the mirror-stage recognition of his own image in the other (Lacan 1).

For me, some years after my high-school mirror-stage epiphany at Stratford, ensconced in graduate school at Northrop Frye's University of Toronto, it was, or it felt, "natural" to turn for my dissertation topic to Shakespeare, and in particular to the green worlds of Shakespeare's last plays, culminating, of course, in *The Tempest*. Like Frye, I treated the play as a romance, and like him in his introduction to the Pelican edition of the play, I found it "a little puzzling why New World imagery should be so prominent in *The Tempest*, which really has nothing to do with the New World, beyond Ariel's reference to the 'still-vexed Bermoothes'" (22-3). Eschewing history (like Frye, I never returned to the question – I didn't think it mattered), I wrote about "imaginative engagement" – the process by which the plays' audiences, distanced from empathetic engagement with character and action, engage their wills imaginatively with the creative process itself, as the plays figure forth an image of what "we" – as universal human subjects – most desire. Years later I found the same process at work in the plays of Frye's disciple, James Reaney, of Stratford, Ontario, whose work, I would later argue, figures forth creative genesis, even though he is perhaps "archetypally" the playwright and poet of local history, for whom the earlier, unknown Native name of the Avon River haunts its present and threatens to disrupt – or reassert – its (anoedipal?) flow.

("You do not flow/With English accents," Reaney wrote, "you do not sound/Like Avon/Or swans and bards" 79.) (Reaney was also, incidentally, as adamant an opponent of the perhaps "archetypally" English Robin Phillips at Stratford as any rubber-gloving John Juliani.) But Reaney seems to have done more or less explicitly and within a single body of work what Len Findlay argues Frye sometimes did inadvertently: he helped us "understand Canada as a set of proto-canonical dramatic productions – predominantly comic and romantic" (292). *Now*, like Findlay, I would "rather liken Canada to a history play" (292). But as Findlay also says, "postcolonial discourse, by virtue of its emphasis on history, politics, 'race,' and the cultural armatures of hegemony, might well have enabled Frye to sound [...] less like an oversanguine Prospero" (304) when he somewhat shockingly argued in 1977, referring to such "back-to-nature" work as Marion Engel's *Bear* and Margaret Atwood's *Surfacing,* that "for Canadian culture the old imperialist phrase 'going native' has come home to roost. We are no longer an army of occupation," he wrote, "and the natives are ourselves" (Frye, *Divisions* 69). "Really?" I hear First Nations playwrights Monique Mojica, Tomson Highway, Daniel David Moses and others saying. And who *is* "ourselves"? (The question for them, perhaps, is not so much Frye's famous concluding questions to the *Literary History of Canada,* "where is here" (Frye, "Conclusion") – they *know* that – but *"who* is here, and how did they get here"?)

It was while working on my PhD that I made my first pilgrimage to England, ostensibly to do research, though the research itself was not really necessary. I was, I now think, in search of authenticity, authority, cultural identity – a position from which, critically, to speak. How could I dare to write about Shakespeare without having visited *the* Stratford-on-Avon, seen the work of the Royal Shakespeare Company, or been to the birthplace of Shakespeare and my own displaced culture? Then, as frequently since, I felt like a fraud – at best a colonial mimic of academic authority that was, I knew in my bones and from the architecture, curriculum, and professoriate of the University of Toronto, fundamentally British. I had not then recognized that by "British" I meant "universal," though my dawning awareness of this was prompted by this trip. In any event, in another flutter of jubilant activity I traveled on my purchased-in-Canada Brit-Rail pass through train stations named after characters in Shakespeare's history plays; and I visited the *real, authentic* towns, cities and rivers after which the colonial imitations and theme parks of Southwestern Ontario were named. I visited Shakespeare's birthplace and his grave (memorizing the verse there, and hoping that my own scholarly dust-digging was not disturbing his bones and invoking his curses: he taught me language, after all, and my profit on't was at that point unclear.) And of course I visited his wife's cottage and all the other "Shakespeare properties" with *real* Tudor architecture, unlike the familiar "Tudor style" of homes and pubs in southern Ontario, with their inauthentic central heating. And I went to Royal Shakespeare Company productions (and bought all the posters, photographs, and souvenir programs) with, then, only a flicker of awareness that at the heart of the company were actors such as the Anglo-Indian Ben Kingsley (born Krishna Bhanji, in Yorkshire) whose actorly authority was based on something other than authentic Englishness. (In fact I saw Kingsley's *Hamlet* at the Other Place, directed by Buzz Goodbody, who had committed suicide for political reasons just before the opening. But I had little awareness of the degree to which the production represented the otherness at the heart of the RSC until much later, when I read Colin Chambers' book, *Other Spaces*. For me, then, it was a peculiarly authentic *Hamlet*, made all the more so by the "real" suicide of its director: "To be or not to be" indeed.) The seed of some destabilizing doubt was planted in me then, but it hadn't risen to consciousness.

Equally central to my visit to England was a trip to London and what I thought of at the time as the very birthplace of my cultural identity: the Tower of London. I did the tour, and it being November I found myself alone in the tiny, haunting Chapel of St. John the Evangelist at the centre of the White Tower, where I had a self-induced mystical experience (and perhaps a replaying of my jubilant but ultimately self-alienating mirror-stage experience). In any case, I was then only slightly haunted by the fact that at this heart of essential Englishness I had discovered what for an anglo-Ontarion was the archetypal other: for of course the White Tower – or at least its central keep – had been constructed (albeit in 1066) by the French. The ironies became somewhat clearer years later while I was visiting Normandy and Brittany – including Juno Beach (the landing site for Canadian troops during the *other* Normandy invasion) and other visible traces of the Canadian presence in the dying days of the Second World War – together with the sites in St. Malo and Mont St. Michel from which Jacques Cartier had departed to "discover" Canada (much to the surprise and annoyance of its inhabitants).

I returned to Canada and continued to work on my dissertation, but also to begin for the first time – perhaps because of some haunting, newly discovered feeling that the English, too, were just English – to read Canadian Literature, which I had not been encouraged by a predominantly expatriate English professoriate to take seriously as a student. (In fact, one of my professors pronounced occasionally that nothing good had been written in English since Milton). I also began, on my return from England, to participate in the theatre, starting with a production of *Macbeth* at the University of Toronto's Hart House

Theatre, and learned that theatre, at least, was less about universal truths than about the specificities of place, time, and audience. And I began over the next several years, mostly lived in New Brunswick (where I learned, among other things, that I had a Toronto accent), to develop something of what I am now arguing is the productively unstable if somewhat schizophrenic critical stance of the postcolonial settler/invader subject working out of two sides of his mouth. At that time I became involved with a small professional theatre company dedicated to the drama of northeastern Nova Scotia; I taught Canadian literature and drama; I created and directed new Canadian work; and I published articles in the field – many of them stridently nationalist or regionalist. Meanwhile, on the other side of my mouth, I directed Shakespeare and Heywood, and worked as an Assistant Director and dramaturg with none other than Robin Phillips at the Stratford Festival, while continuing to publish scholarly articles on the Bard.

Mark Fortier has recently argued that:

> there is always something un-Canadian about being Canadian, that the from-elsewhere is part of the being here. Shakespeare, therefore, is one manifestation of the from elsewhere at work in Canada. As such, Canadians confront Shakespeare as the cultural undead, neither dead nor living, not a person but an other forming part of living personalities... the otherness of the past the remains of which reside here. (342)

This is a position with which I have considerable sympathy, particularly in its insistence, in the wake of dominant discourses of *plus-ça-change* universalism, on the difference, the otherness of the past, and on Shakespeare as one of the ghosts that haunt the collectivity. I do find it politically troubling to group the voice of Shakespeare with those of other "others," many of them individuals and groups considerably less privileged and more materially at risk than "Shakespeare," his dominant-culture constituency, and what he most often represents. But this articulation of Shakespeare as what my Kuna-Rappohonock collaborator Monique Mojica might call "one of the ancestors," remains salutory.

Canada was of course *founded* on what Fortier calls "the from elsewhere" and I call displacement: displacement of First Nations peoples by Europeans, of course, but also displacement of the peasant Irish by the landlords, the English and the potato famine; displacement of the Scottish by their own lairds, the English and the highland clearances; displacement of the Acadians by the English and then again by their epic return from the south; most famously displacement of the British Loyalists by the American revolution; and more recently displacement of a vast range of economic and political refugees and emigrants by intolerable regimes or conditions in their homelands.

Shakespeare *is* perhaps, as Fortier says, one of those many "from elsewheres" that inhabit and constitute Canada. And importantly "Shakespeare" is different things and has served very different functions for the different displaced communities that constitute contemporary Canada. For anglo-Canadian nationalists struggling against the alignment of Shakespeare with the cultural imperialism of the old world, for example, it is easy to overlook the resistant, oppositional, and liberating role that his work has been made to play (often with the aid of translation, as Dennis Kennedy has pointed out) in places such as cold-war eastern Europe in their people's struggles against oppressive regimes. (Tom Stoppard's short play, *Cahoot's Macbeth*, is the best-known dramatic representation of this.) Even within Canada, productions and adaptations of Shakespeare for some communities have served rather than suppressed political resistance – one thinks of American draft resister Stephen Bush's *Richard Thirdtime*, which used *Richard III* in Toronto in 1973 to attack a later "Tricky Dick," Richard Nixon, in the wake of Watergate; or of Robert Gurik's *Hamlet, Prince du Québec* in 1968, in which Hamlet is Québec itself, Claudius *anglophonie* and the federal government; Polonius Lester Pearson; Laertes Pierre Elliot Trudeau; Horatio René Lévesque; and the ghost of Hamlet's father none other than Charles de Gaulle (speaking of ghosts that haunt the collectivity). There was less concern here about reinscribing a universalist Shakespeare as source and authority – or even as a voice of *anglophonie* – than about using Shakespeare for precise (and *anti*-"anglo") political ends. As Leanore Lieblein argues, "Hamlet [in this play] became the voice of a Québec whose legitimate aspiration was national sovereignty" (181).

"Shakespeare," then, haunts different collectivities within Canada differently, and has frequently been used, not only in the service of shoring up but also of destabilizing unitary concepts of Canadian nationhood, even as "Canada" has been used both to reinforce and destabilize unitary concepts of Shakespeare as universal (English) bard. More recently than either of the examples I've cited, both of which come from the height of the (differently) nationalist periods in Canada and Québec, and both of which tend toward binary oppositions, a range of different communities within Canada have entered into negotiations with Shakespeare through, for example, a feminist adaptation of *Hamlet* (Margaret Clarke's *Gertrude and Ophelia*), a lesbian/feminist revisioning of *Romeo and Juliet* and *Othello* (Ann-Marie MacDonald's *Goodnight Desdemona (Good Morning Juliet)*), a First Nations variation on *Hamlet/Macbeth* (Daniel David Moses's *Brébeuf's Ghost*), an African-Canadian prequel to *Othello* (Djanet Sears's *Harlem Duet*), and many others, few of which unequivocally repudiate "the Bard" (though as I indicate in Chapter Five, Michael

O'Brien self-reportedly set out in *Mad Boy Chronicle*, his Viking version of *Hamlet*, "to debase the greatest play of all time" 8) – and many of which (including O'Brien's) coat-tail on his cultural authority.

The now-famous Lewis Baumander production of *The Tempest* at Toronto's Earl Bales park in 1987 and '89), which cast First Nations actors Billy Merasty and Monique Mojica to play a Haïda Caliban and Ariel respectively, may be seen to have participated in such coat-tailing, presenting itself both as an "authentic" production of Shakespeare and a revisiting of the play from an "authentic" (embodied) postcolonial perspective – though Baumander himself is non-Native. Set on the Queen Charlotte Islands on the West Coast of British Columbia, the production was both celebrated as postcolonial critique and criticized for its faithfulness to the colonialist structure of the Shakespearean "original:" it seems, according to Paul Leonard and Helen Peters, that the show reproduced and reified colonial relations in its naturalization of the Prospero/Caliban binary of colonizer and colonized, but managed in Monique Mojica's representation of Ariel as a Trickster figure (supported by the choreography of the late René Highway) to destabilize the play itself and the otherwise assumed moral superiority of the Europeans, onstage and off. The production neither repudiated "Shakespeare" – indeed it relied on "him" for its authority – nor simply reproduced the source play's ideological position: it entered into, and played out, a kind of active negotiation of cultural values *through* Shakespeare, but also through other others, "Native" stories, myths, "ghosts," ancestors, and values, including, most notably, the anarchic, amoral, and unpredictable authority of the trickster/Ariel.

A considerable part of the naissance of Native theatre in Canada since the mid-1980s, in fact, has had ghosted a Shakespearean other at its core, even when this has not been immediately apparent. Tomson Highway's successes in the mid-1980s with *The Rez Sisters* and *Dry Lips Oughta Move to Kapuskasing* – at the main stage of the Edinburgh International Festival and at Toronto's venerable Royal Alexandra Theatre – catapulted Native theatre into the mainstream in part by employing what might be thought of as negotiated dramaturgical forms, Shakespearean and other, some of which he learned while working as a student on productions by the aforementioned disciple of Northrop Frye, James Reaney.

As many have argued, demands for an always and inevitably compromised cultural and racial authenticity and purity most often function in service of the colonial project (as do demands for "authentic" – which usually means Victorian – stagings of Shakespeare). And "Shakespeare" is now arguably as a much part of First Nations, African-Canadian, Québécois, and other non-anglo cultures within

Canada as he is foundational for the dominant anglophone culture. This receives perhaps its clearest articulation in Sears's *Harlem Duet*, as I argue in Chapter Six, below. The play deals with, among other things, the breakdown of the marriage of Othello and Billie, Othello's Black first wife, as he leaves her for "Mona," his white colleague, the brief appearance of whose fetishized white arm is, apart from minstrel whiteface, the only physical representation of whiteness in the play. In a speech that the play does not fully endorse but does allow to stand, Othello argues that:

> My culture is not my mother's culture – the culture of my ancestors. My culture is Wordsworth, Shaw, *Leave it to Beaver*, *Dirty Harry*. I drink the same water, read the same books. You're the problem if you don't see beyond my skin. If you don't hear my educated English, if you don't understand that I am a middle class educated man. I mean, what does Africa have to do with me? (73)

The play itself, by its very source and subject, argues in part that 'my culture is Shakespeare.' As the playwright writes in her Preface to the published script, "As a veteran theatre practitioner of African Descent, Shakespeare's *Othello* has always haunted me since I was first introduced to him. Sir Laurence Olivier in blackface. Othello is the first African portrayed in the annals of western dramatic literature. In an effort to exorcise this ghost I have written *Harlem Duet*" (14). In one scene Billie and Othello, dividing their books and records, peruse such volumes in their collection as *African Mythology, The Great Chain of Being*, and *Black Psychology* – "the scientific foundation for why we're not human" (51). In this context Billie delivers what might be read as a Black woman's response to Prospero's racist appropriation of Caliban, "this thing of darkness I acknowledge mine:" "the *Shakespeare's* mine," Billie says, talking back to the Bard, "but you can have it" (52, my emphasis).

It *might* be read as that, but who might do that reading, and from what position? How does the anglophone settler/invader as critic respond to this work? Years ago, as a PhD student, I had found myself searching for ground on which to stand in relation to a universal English bard whose histories and authenticities happened to me elsewhere and in whom, as in my postcolonial Lacanian mirror, I recognized myself as "other." My first response was to become essentially "Canadian" in a way that I had never been. But then I found myself, Willy-nilly, as it were, aligned with Shakespeare and with colonial authority, addressing, from a position made comfortable by the inherited benefits of the colonial project, the work of *other* "others" within Canada whose cultural, material, epistemological, and historical positionings were not mine, but who seemed to be able to say, as I had not, "the

Shakespeare's mine." What Shakespeare was *mine*, and was *I* willing to surrender it?

Not surprisingly, Gayatri Spivak has something to contribute here, and it has to do with three things: first, with doing one's full, contextualized homework, *in situ*, about what used to be called one's "object of study;" second, with "doing a *historical* critique of your position as the investigating person" (Spivak & Gunew 197): "why not develop a certain degree of rage," she asks, "against the history that has written such an abject script for you that you are silenced?" (197). Third, it has to do with taking "a certain risk." I would suggest that part of that risk has to do with: first, surrendering claims to authority that position the critic as knower, and the historical or cultural "other" as to-be-known – as "*objects* of study;" second, with surrendering concepts of authenticity (with respect to Shakespeare *or* to contemporary cultural communities) that can often accompany spurious claims to historicity; and third, with surrendering modernist notions of what Richard Halpern has called "historical allegory" (1), which efface historical and other difference by consuming the other as part of a universal "us." This is the kind of effacement that takes place in some "modern dress" productions of Shakespeare (or indeed some "modern dress" critical assessments) that seem through selectivity to demonstrate that nothing has changed since 1600, or in some critical appropriations of work emerging from othered cultures, readings that seem to demonstrate a "common humanity" through effacement of significant difference.

I think the unstable third position of the settler/invader subject as critic might ultimately be conceived as a position of collaboration, translation, and negotiation across historical and other difference that is intent, not on the kinds of mediation that smooth over differences, but on keeping difference *alive* (and kicking). But as I become increasingly distrustful of theoretical positionings that allow for material practice to go unchanged while gender, race, and other social positionings are treated as (merely) discursive, or (merely) performed, I increasingly want to take this third position literally, not simply (and comfortably) to construct the critic's relationship with the work *discursively* as one of actual rather than merely metaphorical negotiation, translation, and collaboration. So what am I doing about it now (to return to the autobiography)? Just beginning, I hope, but among other things, as I move beyond the work that is included in the essays that follow, I am learning a great deal by engaging in collaborative work with First Nations playwright Monique Mojica on an anthology of First Nations Drama; with African-Canadian playwright Djanet Sears on the AfriCanadian Playwrights conference and festival and an issue of *Canadian Theatre Review* which will emerge from them; and with a group of women from various backgrounds and positions on a project dealing with

Cultural Memory and the memorializing of violence against women in Canada. This volume represents an attempt to engage in what Gayatri Spivak might call an historical analysis and critique of my own position and the script that history has written for me as a postcolonial settler/invader critic writing in "english,"[1] while focusing on some aspects of ongoing relationship between "Shakespeare" and national identity in "Canada." *Shakespeare and Canada*, then, is an attempt to consider provisionally the role that "producing Shakespeare," broadly understood, plays and has played in producing the contemporary understanding, for individuals and for the collectivity, of Canadian nationhood, subjects, and subjectivities.

---

[1]   See Ashcroft, Griffiths, and Tiffin, 8, on the distinction between "English," as the "standard code" and tool of British imperialist discourse, and "english," "which has been transformed and subverted into several distinctive varieties throughout the world."

# PART I

## SHAKESPEARE AND STRATFORD

# CHAPTER 1

# From Nationalist to Multinational:
# The Stratford Festival, Free Trade, and
# the Discourses of Intercultural Tourism

The "Stratford Story," as it is called,[1] particularly the story of the Festival's founding, has been told and retold in Canada, most often under the auspices of the Festival's official discourse, where it not surprisingly functions, like a kind of institutional autobiography, as justification. According to this narrative, the Festival's first opening night on July 13, 1953 which Herbert Whittaker, the proverbial dean of Canadian theatre critics, called "the most exciting night in the history of the Canadian theatre" (1953/1986: 36) - was a culmination in a long teleological process in the nation and its theatre,[2] an event "as momentous for Canada as the founding of the Old Vic was for England, or the Abbey Theatre for Dublin" (Edinborough, 1954: 50). Full maturity was reached eleven years later in the midst of a controversy over a proposed new *Canadian* flag to replace the (British) Union Jack, when the

---

[1]  "Stratford Story" is the title of a brochure published by the Festival and revised periodically. It is available in the lobbies of the Festival's theatres, and included in reviewers' press packages. J. Alan B. Somerset's *Catalogue-Index to the Festival* is also called *The Stratford Festival Story*. Other versions of "The Story" are told in the National Film Board's documentary, *The Stratford Adventure*; Festival founder Tom Patterson and Allan Gould's *First Stage: The Making of the Stratford Festival*; John Pettigrew and Jamie Portman, *Stratford: The First Thirty Years*; Tyrone Guthrie, Robertson Davies, and Grant MacDonald, *Renown at Stratford*; Guthrie, Davies, and MacDonald, *Twice Have the Trumpets Sounded*; Guthrie, Davies, Tanya Moiseiwitsch, and Boyd Neil, *Thrice the Brinded Cat Hath Mew'd*; Euan Ross Stuart, "The Stratford Festival and the Canadian Theatre;" and Barbara Reid and Thelma Morrison, *A Star Danced: The Story of How Stratford Started the Stratford Festival*.

[2]  Indeed Grace Lydiatt Shaw's book, *Stratford Under Cover: Memories on Tape*, reconstructs in its introduction and organization the entire history of Canadian theatre as a training ground and preparation for the "arrival" that was Stratford. Nathan Cohen commented of opening night, "I don't remember how many times I heard it said 'This is going to put Canada on the theatre map,' or 'we've come of age. We have finally come of age'" (*Toronto Star*, 4 June 1966; quoted in Pettigrew and Portman, 1985, vol. 1: 8).

Stratford Company, led by Canadian actor John Colicos (though directed and designed by the British Michael Langham and Leslie Hurry respectively) celebrated the four-hundredth anniversary of Shakespeare's birth by mounting what Whittaker thought to be a "great" production of *King Lear*: "With this production [...] the nation can rest content. We can hold our head high among the nations of the world in the celebration of Shakespeare's four-hundredth anniversary... Instead of advocating as a design for Canada's flag a maple leaf between two stools, I am now advocating a royal *King Lear* rampant, on a field of Stratford" (1985: 107).[3] Not surprisingly, given this reception, the Festival was eventually (if temporarily) to assume the mantle of Canada's national theatre, and it has served throughout its history as a site for recurring disputes about Canadian nationhood, theatrical and otherwise.[4]

In this chapter I want to use Stratford and "its Shakespeare" as the site for an exploration of contesting versions of Canadian nationalism in the four decades since the Festival was founded, focusing on a few representative "moments" in its history: the founding itself, which I see as the solidification of a delayed colonial celebration of a 19th-century brand of Canadian nationalism configured on an imperialist British model (one that allows Canada's national theatre to be dedicated to the plays of *the* canonical British writer); the "moment" that began with the 1967 celebrations of Canada's centennial and included controversies in 1974 and 1980 over the hiring and replacement as Artistic Director of the British Robin Phillips, in the context of an emergent "localist" (and arguably American-style)[5] nationalism in Canadian life

---

[3]    Whittaker, 1985: 107. Whittaker opens his review noting that "I saw this greatness through a haze of tears that have not dried completely as I write of its success" (104).

[4]    'There is a long history of debates about a national theatre for Canada. See Alan Filewod, "National Theatre/National Obsession," and Denis Salter, "The Idea of a National Theatre."

[5]    In the terms outlined by Loren Kruger in *The National Stage: Theatre and Cultural Legitimation in England, France, and America* (1992: 5) and *passim*, Stratford may be seen to follow the British (and to a lesser extent French) model in which "notions of national culture... sought to mobilize but also to discipline the masses by subjecting them to the dual authority of the centralized state and metropolitan high culture," while the emerging nationalism of the so-called "alternate" theatres in the 1970s followed the American model of "regional politics and local culture" producing *"federated* theatres whose national standing might no longer exclusively depend on the mass presence of the national audience in one place, but which might include a national federation of local audiences." The Canadian debate, however, is somewhat more complex than this polarization suggests, in that the official, "branch-plant" Regional Theatre network was conceived as a national federation of theatres

and theatre; and the current "multinationalist" moment, which extends from the early 1980s to the present, in the context of free trade, "globalization," and intercultural tourism, on the one hand, and an emerging counter-hegemonic political/positional theatre movement and "national interculturalism"[6] on the other.

# I

It is not surprising that Herbert Whittaker should have considered the founding of Stratford in post-war Canada to be a national coming of age, or that a "great" production of *King Lear* – constructed as the greatest play of England's greatest playwright – should have furnished him with an emblem of national maturity. There are two contexts for this. The first, of course, is Shakespeare. In his historical analysis of "The Idea of a National Theatre" in Canada, Denis Salter quotes the British parliamentary call for a national theatre that will be "a British House of which the United Kingdom may be proud, ... a House that will speak to Canada, South Africa, and the Antipodes" (1991: 78)[7] and he notes that Canadians listened to the call. According to Salter, Canadians "could only assume that culture and nationalism were inseparable issues," and "had a tendency to think of theatre as an instrument for the dissemination of high culture, which often meant a repertoire of Shakespeare:"

> As an arbiter of taste, Shakespeare could not be faulted. He was part of a long and enviable acting tradition, he expressed so-called universal, trans-historical values, and he could be readily accommodated to both high and low forms of theatrical culture. Moreover, as an unimpeachable symbol of Old World cultural superiority, he belonged to the Elizabethan age, the period of imperial power to which Granville Barker had so generously likened Canada. Shakespeare, then, by a not unreasonable stretch of the imagination, could be regarded as a Canadian playwright. (1991: 79-80)

Guthrie himself justified the dedication of the repertoire of Stratford to Shakespeare on different, but parallel grounds:

---

disseminating metropolitan culture (constructed as British) from the (dominant) centre to the (culturally impoverished) regions. See Filewod, 1990, esp. 8-9.

6    See Mayte Gomez, "Shifting Borders: A Project of Interculturalism in Canadian Theatre." Gomez distinguishes between the "internationalist" intercultural projects of practitioners such as Peter Brook and Eugenio Barba, which she sees as potentially repressive, and the border shifting intercultural model that she proposes for Canada in the post multicultural era.

7    Salter is quoting *Parliamentary Debates (Hansard)*, vol. 52 (23 April-8 May 1913), 470, also quoted in Kruger, 1992: 127.

In all interpretative arts the classics provide the basis of technical education; they are the only possible artistic measuring rods. For English-
speaking actors, Shakespeare's plays are infinitely the most important of
the classics. No serious actor can consider himself [*sic*] equipped until he
has learnt to grapple with some of the great Shakespearean roles. No actor
need expect to be taken seriously by his colleagues unless he has won their
respect in such roles... Paradoxically, I think it is only out of this that there
will evolve a distinctive style of Canadian theatre... Any distinctive national style, whether of acting, producing, writing or criticizing plays, will
be founded on the [academic and theatrical] study of the classics. (Davies,
Guthrie and MacDonald, 1971: 28)

It occasionally surfaces, of course, that the "distinctive style" that
the Festival fosters is, in Bakhtinian terms, monologic and repressive,
imposing, for example, a clearly class-based "example of Canadian
speech," as Robertson Davies puts it (Davies, Guthrie, and Mac-
Donald, 1971: ii), very much in line with the "purity of the English
language" proffered by Oliver Lyttleton and other advocates of the
British National Theatre (Kruger, 1992: 128).

The second context within which Whittaker's representative enthu-
siasms for Canada's coming-of-age-through-Stratford is the myth that
"Canadian nationhood was won on the battlefield," even if the battlefield was Europe and the myth refers to the First World War (Filewod,
1990: 6).[8] Whittaker's own critical sensibilities, formed during the
Second World War, were those of a kind of Canadian nationalist
cultural dispatcher, "reporting from the front" on the battle for Canadian (post-colonial) nationhood;[9] and Tom Patterson himself, the
founder of the Festival, attributes part of the venture's success to the
"new feeling of self-worth [that] was sweeping the land" in the post-
war years (Patterson and Gould, 1987: 35). But perhaps the clearest
articulation of this context comes from the Massey Report of 1951, the
result of a "Royal Commission on National Development in the Arts,
Letters and Sciences" that was the driving force behind the establishment of arts funding in Canada, the current "mainstream" Regional
Theatre network, and, less directly, Stratford itself. As Alan Filewod
points out, the report introduces its recommendations by stating that

---

[8]    Filewod notes that "the first self-declared National Theatre in Canada" emerged in
       1915, and was greeted "with hysterical rapture" by the Canadian news magazine,
       *Maclean's*, where Arthur Baxter wrote that "in the agony of the present conflict,
       Canada has given birth to a national consciousness... By the living God, we're Brit-
       ish! Canada had found herself" (Arthur Beverly Baxter, "The Birth of the National
       Theatre," *Maclean's Magazine*, 29 Feb. 1916; quoted in Filewod, 1990: 7).

[9]    See Jennifer Harvie and Richard Paul Knowles, "Reporting from the Front: Herbert
       Whittaker at the *Montreal Gazette* 1937-1949 and the *Globe and Mail* 1949-1975."

"we must strengthen those permanent institutions which give meaning to our unity and make us conscious of the best in our national life... Our military defenses must be made secure; but our cultural defenses equally demand national attention; the two cannot be separated." Filewod interprets this, accurately I think, as meaning that "a national arts policy is a necessary defence against un-Canadian Communism."[10]

Patterson's tracing of the origins of the idea of the Festival suggests that Filewod's perception applies directly to the founding of Stratford. While Guthrie's idealist rhetoric called for a Festival that "must demonstrably be a Canadian one," one which "set out to show that Canadian artists could achieve... standards of which they need not feel ashamed" (Guthrie, Davies, and MacDonald, 1971: 26). Patterson speaks of economic and political histories, revealing the class interests that motivated him and shaped his efforts as founder. He first describes with some enthusiasm the machinations of Tom Orr who during the depression used free labor by itinerants and materials from shut-down factories to acquire and build the park system in which the Festival was eventually situated. He constructs Orr explicitly, if ironically, as "an aesthetic Jesus, creating the rock/garden on which I would build my church/ theatre" (Patterson and Gould, 1987: 18-19) after which he goes on to give an account of a depression strike in Stratford which "created a disastrous reputation" for the town, "including that of being the Communist headquarters for Canada." "It was clear," he continues, "that no new industry would want to locate in our town for the foreseeable future" (24).[11] In this context, and that of the impending closure of the CN (Canadian National Railway) railyards, Patterson claims he and his friends conceived the idea of a Shakespeare festival "to save our native town" (26).[12]

The pragmatic basis of the national pride that justified and greeted Stratford at its opening, even early on, was never far beneath the

---

[10]  Royal Commission on National Development in the Arts, Letters and Sciences, *Report* (Ottawa: Queen's Printer, 1951), 275, quoted in Filewod, 1990, 8.

[11]  Patterson adds a rather unsavory anecdote (which he calls "quite charming") about a former strike leader (whom he names) who later returned to Stratford – hat in hand and shamefacedly, in Patterson's construction – to sell a wax treatment for the stage. Patterson can barely contain his glee in noting "how the mighty [*sic*! – this *was* the depression] socialists had become capitalists, just two decades later" (25).

[12]  Ironically, the "national dream" that in Canada was the railroad in the 19th-century was to be replaced in Stratford by an equally compelling national dream of theatre. *The National Dream* is the title of a popular history of the building of the railroad published in two volumes by Pierre Berton in 1970 and 1971 and made into a television mini-series on the (federally funded) national network, the CBC, starring Stratford's perennial Canadian leading man, William Hutt, as Sir John A. MacDonald, Canada's first Prime Minister and "father of confederation."

surface. Guthrie was anxious for an opportunity to produce Shakespeare on his own terms and his own stage, and he found such an
opportunity in Stratford. As he wrote to Alec Guiness, "Canada is
busting with money &, more importantly, busting with a sort of
XX[th] century *nationalism* – they want to scrawl their names on the wall
of history. Everyone knows it's now too dangerous to do that in terms
of military glory and territorial acquisition – *faute de mieux* [!] one
must be content with another sort of immortality" (Guthrie, 1952).
Michael Langham, whose production of *Henry V* in 1956 was perhaps
the most cynical attempt to exploit the rhetoric of national unity –
Langham recruited Québec actors to play the French, and marketed the
production as a rapprochement of Canada's two solitudes[13] – has
admitted that "there was never anything Canadian about Stratford. [...]
That was a diplomatic thing Guthrie cooked up" (Corbeil, 1982). As
early as 1954 Guthrie admitted, "I don't know how far it may be
possible to interpret a classical play in a distinctively Canadian way"
(Davies, Guthrie, and MacDonald, 1954: 166).[14]

Even publicly, if the overwhelming majority of press clippings in
the Stratford archives reveals the discursive dominance of the high-
culture nationalist myth, there were occasional voices – most notably
that of the *Toronto Star* critic, Nathan Cohen – that drew attention to
the fact that the emperor may have had great costumes, but was wearing no clothes.[15] In 1954 Cohen warned about the Festival's potential
degeneration into "just another summer theatre venture, with special
overtones of snobbery" (Edmonstone, 1977: 227). In 1955 he noted

---

[13]    It would be interesting to compare Langham's nationalist interpretation with that of
       Olivier. Also interestingly, a comparable but very different experiment from
       Langham's was attempted in 1988, when Saskatchewan's Gordon McCall and
       Québec's Robert Lepage collaborated on an outdoor production of *Romeo and
       Juliet(te)* using Québécois and English Canadian actors as the Capulets and
       Montagues respectively. This production subsequently toured Canada, including
       performances in Stratford (though not at the Festival). Unlike Langham's *Henry V*,
       however, the McCall/Lepage *Romeo* was fully bilingual – the Capulets spoke
       French except in their contacts with the anglophone Montagues – and its outdoor
       staging on a stretch of pavement representing the Trans-Canada highway lent an
       explicitly pop-culture feel to the show. And of course in *Romeo and Juliette* the
       French were not ignominiously defeated in battle by the English.

[14]    Euen Ross Stuart points to Guthrie's opportunism and considers in some depth the
       relationship between the Festival and its Canadian context. I am indebted to him
       throughout this section.

[15]    See especially Cohen's article, "Stratford After Fifteen Years" and Wayne
       E. Edmonstone, *Nathan Cohen: The Making of a Critic*, 224-30. It is important,
       however, to note Cohen's initial enthusiasm for the Festival, which he saw as mark-
       ing "the beginning of an exciting and vastly hopeful chapter in our theatre history"
       (quoted in Edmonstone, 1977: 215).

that "socially, the Festival is now entrenched. [...] Artistically [...] it is hell-bent for sterility," and that, after all, "there is no such thing as a Canadian style of doing Shakespeare" (Edmonstone, 1977: 229-30).

The founding of Stratford, then, was discursively constructed as the founding of a Shakespearean National Theatre in Canada after the British (imperialist) model, in which Shakespeare was used to serve the interests of cultural colonization by a dominant – and on occasion explicitly capitalist (or anti-communist) – elite. Canadians provided the capital, and the labor, but the lead roles both onstage and off were played by the British.[16]

## II

The second "moment" that concerns us here begins in 1967, Canada's centennial year, in which Stratford announced the appointment of its first Canadian artistic directorate,[17] and the Festival with the National Arts Centre in Ottawa jointly announced that the company would henceforth be called "The Stratford National Theatre of Canada," operating out of Stratford and the Nation's Capital. (This merger never happened, though in 1973 the company toured Europe – not Canada – under that name, performing no Canadian plays.) This moment extends through the early years of the profoundly (if also opportunistically) nationalist alternative theatre movement in Canada, inspired and populated in part by the 1960s "counter-culture" movement and American resistance to Vietnam;[18] and it continues through the nationalist outcry that accompanied the hiring of an English Artistic Director, Robin Phillips, in 1974, culminating in the reprise of that outcry surrounding the proposed hiring – blocked at the Cabinet level by Immigration Canada – of Britain's John Dexter to replace Phillips in 1980.[19] It also extends through the Trudeau era of strong

---

[16] In the season, Guthrie used only four non-Canadian actors of eighty in the company, and much was made of this. These four, however, played leading roles (or, as Guthrie said "carried a great deal of the weight" [Davies, Guthrie, and MacDonald, 1971: 29]). Moreover the director, designer, and the heads of all the technical departments were from Britain.

[17] Jean Gascon and John Hirsch were appointed joint artistic directors, but the arrangement only lasted for the 1968-69 season, after which Hirsch left and Gascon remained to hold the position alone.

[18] See Denis Johnston, *Up the Mainstream: The Rise of Toronto's Alternative Theatres*, 30-50, and Diane Bessai, *Playwrights of Collective Creation*, 34.

[19] The outcry in 1980 was in fact not simply over the proposed hiring of Dexter, but over the cavalier firing of the so-called "gang of four" – Pam Brighton, Martha Henry, Urjo Kareda, and Peter Moss – the artistic directorate who had been appointed after Phillips's resignation but before the Board learned that Dexter was available. See Martin Knelman, *A Stratford Tempest*, 96-110.

centralist federalism, together with bilingualism, biculturalism, and eventually official multiculturalism in Canada.[20] These were of course also the days in which Trudeau unilaterally invoked the War Measures Act to quell a different (but parallel) kind of nationalist uprising in Québec (the so-called separatist movement), and in which he made a name for himself as a statesman on the so-called "international stage."

Accounts of this period at Stratford are legion and typically polemical, and they tend to construct a drama of conflict between "nationalist" and "internationalist" positions. Thus, on the one hand the nationalist hordes are seen to be villainously attacking the temple of transcendent art in which all Canadians should take pride; or on the other the arrogant British are accused of colonizing what ought to be a "purely" Canadian institution, using Canadian public funds to produce British high culture. What has to be taken into account in analyses of the history of the Festival in this period is the parallel history of Canadian *drama*, and of the founding and growth of a series of small theatres across the country that were dedicated to Canadian plays and Canadian artists. 1967, Canada's centennial year, is often constructed as a turning point in the history of drama in Canada, the year in which George Ryga's *The Ecstasy of Rita Joe* was produced at the "mainstream" Vancouver Playhouse, John Herbert's *Fortune and Men's Eyes* "made it big" in New York, and James Reaney's *Colours in the Dark* premiered at the Avon Theatre at Stratford.[21] The following year saw the founding of Theatre Passe Muraille, the first and most influential of the so-called "alternate" theatres in Toronto that were to serve as the focal points for nationalist sentiments in the Canadian theatre community throughout the 1970s.[22] Nineteen sixty-eight also saw "Trudeaumania" and Pierre Eliot Trudeau's first election to the office of Prime Minister. Stratford and Shakespeare in this period served in

---

[20]    For a history and analyses of these policies and their discursive construction of a dominant-*cultural* "us" (French and English) as opposed to an *ethnic* "them," see Gomez, 1993.

[21]    The clearest statement of this construction of 1967 is in the preface, introduction, and organization of the influential first edition of Jerry Wasserman's anthology, *Modern Canadian Plays*, but the assumption is made in most surveys of contemporary Canadian drama and theatre.

[22]    For a history of the "alternate" theatre movement in Toronto, see Johnston, 1987. See also Alan Filewod, *Collective Encounters: Documentary Theatre in English Canada*; Filewod's entry on "Alternate Theatre" in *The Oxford Companion to Canadian Theatre*; and Renate Usmiani, *Second Stage: The Alternative Theatre Movement in Canada*. There are many good articles on specific aspects of Theatre Passe Muraille, but for general accounts of the early years see Bessai, 1992, 31-132; Judith Rudakoff, "Theatre Passe Muraille;" and Brian Arnott, "The Passe Muraille Alternative."

the emerging alternative theatre movement primarily as sites of frustration and disenchantment that would come to the surface in 1974 with the appointment of Phillips.[23]

Arguably, however, that frustration grew less out of an idealistic nationalism than a pragmatic populism and an effort on the part of young Canadian theatre artists to find work. It is significant that while the Massey Commission and the founding of the Canada Council shaped the early funding and development of the (mainstream) Regional Theatre network and Stratford, it is generally agreed that (minimum-wage) federal job-creation grants rather than "Arts Funding" were what enabled the founding and early survival of the small alternative theatres, which at least at first were more populist and "counter-cultural" than nationalist. It is also significant that as Denis Johnston points out, the "Opportunities for Youth" (OFY) and "Local Initiative Program" (LIP) grants that funded these companies represented "a government strategy to reduce unemployment *and disaffection among young adults*" (1987: 7). If Stratford during these years was perhaps more "Canadian" than it had ever been, with a Canadian artistic director and producing at least a few Canadian plays, it was nevertheless entrenching itself as the Canadian home of high culture, where Governors General attended openings in limousines, accompanied by triumphant fanfares and booming canons. Meanwhile, Theatre Passe Muraille's founder, Jim Garrard, with conscious class coding, was announcing his intention to make theatre "as popular as bowling" (Shain, 1969);[24] and his successor, Paul Thompson, was claiming that "the really interesting people are the ones who don't go to theatres" (Wallace, 1974: 64). "If Shakespeare were living today," Thompson claimed, "he would not be working at the Festival, he would be doing what Passe Muraille is doing" (Arnott, 1978: 111).

The stories of the outcry over Phillips's appointment and replacement in 1974 and 1980 are too numerous and too familiar to reiterate.[25]

---

[23] Nevertheless, a surprising number of the major figures in the alternative theatre movement in Toronto and in Canada worked at Stratford for a season or two. Some, such as Tom Hendry, worked there as administrators, but most as Assistant Directors – notably John Juliani, who famously (and using a rubber glove) challenged Robin Phillips to a duel on the latter's arrival as Artistic director in 1974 (see Robin Phillips, "On Being Invited to Canada," 64); and Theatre Passe Muraille's Paul Thompson, who later directed that theatre's anti-Stratford satire, *Shakespeare for Fun and Profit* (1977).

[24] Also quoted in Robert Wallace, *Producing Marginality: Theatre and Criticism in Canada*, 76.

[25] They are most clearly told in Knelman; in Pettigrew and Portman, vol. 2, (43-58 and 187-232); and in *Canadian Theatre Review* 30, particularly Boyd Neil's "A Chronology" (25-33).

What is significant here is that this period saw parallel and mutually
exclusive lines of nationalism develop in Canada.[26] Many Canadians
took great pride in Phillips's accomplishments at the Festival, quoting
the near-unanimous view of British and American critics that the
company was in the same league as Britain's Royal Shakespeare
Company and National Theatre.[27] Meanwhile, nationalists of a different stripe were pointing with equal pride to the significant successes of
a localist Canadian drama emerging "from the colonial twilight,"[28]
building an alternative theatre (albeit often based on American models), and rejecting the value or relevance of proving ourselves as a
nation on the battlefields of Shakespeare.

The significant successes of shows such as Theatre Passe
Muraille's famous collective creation, *The Farm Show*, came not from
a British imperialist impulse to unite the country under one flag, one
proper accent, and one world-class standard of classical theatre, but
from a populist assertion of the value of place, of "ordinary people,"
and of regional and local cultures and accents.[29] Paul Thompson's
paradigmatic Passe-Muraille model of collective creation – which I
suspect owes at least as much to his training in France with Roger

---

[26]   In a letter to the Stratford Board, published in *Canadian Theatre Review* 3, a group
       of Canadian directors (Bill Glassco, John Hirsch, Martin Kinch, George Luscombe,
       Leon Major, Henry Tarvainen and Keith Turbull) lamented the fact that "the theatre
       we represent is taking one direction, and Stratford another:"

       Canadian theatre is now working consistently to present world theatre in Cana-
       dian terms, to reveal truly Canadian sensibility, and to advance, under the best
       circumstances at its command, Canadian plays, and the work of theatre artists in
       every field. The time has come when we have a right to expect leadership from
       your theatre, which is the national theatre of our country whether it accepts that
       title and the accompanying burdens or whether it does not. Your theatre receives
       the largest public subsidy of any theatre in Canada, and we think the time had
       come for some public statement as to its function and its plans for fulfilling that
       function. (34)

[27]   See Stuart, 185.

[28]   "From the Colonial Twilight" is the title of an article by Alan Richardson and Don
       Rubin which responds to the 1980 controversy at Stratford by constructing an ar-
       gument based on "Love of Country" articulated in what seems to me to be a pecu-
       liarly American rhetoric of patriotism. Rubin, the editor of *CTR* from its founding
       in 1974 until 1983 and at the forefront of the nationalist outcries in both 1974 and
       1980, was born and raised in the United States, and like many actors, directors, and
       writers in the alternative theatre movement, came to Canada in 1968 during the
       Vietnam War. For a discussion of Rubin's role and influence, see Ira Levine, "The
       Critic as Cultural Nationalist: Don Rubin at the *Toronto Star* 1968-1975 and the
       *Canadian Theatre Review* 1974-1983."

[29]   In contrast to Robertson Davies, who wanted to see a standard set at Stratford for
       proper Canadian speech, Thompson regularly shocked actors at auditions by asking
       them to do five Canadian accents. See Bessai, 1992, 37.

Planchon as it does to his Canadian birth and upbringing – is ideologically opposed (on grounds other than nationalism) to the hierarchical, high-culture model that in Canada achieved its apogee at this period at Stratford. While, as Diane Bessai points out, the model of theatrical development used to fund the arts in Canada (through the Canada Council) "was based on the concept of a homogeneous national theatre" (1992: 25),[30] Passe Muraille, in both theory and practice – the company was directly involved in the founding of several small, alternative theatres from Newfoundland to British Columbia – invoked a model of national(ist) (versus National) theatre that consisted of a multiplication of localist companies. In 1977, Thompson and Passe Muraille mounted *Shakespeare for Fun and Profit*, a satiric critique of Stratford's high-culture Shakespeare, the title of which suggests that the dispute also had an economic dimension.

Similarly, what was often overlooked in accounts of the 1980 crisis, as questions of John Dexter's nationality took the foreground, was the fact that, faced with the erosion of its industrial base, the economy of the town of Stratford had come to *depend* upon the Festival that Tom Patterson had founded, in part, to make Stratford safe for capitalism.[31] What tends to be overlooked, then, in the construction of this period as a postcolonial nationalist struggle to let the Canadian voice be heard through the production of Canadian *plays*,[32] is the fact that so much of the struggle at the time was between contesting *views* of nationalism, economics, and cultural production, views that were rooted in questions of class. After LIP and OFY grants – grants to *workers* rather

---

[30]  Bessai goes onto point out that in the official discourse in which the Council participated "the 'regions' in relation to [Toronto and Montreal] were already beginning to sound like the British 'provinces' in relation to London" (25-26).

[31]  Playwright Michael Cook, who was living in Stratford at the time, noted that, in 1980,

> while Canada's artistic community roared in outrage at moves by the Stratford Festival board, the inhabitants... reeled in a state of near panic, noting that "Its manufacturing industries [were] suffering..., [and] its citizens ha[d] for some time been aware that unless a broader economic base can be found the town will simply become a service agency for the Festival... It's very difficult to get excited about pristine artistic standards when your throat is about to be cut. (1991: 12-13)

[32]  It is interesting at this point to recall Guthrie's argument in 1953 that

> People may go on writing and producing realistic comedies of Canadian life [the only kind of Canadian play Guthrie could or would imagine]; but these, I believe, will remain mere copies of a naturalistic theatre which is essentially the product of 19th-century culture in Europe, and is already bygone. Any distinctive national style... will be found on the study of the classics. It will only be, in my view, by evolving a distinctively Canadian comment on the classics that any satisfactory native dramatic style will be achieved. Such comment will occur not only in criticism but in performance. (Guthrie, Davies and MacDonald, 1971: 28)

than to "The Arts" – had long-since dried up, and as the original alter-native theatres began to receive *arts* funding, the socially radical populism that had motivated their founders was virtually forgotten, their potential for political intervention was appropriated, and they lost their "alternative" label. They began, finally, to produce Canadian plays with high-culture aspirations, to inaugurate subscription seasons, and to install corporate boards of directors. One of them, Toronto Free Theatre, even began offering summer productions of Shakespeare in Toronto's High Park.[33]

The debates surrounding Stratford and Canadian theatre during this period exemplify the dangers of appropriation posed by nationalisms in post-colonial cultures, particularly of settler colonies:[34] initially em-powering and subversive, such nationalisms are always in danger of appropriation by the so-called "internationalist" dominant culture. By opportunistically waving the flag, these alternative companies may have drowned the politically alternative baby in the nationalist bath water.

In any case, if the first-moment founding of Stratford represented the founding of a National Theatre in Canada, the struggles surround-ing my second moment represent a polarization of ideologies, as colonialist discourses of international high culture were confronted by attempts to found a populist national(ist) theatre as a post-colonial and counter-hegemonic gesture of resistance.[35] At this point in Canadian

---

[33]   The funding councils required corporate-style boards before awarding grants. See Alan Filewod, "The Life and Death of the Mummers Troupe" for an account of how one important alternative theatre was eventually destroyed in part by its not fitting funding categories. The history of Toronto Free Theatre is also instructive in this regard. The company was founded with public funding and for ideological rea-sons of access initially charged no admission prices (see Johnston, 1987, 170-96). This policy didn't last, and eventually the company, under artistic director Guy Sprung, merged with the "mainstream" Centrestage company in 1987, and was re-named "The Canadian Stage Company," its new name reflecting its national ambi-tions and self-image. Three years after the merger, however, the company's board of directors fired Sprung against the protests of Toronto's theatrical community, and has since mounted a typical "mainstream" regional theatre season.

[34]   For the distinction between "settler colonies" such as Canada, Australia, and New Zealand (not to mention the United States) and "invaded colonies" such as India or Nigeria see D. E. S. Maxwell, "Landscape and Theme," *Commonwealth: Unity and Diversity within a Common Culture*, ed. John Press (London: Heinemann, 1965), discussed in Bill Ashcroft, Gareth Griffiths and Helen Tiffin, *The Empire Writes Back: Theory and Practice in Post-Colonial Cultures*.

[35]   This is not the place to discuss Québec, but it is worth noting, perhaps, that Qué-bec's alternative "jeune théâtre" was similarly nationalistic (though "nation" in this case meant Québec itself), and if its political thrust was clearer, it has, arguably, been similarly appropriated by what I think of as the "corporate nationalism" that has increasingly stranded the *indépendantiste* left wing.

cultural life "Shakespeare" represented "internationalist," high-culture "standards" that many felt needed to be shelved – at least temporarily – if Canada were to get on with the work of building a culture. There were few productions from the Shakespeare canon in this period outside of Stratford and the (branch-plant) Regional Theatre network.

## III

The third "moment" from the early 1980s to the 1993 Stratford season, the last in the Artistic Directorate of British-born David William, and the last summer in power for the Brian Mulroney-led Progressive Conservative federal government, a government which favored decentralization, privatization (which for our purposes means commercial theatre, primarily in Toronto), and increasing rapprochement with the United States. Mulroney's years in office were framed by an election promise not to engage in free trade negotiations with the US – you don't go to bed with an elephant, as Mulroney (quoting Trudeau) said at the time – and the completion of the first years (and first major job losses) of the fully-implemented Free Trade Agreement (FTA), together with parliamentary approval of a new, improved North American Free Trade Agreement (NAFTA).

In the realm of the arts, the Mulroney years were marked by increasingly severe erosion of public support, in principle and in practice, particularly as the principle of arms-length funding was increasingly replaced by direct funding, corporate partnerships, and the principle of matching grants. Not surprisingly, a company such as Stratford, which already receives by far the largest grants from government of any Canadian theatre ($2,477,000 in 1993), is considerably more likely to be able to arrange corporate partnerships, and therefore to win matching grants from government, than is, say, a small, activist gay theatre company such as Toronto's Buddies in Bad Times. And they do. Stratford productions in 1993 were all sponsored by corporations such as Dofasco, Price Waterhouse, National Trust, Union Gas, and Imperial Oil. Meanwhile, Buddies in Bad Times, together with the rest of the Canadian theatre community, was faced with a federal Cabinet Minister, Otto Jelinek, who threatened to "tamper" with the principle and practice of arms-length funding. "Some of these ridiculous grants make me want to bring up," he said to one group of businessmen, referring to the "fact" (he distorted the amounts) that "$10,000 went to fund a production called *Love Darts*, and Buddies in Bad Times got $60,000 to stage *Drag Queens on Trial*. That's homosexuals, I take it" (quoted in Knowles, 1990: 9).

At the same time, the increasing multinationalism that the FTA and NAFTA represent – which the economists call "globalization," but which from a Canadian perspective seems like the increasing incapacity or unwillingness of government to counter the interests and hegemony of multinational corporations – was balanced (unequally, of course) by increasing activity in the "particularist"[36] feminist, gay and lesbian, Native, African-Canadian, and what I want to call "post-official-Multiculturalism" theatre communities in Canada, including those in rural and outlying geographical areas. In this period Shakespeare dwindled in importance at Stratford, to the point at which, by 1993, only 3 productions of a total 10 were of Shakespeare (versus a high of 7 of 13 in 1979), while his plays at the same time became the site of various anti-hegemonic attempts at (re)appropriation outside the Festival. This heterogeneous activity has issued, among a great many other things, in such productions as Black Theatre Canada's "Caribbean" *A Midsummer Night's Dream* (1983), Skylight Theatre's native-Canadian *Tempest* (1987, 1990), Theatre Columbus's "clown" *Twelfth Night* (1990), Theatre Under the Bridge's urban *Romeo and Juliet* (1993) – staged under a bridge in post-industrial downtown Toronto – and Necessary Angel's cross-cast *Lear* (1994), together with an outbreak throughout the same period of Shakespearean production in Québec – unheard of in the 1960s and 1970s – including "l'événement Shakespeare" in Montreal in 1988,[37] and most recently prominent Shakespearean reinterpretations by Robert Lepage, who is being hailed (and hired) internationally as the new (intercultural) Peter Brook.

The most interesting of these "particularist" productions, such as the Skylight Theatre *Tempest*, which was set on the Queen Charlotte Islands off the coast of British Columbia and cast Native Canadian actors as Ariel and Caliban, have been explicitly read as post-colonial critiques, in this case of the settler colony's past and present mistreatment of its indigenous peoples.[38]

Also prominent among these reappropriations of Shakespeare have been adaptations, revisions, and theatrical contestations that range from Peter Eliot Weiss's environmentally-staged *Haunted House Hamlet* (1986); through Carbone 14's celebrated version of Heiner Müller's *Hamletmachine* (1988); Margaret Clarke's feminist *Gertrude and*

---

36    For an account of some of this activity, and the introduction of the term to Canadian theatre criticism, see Wallace, 1990, 7-18. Wallace attributes the term to Richard Schechner, "Race Free, Gender Free, Body-Type Free, Age Free Casting," where it is described in the sense he uses it, and I use it here. It had appeared earlier in Canada, however, when Paul Thompson, in Ted Johns, "An Interview with Paul Thompson," preferred it to "regionalism" to describe what I have been calling the "localist" impulse of my second "moment" (quoted in Bessai, 1992: 126).

37    See Marianne Ackerman, "L'Événement Shakespeare."

38    See Helen Peters, "Towards Canadian Postmodernism."

*Ophelia* (1993); Normand Chaurette's *The Queens* (1991 in French, 1992 in English), an "explosion" of the chorus-of-women scene (IV.4) in *Richard III*; and Pow Pow Unbound's provocative (post-?) feminist deconstruction of the same play in *Horrible Night of a Man of War* (1992); to the now well-known *Goodnight Desdemona (Good Morning Juliet)* (1988, 1990), by Ann-Marie MacDonald (discussed in Chapter Six). MacDonald's play, which emerged out of Toronto's feminist Nightwood Theatre, not only staged an enactment of "resisting reading,"[39] but it also explicitly (if lightheartedly) engaged issues of representation emerging from the overwhelmingly (for women) hom(m)osocial working environment at Stratford. As the central character, Constance Ledbelly, remarks of Romeo, Mercutio, and "the boys,"

> Those guys remind me of the Stratford shows I've seen,
>
> Where each production has a Roman bath;
>
> the scene might be a conference of state,
>
> but steam will rise and billow from the wings,
>
> while full-grown men in Velcro loin-cloths speak,
>
> while snapping towels at each other.
>
> Why is it Juliet's scenes with her Nurse
>
> are never in a sauna.
>
> Or 'King Lear': imagine Goneril and Regan, steaming
>
> as they plot the downfall of their Dad,
>
> while tearing hot wax from each other's legs;
>
> Ophelia, drowning in a whirlpool full
>
> of naked women. Portia pumping iron –
>
> [*A woman screams within. Male laughter*]
>
> [*verge of tears*] I want to go home. (MacDonald, 1990a: 55)[40]

Pow Pow Unbound's *The Horrible Night of a Man of War*, though it did not explicitly address Stratford, was directly subversive in its treatment of both space and gender. The show, staged at Buddies in Bad Times theatre with four women, a transvestite Buckingham, and a

---

[39] See Mark Fortier, "Shakespeare with a Difference: Genderbending and Genrebending in Goodnight Desdemona." Significantly, I think, Fortier is discussing the first version of the play, produced by Nightwood, before its subversive feminism was to some extent contained and neutralized by revision and remounting at Canadian Stage, the National Arts Centre, and elsewhere in 1990. See Richard Paul Knowles, "Reading Material: Transfers, Remounts, and the Production of Meaning in Contemporary Toronto Theatre."

[40] For a feminist post-colonial analysis of *Goodnight Desdemona* that considers this passage, see Ann Wilson, "Critical Revisions: Ann-Marie MacDonald's *Goodnight Desdemona (Good Morning Juliet)*."

(frequently) naked and (always) vulnerable Richard, was mounted in the centre of a room on a square platform with curtains facing the surrounding audience on all sides. It offered obstructed views of the action and disruptions of linear focus, while staging such startlingly transgressive moments as a "wooing" scene in which Richard was hurled about the space by the penis, at the mercy of an anything-but-passive "Lady" Ann.

All of these productions in their different ways (re)appropriated Shakespeare for their particular(ist) communities in ways that are unavailable to directors at Stratford, given the material conditions, institutional discourse, and construction of the audience that obtain there. Stratford during this period put most of its efforts into competing with the new and burgeoning commercial theatre scene in Toronto, which consisted at the time, and since, primarily of so-called megamusicals.[41] When directors such as Michael Bogdanov (*Measure for Measure*, 1985) or Joe Dowling (*A Midsummer Night's Dream*, 1993) *did* attempt to mount interventionist critiques, they ran up against the constraints of their stages, the training and presuppositions of their actors, and the organizational and discursive structures of the Festival as Institution. The resulting productions were often unsuccessful in their own terms as well as in the eyes of a critical fraternity (*sic*) that is overwhelmingly conservative.

Bogdanov is probably the best-known self-described socialist director of Shakespeare, and his political project is well known. His productions are replete with signs, songs, interpolated prologues, eclectic costuming, and other "Brechtian" alienation devices, and they take political stances that attempt to expose the plays' authority figures as capitalist goons. In his *Measure for Measure* at Stratford in 1985, the Duke and Angelo were dressed in tailored business suits, the Duke was prone to admiring himself in the mirror, and Angelo reached orgasm after delivering his "plainly conceive, I love you," to an Isabella he had cornered against a desk.

It was part of Bogdanov's project to make members of Stratford's predominantly white, upper-middle-class audience feel complicit in the depravity of their onstage counterparts. Before the production opened, an extended prologue introduced the audience to a Viennese underworld of pimps and prostitutes, who circulated in the lobby handing out business cards, and roamed the house inviting spectators to the onstage "club" to dance with exotic figures of uncertain gender. The

---

[41]   In 1993, as against the three Shakespeare, the Festival mounted two musicals – *Gypsy* and *The Mikado* – together with *A Midsummer Night's Dream* and *The Imaginary Invalid* virtually reconceived as musicals.

club, of course, was the script's underworld, and this opening attempt to implicate the audience in its dubious pleasures was revived immediately before the interval, when a highly erotic strip – reviewer Ray Conlogue described it as "a stripper unzipping herself while crooning fellatiously [*sic*] into a bullwhip microphone" (1985) – was interrupted just before its climax by the sirens and flashing lights of a supposed police raid.

The problems here are clear. Far from feeling implicated as voyeurs or, in the prestage show, participants, most audience members, who after all had come to see "Shakespeare at Stratford," reacted with either detached amusement – "isn't it clever" or embarrassment. The police raid was greeted with relief, nobody *wanted* the stripper to go any further (not at Stratford!), and of course the audience *wasn't* hustled off to prison, but to the comforts of the Festival Theatre lobby, its bars, and its gallery of past triumphs.

There were similar problems in the last act, where the Duke's return was staged as a television press conference. As a brass band played (incongruously in Canada) something resembling "Hail to the Chief," the Duke and Angelo stepped out to the balcony – clearly centre of power, at the precise centre of the theatre building – flanked by armed guards. We heard the whir of a helicopter, flashes popped, and the house lights came up to reveal microphone stands in the orchestra aisles, at which the audience was invited to present grievances. Isabella, Mariana, Lucio, and Friar Peter entered through the house and used the microphones to speak across the huge gap – the empty stage floor, the surrounding gutter, and a dozen rows of seats – between the people and the seat of power; Lucio shouted his interruptions from various positions in the house. The platform party spoke to imagined cameras, never to their questioners.

This interesting attempt to use the configurations of power represented in and by the stage almost worked, but the production's politics were consistently undermined by the conspicuous consumption on display in the sets and costumes (together with the rich wood backdrop of the stage and its facade), by the overwhelming weight of the Festival as a cultural institution, and by the traditional training of actors who insisted on drawing upon their sense memories and such to play empathetic, individualized "characters" as unified subjectivities.[42]

---

[42] There has not been a great deal of analysis of the ideologies inscribed in actor training, which for the most part presents itself as neutral and value free. For a discussion of the dominant schools of voice training for Shakespearean actors, however, see Richard Paul Knowles, "Shakespeare, Voice, and Ideology: Interrogating the Natural Voice;" and for an analysis of training at the English section of

Stratford in 1985 was trying to crawl out from under a serious financial crisis, including a barely averted strike by its maintenance workers and the resignation of its two leading designers, partly out of concerns about financial extravagance.[43] The average production budget in the season of Bogdanov's socialist *Measure* was approximately $1 million. The show was sponsored by American Express, a fact featured in a programme that included glossy ads for Cadillac cars, Victoria and Grey Trust, IBM, and the Royal Bank. Finally, the production was mounted within the hierarchical organizational structure of the Festival and the professional theatre in Canada, in which the corporate-style board of directors is at the top, the artistic director and business manager directly beneath, the director of the production below them, and the actors, implicitly constructed as both the worker bees and to-be-looked-at products, are the bottom rung of a theatre configured as a corporation, with traditional corporate goals and ideologies. It is difficult to see this structure as revolutionary, but it is inscribed in the productions, whatever their thematic content. Within this formulation, the audience is constructed as the passive consumers of an artistic and intellectual product, lavishly built for its pleasure by a labor force of actors and technicians, and delivered through slick advertising and the culturally affirmative discourse of Stratford as "big business:" the Festival is the largest theatrical institution in North America, by 1993 employing 750 people, with a total annual budget of approximately $25 million and fixed assets of over $40 million. All of these figures have grown exponentially since, as have ticket prices.

It is important to note, not simply the construction of Stratford's audience as high-culture consumers of productions for which ticket prices ranged from $34.50 to $49.50 in 1993, but, most significantly, the degree to which the Festival was by then taking part in the international discourses of "globalization" and multinationalism, which dominated the business pages of newspapers and magazines in the early years of the decade, and which have crippled the power of governments to implement national social or cultural policy ever since. Corporate sponsorship of the season's shows at Stratford was notably multinational – from Dofasco to Price Waterhouse – and I have noted in Chapter Two, that program advertisements were targeted at an intercultural consumer market. I also draw attention there to an ad that appeared in every program in 1993, as well as elsewhere in Festival

---

Canada's National Theatre School see Denis Salter, "Body Politics: English-Canadian Acting at NTS."

[43]   See Stephen Godfrey, "Disillusioned designers quit Stratford."

publicity, which invited the theatre's "patrons" – particularly those who may be "traveling by corporate jet" – to relocate to Stratford.

Not surprisingly, this discursive context had a demonstrable impact on the 1993 productions, and on the ways in which they were read. Set against the struggling interculturalism of the fledgling "particularlist" theatre community, Stratford's shows clearly served a different kind of border crossing, one that might most accurately be called "intercultural tourism." As Chapter Two demonstrates, the colonizing gaze of the audience in the 1993 season, constructed by that discourse as white, male, and middle-aged corporate "patrons," rested comfortably on comically appropriative anglo-saxon actors in "yellowface" (*The Mikado*); on an erotically exotic, archetypally "orientalist,"[44] and of course feminized Egypt (*Antony and Cleopatra*); on generic and vaguely African primitivist masks and straw headdresses (*The Bacchae*); and on appropriated and dehistoricized black American street culture treated as generic video-pop (*A Midsummer Night's Dream*).

My third "moment" in Stratford's history, then, has to do less with the founding of a National Theatre or national theatre(s) in Canada, than with the founding of a multinational theatrical corporation as an instance of (what I think of as) corporate colonialism in a post-national world, in which emerging post-colonial interculturalisms struggle to resist appropriation as markets or as raw materials in the now dominant discourses of free trade, "globalization" and "the world economy." Shakespeare, who had earlier been either The Model for a National Theatre of "world-class standards" (or the test against which Canada must prove itself); or the imported "internationalist" enemy of those searching for a counter-hegemonic national drama (and national identity); or the "high-culture" icon against which populist practitioners struggled was now one of many sites of contestation between conflicting views of interculturalism: the corporate bard, appropriated in the service of globalization, versus the lower-case shakespeare[45] script as pre-text and the shifting site of *anti*-hegemonic, "particularist" subversion.

---

[44] See Edward Said, *Orientalism*.

[45] I am adapting the idea of lower-case Shakespeare from post-colonial theory, where "English," as "the language of the erstwhile imperial centre," is distinguished from "english" as a post-colonial hybridization "which has been transformed and subverted into several distinctive varieties throughout the world." See Ashcroft, Griffiths, and Tiffin, 1989: 8.

# CHAPTER 2

# Shakespeare, 1993 and the Discourses of the Stratford Festival, Ontario

At the entrance to the Festival Theatre at Ontario's Stratford Festival in the 1993 season, between the ticket-taker and the three central aisles where reviewers are seated, there was a framed excerpt from Eric Bentley's afterword to Stark Young's book, *The Theatre*. The passage was retitled, prominently and in bold-faced type, "**So What Is Required of the Theatre Critic?**" I quote the passage in full as it presented itself to Stratford's audiences and reviewers:

> The perspicacity to read the idea in the performance, and the tact to sense if it is fully expressed and in what details, by what means, by what surprising line readings, by what unpredicted movements. What the critic must not do is accept or reject these movements, these line readings, on their own – as being traditional or the reverse, as being handsome or brilliant or the reverse. He [*sic*] must see them, feel them, as part of a pattern, the pattern that expresses (if all is well) the pervasive idea.

> I am re-stating what I have taken to be the two main principles of Stark Young's theatre criticism. In essence they are traditional, even perennial, nor are they unduly complex. Nonetheless they remain beyond the grasp of most dramatic critics, who seem incapable of the discipline required, the intellectual labour required, and instead blurt out their immediate reactions to the separate parts of the theatre occasion. They register only a brute response to each moment, or perhaps only to certain moments, the moments when they are awake. And since such waking moments follow minutes of somnolence, one senses the lack of connection with what has been going on. Our critics are accustomed to let themselves be as passive as the most helpless, hapless spectator. "Show me!" "Entertain me!" Alas, extreme passivity simply inhibits all real artistic experience. (1986: 138)

Setting aside Bentley's notions of unity and intended meaning, his generalizations about sleepy reviewers, and his condescension to audiences – helpless, hapless, and passive as he may think them to be – the fact of Stratford's reproduction of this passage, recontextualizing it and putting it on display for reviewers and audiences alike – in effect making it part of the public discourse of the theatre – is remarkable.

It is within the context of that discourse rather than "the" perceived "idea of the performance" or the presumed "pattern that expresses… the pervasive idea" that I want to consider the productions of the 1993 Festival; and this discursive context is too often and too easily ignored in reviews and analyses of productions of Shakespeare at Stratford and elsewhere. I want to ask in this chapter what, and more importantly *how* Shakespeare *means* at the Stratford Festival, and what is produced in producing Shakespeare there. This involves an analysis not simply of the productions "in themselves" (as if such a thing were possible), but of the discursive and material contexts from which those production emerged, not all of them as blatant in their attempts to control and contain audience and critical response as the passage quoted above.

The poster for the 1993 season at the Festival, which also served as the cover for the season brochure and various other publicity materials, consisted of four glowingly golden geometrically-shaped artifacts: a solid, rectangular neoclassical portico; a circular Victorian clock with Roman numbering but without hands; a curvilinear Renaissance-style cupid with a bent, semi-circular bow; and a triangular and apparently "*japoniste*" fan made from the folded manuscript of a musical score. All of these icons were photographed in soft focus, floating freely against an ethereal background of purples, blues and pinks that resembled blue backlighting refracted through fine crystal. The poster conjured romantic, nostalgic, and of course ahistorical images of a timeless, mythologized, and idealized "past," untouched by historical specificity, and united in a glow of transcendent and golden iridescence. The individual icons were vaguely suggestive of the season's shows: Euripides' *Bacchae*; three plays by Shakespeare; two classic French comedies; *The Importance of Being Earnest*; two musicals, including *The Mikado* (though both *A Midsummer Night's Dream* and *The Imaginary Invalid* were also virtually reconceived as musicals); and a new Canadian history play. But taken as a whole, and taking into consideration the solid gold Roman-style type used for the poster, as reminiscent of the letterheads of distinguished boards and corporations as the neoclassical portico was of the facades of Canada's most august financial institutions, the poster offered escape to an idealized and comforting transcendence, coupled with a reassuringly corporate sense of security, comfort, and even luxury. This is the visual imagery that framed the discourse of the Stratford Festival in 1993, and it was among the most effective in silently shaping the ways in which the Festival's audiences received the season's shows.

This is true partly because many of the shows, notably Artistic Director designate Richard Monette's *Antony and Cleopatra* and outgoing Artistic Director David William's *Bacchae*, echoed, in their set and costume designs and their publicity photos, the visual imagery of the poster. As prominent, indeed, as the poster imagery was a gloriously rich and golden publicity photograph of the appropriately-named and exaggeratedly buxom Goldie Semple, playing Cleopatra, in the encircling embrace of her Antony, the leonine (if prosperously paunchy) Leon Pownall. This photograph graced the cover of the season's souvenir program and other Festival souvenirs and publications, and reinforced the poster's rich sense of romantic nostalgia. The productions themselves resonated within this context as period and place blended together in a kind of intercultural tourism for cross-border tourists (34% of the Festival's box-office in the 1993 season was from direct sales to the United States), which manifested itself most clearly in the "yellowface" Japanese of *The Mikado*, in the textbook orientalism of *Antony and Cleopatra*'s erotically exotic Egypt, depicted as an almost archetypal white male fantasy;[1] in the generic and vaguely African primitivism of the masks and straw headdresses of the *Bacchae*; and even in the appropriated punk and rap of the African-American street-culture forest of *A Midsummer Night's Dream*, which the production treated much in the same way as the script treats India – as exotic fodder for the appropriative voyeurism of a dominant, tourist audience. But then, as actor Lorne Kennedy admitted in the promotional "Festival Edition" of the Stratford *Beacon-Herald*, commenting on the quintessentially British production of *The Importance of Being Earnest*, Artistic Director David William, the play's director, *is* "a living fossil" of that play's milieu. "He has a direct connection with these people and he's a cultural imperialist anyway" (Lorne Kennedy, 1993). Many in Canada remember, too, William's unashamed claim, when he was first appointed to his position, that elitism, in its cultural and intellectual senses, is not a dirty word.

The larger discursive context within which the 1993 season produced its meanings resided in various brochures, press releases, and other written material; in the physical environments of the Festival itself, including audience amenities, gift shops, and ancillary spaces as well as the performance venues; and of course in the season's repertoire and individual productions.

It is immediately apparent that the written discourse of the Festival in 1993 was universalist, individualist, essentialist, and literary. It was, as the Festival's Literary Manager, the late Elliott Hayes, wrote in the season's souvenir program, "all embracing," constructing itself as the embracing subject positioned to welcome, comprehend, and contain all

---

[1]   "Textbook orientalism" refers to Edward Said's classic study, *Orientalism*, concerning the scholarly construction of "the Orient" as mysterious, exotic, feminine, unchanging, and ultimately inferior to "the Occident."

aspects of humanity and all human cultures, which are silently constructed as the objects of that consuming subjectivity. What the Stratford Festival "can offer the world," according to Hayes, is "the broad
spectrum of dramatic literature and all its various mutations on the
theme of what it means to be human." He presented the season's
productions variously as "dramatic constructions [that] attempt to
elevate the tragic elements of our daily lives to a mythic level," or to
"emphasize the universal nature of theatre in a profound and very
tangible way," but that can present only the empathetic and usually
psychological "struggles" of individual characters, not point toward
social solutions, since "art, as religion, can offer no certifiable answers.
The artist and the orthodox minister can only offer articles of faith. We
accept or reject their offerings according to our own experiences"
(*Stratford Festival 1993 Season*). The universalist/individualist discourse, and its effacement of the historical and social, together with the
envisioning of any social change that they might offer, could hardly be
more thorough.

Hayes concluded his address with a virtual summary of the neo-
Aristotelian, ahistorical, and culturally affirmative qualities of the
Festival's discourse. He expressed his hope that, "For some – for
many, perhaps – there will be a cathartic moment in the theatre when
tears or laughter will bring you to understand that none of us are [*sic*]
truly alone. Euripides – Shakespeare – Molière – Oscar Wilde – are
separated by thousands of years, but here at Stratford they are contemporaries." Clearly, within this context, and congruently with the most
conservative theories of the cathartic functioning of great art, few will
leave the theatre in a subversive, activist, or even socially-conscious
frame of mind, whatever they may see on the Festival's stages.

The most widely circulated of the season's contextualizing texts
was David William's "Welcome to the 1993 Season," reprinted in
slightly varying forms in the season brochure, in all of the season's
programs, and in the large and glossy souvenir program, where it is
expanded slightly, printed under a photograph of William reclining in
casual elegance in a colorful cotton sweater and corduroy slacks, and
where it is entitled a "Message from the Artistic Director." In each of
its manifestations William's message is clear: we are to see at the 1993
Festival a clearly balanced, binary, and unthreatening exploration of
"Order versus the anarchy of Instinct; super-ego and id; sense and
sensibility; Apollo against Dionysus," universal and transcendent
themes all, and all designed to "appeal, we hope, to all heights of
brow" as "a season that will sustain and divert" – and clearly *not*
disturb – audiences who are welcomed both as "returning patrons [*sic*]
and… new friends" (William, 1993). Many of the "returning patrons"
(corporate and individual) are listed as donors in the back fourteen

pages of the souvenir program under no less than nineteen categories, ranging from "Major Sponsors" and "President's Club" through "Centre," "Main," and "First Stage;" "Diamond," "Gold," and "Silver Stage;" to "Playwright's Circle," "Supporting" member and "Supporting Plus;" and finally to various kinds and degrees of benefactors and associates identified by dollar amount, type, and kind of donation (*Stratford Festival 1993 Souvenir*). The new "friends," too, were presumably able to afford the Festival's skyrocketing ticket prices, ranging (except for various promotions) from $34.50 to $49.50 (prices have more than doubled since) and ranked in equally hierarchical order, with the cheaper seats on the extreme periphery of the theatres, where sightlines and acoustics can be appalling.

These prices are difficult to justify at a publically subsidized, not-for-profit theatre, particularly when the high-priced sections had tended to expand over the years, pushing the rest further and further to the margins, and when what had been the less-expensive seats at the Tom Patterson Theatre (formerly the Third Stage) had moved into line with those at the "main" stages. The Canadian government arts-council grants are justified by the theatre, however – in information sheets included in press packages and in the souvenir program – on the grounds of the jobs and tax revenues generated, and on the grounds that those grants amount to only 10% of the Festival's annual revenue. From a theatregoer's or theatre worker's point of view in Canada, however, when they amounted to by far the largest grants given to any theatre in the country, and when that theatre has staged more American musicals than Canadian plays, the $2,477,000 granted to Stratford in 1993 seemed like subsidizing the rich – and the rich American tourist at that.

How did all of this shape meaning in the Festival's productions of Shakespeare, as "patrons" or potential patrons arrived clutching their $49.50 tickets, each of which prominently displayed the name of that production's corporate sponsor: Dofasco Inc.; Price Waterhouse; the Bank of Montreal; National Trust; Union Gas; Imperial Oil; and so on? How did the productions *mean* for audience members sitting in plush seats that sported brass plaques acknowledging their individual or corporate donors, and reading programs full of upscale and globally "intercultural" (or multinational) advertising for Parisian watches, Jamaican rums, Japanese electronics, Ralph Lauren clothing, and American luxury cars named after Spanish cities? How was meaning shaped by the ad, which appeared in every show's program, inviting the theatre's "patrons" to relocate to Stratford, where "the quality of life is unmatched in North America," particularly for those who may be "travelling by corporate jet?" and are desirous of having "'just-in-time' proximity to major Canadian and American markets"? In other words, how did the discourse of the Festival construct its audiences?

Clearly Stratford in 1993 imagined its "patrons" into being as well-to-do consumers; as having money and leisure to spend on "the finer things of life" reserved for those with privilege and position, including fine cars, fine restaurants, and the fine arts; and as "cultured" people who were constructed in the festival president's "Salute to Corporate Sponsors," printed in the season's programs, as being capable of recognizing "the enduring role of the arts today," arts which serve "as a testament to the creativity in us all." (Not incidentally, "us all" is represented by the accompanying photographs of the corporate sponsors as exclusively white, male, and middle-aged.) Finally, and above all, Stratford's audiences were constructed as successful people, partners in the success of the theatre itself, which, we were told by Elliott Hayes, "asserts itself as an institution which has been built – and continues to build – on the successive achievements of individual artists." And as we were told in the "Visitor's Guide" to "1993 Festive Stratford" and elsewhere, the Festival "began in a tent in 1953 and is today the largest repertory company in North America, performing on three separate stages and ranked among the great theatres of the English-speaking world." Indeed, according to a brochure called *The Stratford Story*, the Festival is more specifically "ranked among the *three* great theatres of the English-speaking world" (my italics), in spite of having been "founded in a country where indigenous professional theatre was rare, if not largely unknown," a cultural "vacuum" which without the "vision and perseverance" of a few entrepreneurs (and the help of a few high-profile "consultants" from Britain) might shamefully have remained as "simply another sleepy small town in Ontario." Clearly, then, Shakespeare at Stratford in 1993 was constructed and read as an intercultural, multinational, and historically transcendent product presented for the pleasure of a privileged and culturally dominant group of consumers for whom "globalization" meant market access, and for whom cultural production was undertaken for the benefit and advantage of those who could afford it.

\*\*\*

There was, of course, another set of material conditions through which meaning was produced at Stratford in 1993, conditions that shaped and circumscribed the ways in which directors, designers, actors, and technicians functioned there. Some of these, such as the training and experience of theatre professionals in North America and Britain are not unique to Stratford, except perhaps in the unusually diverse combination of backgrounds from which the Festival tended to draw. It *is* perhaps worth noting in passing, however, that many of these training methods and processes – such as the Cicely Berry/ Kristen Linklater/Patsy Rodenburg schools of voice training, the Alexander technique and other physical and movement methods, all affirmed by the Festival's corps of eight voice and movement coaches – reinforced the psychophysical and linear conceptions of character, motivation, and action that are already culturally privileged and deeply inscribed in theatrical discourse.[2]

Material conditions specific to the Festival in 1993 included the physical and technical circumstances operating at the three theatres and their auditoria, the functioning of the Festival as a repertory company, and the various traditions, procedures, and processes, organizational and administrative, which had developed at Stratford over its (then) forty years of operation. The company, not unusually in Canada, is organized along hierarchical, corporate principles, with a Board of Governors dominated by businessmen overseeing the finances and appointing the Artistic Director and General Manager, who report and answer to the board. The various departments for which they are responsible are then run by department heads, managers, and supervisors, in a system that constructs the creative teams in familiar ways as the working class of the theatre, producing and marketing the Festival's shows (and often even themselves, as "stars," "personalities," or "attractions") as products for the consumption of the paying customer. If this seems unsurprising, even normal procedure for a major theatre in the dying days of the 20th century, that is perhaps a measure of the degree to which consumer capitalism has become the unquestioned and unquestionable "common sense" of the "cultural industries" and the "arts sector," where creative exchange and communication have degenerated with the increasing commodification of culture to the level of commercial exchange. And this structure was and remains deeply embedded in what the "employees" of the Festival do, what is presented on stage, and how audiences understand it.

Stratford was and is not only first and foremost a business; it is also important to realize that as the largest theatrical institution in North America it is *big* business. In 1993 the Festival employed 750 people, had a total budget of $24,711,000 (CAN), and had fixed assets with an insured value of $40,381,500. And as in all institutions of its size, there is a certain institutional, structural, and procedural inertia that obtains, and that can defeat even the best-intended creative efforts at change, resistance, or subversion. The physical plant alone, and the corps of some of the world's best designers, technicians, carpenters, painters, cutters, tailors, decorators, jewelers, milliners, shoemakers, wigmakers,

---

[2]     See Knowles, "Shakespeare, Voice, and Ideology."

propmakers, composers, musicians, electricians, and crew, all require employment, even on productions that might be better served by more simple or austere technical support. The sheer quality of the work done by Stratford's staff – and the expectation for excellence-on-parade that this has created over the years – creates a situation in which the "to-be-looked-at-ness" of what is presented can only serve to construct the audience as passive consumers, patrons, or investors who must be satisfied that their money has been well spent.[3] If the discourse of the festival constructed, and continues to construct its audience as white, well-to-do, male, and monolithic, then, the excellence of its physical plant constructs the objects of their gaze as products for perusal and consumption. In 1993 that gaze rested comfortably on a remarkable number of women in lycra body suits – the chorus in the *Bacchae*, for example, and Titania in the *Dream* – together with the scantily-clad strippers of *Gypsy* and the "marquee" breasts of Goldie Semple's Cleopatra, which were made the centre of focus through her costumes to the degree that they became the central theme of the show. Aligned with the interculturally "exotic," which was of course gendered female, this objectification of women's bodies was both a contribution to and a product of the Festival's discursive construction of its audience.

If the Stratford Festival functions administratively and ideologically as a corporation, however, or as a factory of arts, it also functions theatrically as a repertory company, in 1993 mounting on its three stages ten full productions, one small-scale trilogy, and several special events. This, too, has many implications for the mounting and meaning of its shows. The repertory system is often celebrated, and justly so, for the ways it can create a healthy company atmosphere, a modicum of job security for theatre workers who are often itinerant and market-dependent, and a creative context in which actors' and others' work on each show imaginatively feeds the other shows on which they work, as various kinds of cross-fertilization feed the creators *and* "consumers" of the shows. To some extent this is true. In 1993, for example, intriguing resonances were created, for the actor and for audiences, between Colm Feore's reptilian Oberon in *A Midsummer Night's Dream* and his fluidly potent (if incongruously masked) Dionysus in *Bacchae*. For Shakespeare the most interesting and (to me) surprising of the resonances created between productions in 1993 had to do with *King John*, directed at the Tom Patterson Theatre by Robin Phillips, and Monette's *Antony and Cleopatra*, and many of these resonances were created or enhanced by the fact that the shows shared many actors. The casting of

---

3    "To-be-looked-at-ness" is a coinage of feminist film theorist Laura Mulvey, in her
     seminal 1975 article, "Visual Pleasure and Narrative Cinema."

Goldie Semple as both Constance and Cleopatra, for example, highlighted the plays' parallel uses of messenger scenes in which strong women receive the news of their personal betrayal by powerful men for political reasons. Similarly, the situation of *King John*'s Blanche, torn apart by her conflicting loyalties to her husband and family, gained resonance from the precisely parallel circumstance of *Antony*'s Octavia. While in the Phillips production Michelle Fisk's Blanche was quite literally at the centre of an effectively emblematic tug-of-war involving the full company, however, the same actor's Octavia was as abandoned by her director as her husband, and left to play the traditional Stratford simpering woman of the tragedies. Other resonant details included the intriguingly different portraits of practical men presented by Stephen Ouimette as Philip the Bastard and as Caesar; the moments in each play in which deserters are themselves betrayed by their new commanders; and even the parallel employment of upstage muslin curtains as backdrops, scrims, and discovery spaces.

Finally, of course, even outside of the single season's repertory, return visitors to the Festival themselves create resonances by following individual actor's careers, building a memorial repertory of roles (or even of recycled costumes and furnishings), and taking note of such things as the reappearance in 1993 of Stratford's previous King John, Edward Atienza, in the role of a peevishly sleazy Pandulph, or of the evocative echoes in Colm Feore's Oberon of his earlier roles as Iago, Iachimo, and Richard III. Such things may be considered to be accidental or irrelevant, but judging by overheard conversations in lobbies and bars, they form a considerable part of most audiences' experience of the plays.

There are constraints to this too, however, some of them more apparent to audiences than others. Casting at Stratford, for example, is a complex procedure, as each director is allowed to hire a minimal number of actors, who then become part of the company's pool, the bulk of which is hired by the Artistic Director and the "resident director," Robert Beard in 1993. It is from this pool that the majority of roles in each production is cast, after, of course, the labyrinthine complexities of scheduling for shows and rehearsals are taken into account. This can work to actors' and audiences' advantage, as it did when Robin Phillips, in his days as Artistic Director (1974-1980), most often took the career needs of his actors and the experience of his audiences into account in taking personal responsibility for the casting of each season. (But then Phillips tended to himself direct an unprecedented and unsurpassed percentage of each season's shows.) These casting procedures and constraints can also, however, create awkward situations in which directors work with actors they might not otherwise have cast, and actors find themselves stretched in uncomfortable and unhealthy ways, particularly when, as in 1993, the demands of Broadway-style musical theatre and the classical repertory make conflicting claims. The combination of Pompey in *Antony and Cleopatra* with Herbie in *Gypsy* (Peter Donaldson's roles in 1993), can hardly be considered to be healthy cross-fertilization.

There are other, even less apparent rules of repertory as well, rules that are no less constraining. Lighting, for example, is a complex proposition at Stratford, when in 1993 an instrument hang at the Tom Patterson Theatre (the Festival's "third" space) was shared among five shows (including one trilogy) by five different lighting designers, plus a "special-event" "Words and Music Series" of six different evenings. Even at the well-equipped Festival Theatre, where four different designers shared a grid for four very different shows, a certain "house style" almost inevitably obtained, particularly given the significant time constraints on the hands-on use of the busy theatre. At Stratford that style tends to be dictated by the tastes and practices of Michael Whitfield, in 1993 in his twentieth season at Stratford and serving as Resident Lighting Designer. Whitfield's work, for the most part, carries on a tradition of mottled gobos (patterned screens slotted at the front of lighting instruments) and textured atmospherics established by his predecessor, Gil Wechsler, a tradition that tends to create or support a style of heightened theatrical naturalism. The results can be an accommodating softening of a directorial concept, as when in 1993 the potentially subversive and hard-edged pop-rock forest of *A Midsummer Night's Dream* was made more comfortable and more conformative by forest lighting that attempted to reproduce on the facade the polka-dot patterning applied to the stage surface, but through the use of softening, almost dappled gobos ended up consorting better with Mendelssohn than Motley Crüe, the production's apparently intended inspiration. There is a long-established procedure and technique for lighting at Stratford, and without the informed insistence of a passionately committed director or designer – and at least one director at Stratford in the past has notoriously left the lighting, level-set rehearsal to stage management – that tradition carries the day almost without question.

Quite apart from Stratford's repertory system, of course, the theatres themselves and their stages are the most visible and most significant material conditions for the production of meaning at Stratford. In 1993 the Festival operated three theatres. The Avon, seating 1,107 was the company's "second stage." It housed Stratford's only proscenium, was not used for Shakespeare, and can be passed over fairly quickly here. It is worth noting, however, that as the traditional Stratford home not only of Gilbert and Sullivan, but also of financially risky productions of new work or of challenging plays by Ibsen, Chekhov, and Strindberg, it was disappointing in 1993 to see it used exclusively for

*The Mikado* and *The Importance of Being Earnest* (the other two theatres were used for four and six productions respectively), both unimaginative if logical choices for this space, and both expected to be money-makers.

*Antony and Cleopatra* and *A Midsummer Night's Dream*, together with *Gypsy* and *The Imaginary Invalid*, were mounted on the so-called "Elizabethan-style" thrust stage of the Festival theatre, for which Stratford is famous. There is a fiction popular among followers of J.L. Styan and his book, *The Shakespeare Revolution*, together with the publicity offices of Elizabethan-style theatres that thrust stages, as "empty spaces," are not only "authentic" in some transhistorical sense, but are also genuinely *empty*, neutral, "audience-friendly," and there-fore democratic. These spaces, the publicity goes, allow "Shakespeare" to speak directly, as he did to his original audience, to "speak for himself," and be interpreted freely by audiences unburdened by the intrusion of inappropriate scenic decoration. But ideology abhors a vacuum, and there is no such thing as an empty space. Empty spaces are to the theatre what "common sense" is to critical practice: vacuums to be filled by the unquestioned because naturalized assumptions of ideology.

The Festival stage is a good example. Designed by the late Tanya Moiseiwitsch and built in the 1950s, the stage is very much the product of its time. With its clarity of line and its solidity, its air of dominance, permanence, and authority, the stage is a perfect, internally coherent, and self-contained monument, not to Elizabethan staging, but to post-war modernism. Whether used as Tyrone Guthrie and Michael Langham have used it, as a series of rostrums for proclamations in turn by highly theatrical characters; or as Robin Phillips has, to draw audi-ences into identification with naturalistically conceived characters and societies; the stage and the auditorium that surrounds it impose physi-cal conditions that once again construct audiences as the passive consumers of the production as product, and support the replication of capitalist and patriarchal structures.

Power is located stage centre at the Festival Theatre – the central pillar of the stage is at the precise geometrical centre of the original building – whence it radiates centrifugally throughout the auditorium, nodding intimately towards the $49.50 seats in orchestra aisle six, but growing increasingly distant towards those seated more cheaply on the peripheries or in the balcony, where sightlines and acoustics are seri-ously flawed. Whatever the *thematic* content of the productions – which is often a soft-core and self-congratulatory liberalism – any potentially transgressive material that is present is contained and neutralized by a stage and a building that are, to a large extent, them-selves the message.

Power was very much in evidence as a central subject of Richard Monette's *Antony and Cleopatra* and Joe Dowling's *A Midsummer Night's Dream* in 1993, both of which concerned themselves more or less directly with power relations and power structures between men and women. In *Antony and Cleopatra* the audience was clearly constructed as male, and their subject position was aligned with that of Antony. The program's plot summary began, quite literally, with "Antony," and the production changed the first line of the script from "this dotage of our general's" to "this dotage of our Antony's," no doubt for clarity. The story was then told in both the summary and the production from the point of view of what Harley Granville Barker, in a passage used for the program note, calls "the once triumphant man of action, [its] hero." As a side-bar to the plot summary, in bold-faced type, the program quotes Antony in Act IV, Scene 14, "I made these wars for Egypt, and the queen, whose heart I thought I had, for she had mine," constructing Antony and Cleopatra as subject and object respectively, and reinforcing Granville Barker's note that "truly it is [Antony's] passion for Cleopatra that is his ruin" (*Antony*). Similarly, the director is quoted in the Festival edition of the local newspaper, the *Beacon Herald*, as saying that "the play is about the conflict between duty and desire" (presumably Antony's), and that it "shows the dissolution of Antony's powers to command" (Monette, 1993). In the same article, however, Monette mystifies and naturalizes his reading as neutral and value free by insisting that "I've chosen to balance the play and not interpret the play" (Monette, 1993).

Antony was played by Leon Pownall in a physical form and actorly fashion not easily distinguishable from his earlier performances as Henry VIII at Stratford, or even his incarnation as Long John Silver there in 1991. An ageing and overweight sensualist going through mid-life crisis, Pownall's Antony was dressed by designer Stephanie Howard, "sometimes [...] like Lawrence of Arabia and sometimes like the Sheik of Araby," as the *Beacon Herald* puff piece itself put it ("*Antony*," 1993). In the same newspaper, Pownall claims to see Antony as having "gone native," and he describes "the exquisite romance and lifestyle of the East" in textbook orientalist terms ("*Antony*," 1993). Clearly this Egypt, represented through the eyes of Antony (and of course Enobarbus), functioned for both the audience and for the characters as a white male fantasyland, where exotic, passionate, and foreign women, some of them Black (but not Cleopatra),[4] exist for the

---

[4]    For a discussion of representations and casting of Cleopatra's attendants as women of color, but rarely, in spite of historical evidence and critical argument, Cleopatra herself, see Carol Chillington Rutter, "Shadowing Cleopatra: Making Whiteness Strange."

sole purpose of transporting "us" beyond the mundane worlds of Caesar, the economy, and affairs of state. Lurching, pompous, and blustery, this Antony was not himself very attractive (I overheard one man ask his companion at intermission what Cleopatra saw in him), but was perhaps an appropriate surrogate for playing out the fantasies of an audience already constructed by the discourses of the Festival as white, male, and middle-aged.

Goldie Semple's Cleopatra was appropriately conceived and costumed to fit the needs of her Antony and her audience. Her outrageously lavish clothes and accessories were for the most part generically exotic rather than specific to any particular place or historical period, appropriating "the other" as represented by rich fabrics and "eastern" fashions in much the same way as the same season's *Bacchae* followed the modernists in appropriating generically "primitive" and "African" masks and materials. According to the *Beacon Herald*, Semple herself saw Cleopatra, not surprisingly, as "passionate," "sensual," and "seductive," "attuned to Eastern intuition as opposed to western logic [...], and to a place which is more sensual and imaginative" ("*Antony*," 1993). And if there was more bluster and bust than sex or sap in the relationship between these lovers, at least, in death, "they both transcend," as Semple said, and the fantasy was made both safe and metaphysical. As the audience filed out of the theatre, Antony and Cleopatra could be heard, voice over, replaying their earlier love scenes, presumably rejoined in an eternal gaudy night in Cydnus.

Apart from the Egyptian locations, the production was set by designer Stephanie Howard in a vaguely defined late 19th or early 20th century, with much use of uniforms to differentiate among the armies. Taken as a whole, the costumes suggested an uncomfortable meeting of the Arabian Nights with fascist Italy, which was openly evoked by the uniforms, troop formations, and massive desks (with black telephones) employed for the Roman scenes. This choice, together with the focus on Antony as subject, tended to reduce the talented Stephen Ouimette as Caesar to sneering caricatures of a cartoon dictator. The design had the quality of work by someone who had seen but not understood Robin Phillips' Edwardian settings for Shakespeare, picking up moments but managing them badly, and eschewing both Phillips' historical specificity and the overt and confrontational eclecticism of, say, the Bogdanov/Pennington *Wars of the Roses*, the costumes for which, ironically, were also designed by Stephanie Howard.

Joe Dowling's *A Midsummer Night's Dream* was more thoroughly eclectic than Monette's *Antony*, and more potentially unsettling of audience complacencies. Dowling's Athens combined modern-dress suits for the Duke and his security people with more-or-less Austro-Hungarian uniforms for Demetrius and Lysander that looked to have been pulled from old *Much Ado* stock, adding "roaring twenties" outfits for the mechanicals. His forest, however, was an inflatable rubber and lycra melange of erotic exotica with extensive music and dance deriving primarily from American street culture and the world of rock video.

The stage arrangements and blocking were all dictated by the presence in the forest scenes of a few large, inflatable rubber set pieces, costing $15,000 (Canadian) to build, and inspired by the inflatable emergency exit ramps in commercial aircraft. Most observers and reviewers recognized these as male and female genitalia (though at least one academic I spoke with saw them as the ingredients of a ham and Swiss cheese sandwich). In any case, a large, ribbed, and certainly phallic trunk rose from the stage floor to the balcony, connecting a more globular blob on the stage proper to the vaginal folds of another on the balcony level, which was used for entrances and exits. The balcony piece was suggestively effective as Titania's bower, particularly when she led Bottom there in III.1, but it was at best confusing elsewhere to see Puck and others crawling through its opening to make entrances and exits. The phallic trunk, on the other hand, was used primarily by Colm Feore's reptilian, bat-like Oberon, who on occasion hung from it by one hand, scuttled up its shaft, or slithered quickly down the shank. Meanwhile, the testicular blob, stage centre, served as forest floor, pillow, grassy knoll, and other sylvan sites, but was distractingly prone to causing sleeping lovers' heads to bounce about while Puck and others walked upon it as the forest floor.

The set, then, designed by Hayden Griffin, seemed finally to be an example of what happens when a single concept, however provocative and technically innovative, gets out of hand. In spite of an at times jarringly abrupt juxtaposition of styles and periods; in spite of the transgressive sexuality of the forest's eroticism, including transvestite "fairies" as back-up singers for the spotted-snake lullaby to Titania; and in spite of an unusually attractive cross-dressed Thisbe; the design not only caused incidental constraints and distractions in the forest scenes themselves, but it also detracted from the scenes at court. There was the need, at the outset, to disguise the blobs' uninflated presence through the use of an obtrusive red canopy and guy-wires; and at the end to leave one blob onstage at court, illogically, though perhaps with deliberate intrusiveness, to serve as set piece for the play-within. The design also encouraged a tendency in the acting and conception of the production to let the audience off the hook, partly because of tongue-in-cheek acting in roles such as Bottom (Ted Dykstra), and partly because of the evident lack of logic in *this* Oberon's attempting to help the lovers. There was no felt need to take the whole thing seriously.

There is no question, however, that the forest dominated and dictated the terms for the production, and as a site for potentially creative or even subversive anarchy this could have been productive. The first scene at the court was full of tension between a tyrannical Theseus and "his" Hippolyta, whose long, silent, and upstaging descent from the balcony and cross over the stage to kiss Hermia signalled dissension clearly, even before her peremptory exit on "Come my Hippolyta," which left Theseus publicly embarrassed for "what cheer my love." And the later cutting of "the lunatic, the lover and the poet" suggests that great constancy was not something for which the production was striving. Although the Duke and his captive Queen seemed to pick up in Act IV, scene 1, where they left off earlier, unchanged until Hippolyta forced Theseus to overrule Egeus, making a point, then, of taking his arm on his Act V reprise of "Come Hippolyta," the resolution did come, seemed to come too easily, and was apparently unrelated, except through plot parallels, to the transformations of the night. Finally, the reasons for Hippolyta's willingness to marry and reconcile with Theseus, like those for Titania's reconciliation with Oberon, were both unclear and problematic, imposed, disappointingly, by the conventional comic structure, which was treated with Stratford's usual reverence. In any case, the potentially interesting strength of Hippolyta dissolved at the end into the kind of soft-core and token feminism that can generally render liberal feminisms ineffectual.

The forest scenes did not, however, seem to be mediative in conception, though they ultimately served that function almost in spite of themselves. Presided over by a gyrating Puck dressed in a fringed electric blue and yellow body suit with matching yellow face and frizzy blue hair, these forest scenes might best be described as, "The Story of the Night: the Musical." Drawing on commercialized street culture, rock video conventions, and what I think of as "designer punk," Keith Thomas's musical score and John Broome's choreography blended and appropriated the violent social voice of rap and contemporary dance music – the electronic "sampling" of "rock the ground" was a brilliant moment – with the softer, earlier tones of 1950s "do-wap" (dew lap?), together with the occasional foray into, among other things, torch songs, blues, and something sounding suspiciously like Andrew Lloyd Webber. The sound track was for sale in the lobby.

What could have been a frenetic and subversive upheaval at the centre of the play – the quarrel between Colm Feore's Oberon and Lucy Peacock's Titania was violent, and their reconciliation violently erotic – was contained somewhat too comfortably by the exploitative commercialization of black street culture, the colonizing gaze of an audience constructed as consumers, and the lethal embrace of the stage, its institutions, and its traditions. There were elements, such as the ugly intrusiveness of the inflatable forest set-piece into the otherwise elegant court in Act V, in which one could sense the potential of genuinely disturbing subversion of Stratford's high-culture traditions. But overall this potential was contained and neutralized by the elegance of the stage's rich natural wood, especially its rich upstage facade (a containment which the designer tried with only partial success to circumvent by applying plastic polka dots to the stage surface and projecting matching polka-dot patterns onto the facade with light); by the poise and grace of actors who had trouble assuming an ugliness they were not trained to; by the mellifluousness of the sound system; and by the sheer quality and conspicuous cost of the set pieces, costumes, and masks.

While actors gushed in interviews about the "pumping eroticism" of the production ("*Midsummer*," 1993) suggesting that it would shock, surprise, and even disturb audiences, Dowling drew upon the old chestnut, Jan Kott, to talk about the contemporaneity of the text which would, he assured us, be "spoken as it is" ("*Midsummer*," 1993). For all of the rhetoric of contemporary relevance, and for all the promised pop-culture irreverence and socially subversive sex, the underlying discursive construction was universalist and conservative, and this conservatism was reinforced by an otherwise incongruous program note from G. K. Chesterton on the structural perfection of the play. The forest, according to Dowling, evokes a Nature that "doesn't change," and a sexual imagination that "we all have" ("*Midsummer*," 1993). The final blessing, delivered throughout the auditorium by means of a syrupy choral song, with solos by an Oberon who by virtue of his murky make-up and glittery top hat resembled a chimney-sweep refugee from *Mary Poppins*, was a sentimental reversion to a Disney-esque fairyland whose power to disturb had long-since been contained.

All this, of course, is familiar and discouraging – what Alan Sinfield has taught us to think of as "Shakespeare-plus-relevance" (1985: 176). The eclecticism of the design was ultimately evasive, then, resembling in its ahistoricism as well as its eclecticism the excesses or irresponsibilities of much depoliticized North American postmodernism. The production's ultimate message seemed to be, "see how hip we are? Shakespeare isn't *really* so stuffy: you can feel cultured and hip at the same time!" Puck's epilogue, on the production's lack of offense, was entirely accurate.

Stratford's Third Stage, renamed the Tom Patterson Theatre in 1991 in honor of the Festival's founder and in acknowledgement of its first-stage prices, has traditionally been less likely than the Festival stage to be bound by the dead hand of the past or the constraints of genteel expectation. Housed in a converted barn-like building beside the Stratford lawn-bowling club, and seating a capacity of 500 in 1993 (less than 25% of that of the Festival theatre), the Tom Patterson has little of the air of authority and permanence of Stratford's other stages; in fact, it reverts each winter to its off-season role as a badminton club. The venue has been in use by the Festival for new or experimental works or workshops since 1971, and has through much of its theatrical history been the home of the Young Company, who staged Corneille's *The Illusion* there in 1993. This tradition creates at least an atmosphere of less constraint than obtains at the other stages. It has also created a "third-stage" audience that, in theory at least, is more adventuresome than at the other theatres, more willing to take risks on new work, such as the 1993 production of Canadian playwright Sharon Pollock's *Fair Liberty's Call*; on small-scale shows, such as the three-play, one-man *Wingfield Trilogy* in 1993; or on "difficult" plays, such as *The Illusion* or *King John*.

In 1993, for *King John* at least, the sense of interpretative freedom was reinforced by the fact that Robin Phillips, the play's director, was artistic director of the Festival from 1974-1980, and was in 1987 the original designer of the modular stage since housed at the Tom Patterson, though it was modified and softened somewhat by Debra Hanson, the Festival's Head of Design in 1993. Phillips did his best to restore the extended thrust that he designed in the late 1980s to its original shape and dimensions, and through paint to a color resembling its original austere bleached pine. As designed, and as used for *King John*, it was a remarkably uncompromising space, which provided audiences with an astonishing range of extreme perspectives on the action, and exposed flaws and hesitations mercilessly. As Phillips uses it, this is among the most challenging stages in the world.

In *King John*, Phillips used it to create, as both set designer and director, and with the help of Ann Curtis's costumes, an internally coherent, historically precise, and theatrically stylized world of the Europe leading up to and engaged in the First World War. If Dowling's *Dream* was failed or half-hearted postmodernism, however, Phillips's *King John* represented the successful, clear, perfectly realized, and ultimately closed *modernist* vision of one of the few Canadian directors with, like most modernists, a recognizable individual aesthetic, one that was precisely served and supported by the austere elegance of the restored third stage. For this production, for better or worse, the material context worked to reinforce the production's aesthetics and politics rather than to subvert them, as in Dowling's *Dream*.

Like many modernist works, Phillips's *King John* was at least in part and at least implicitly about power, form, the power of form, and the forms of power. The period setting, not coincidentally, coincided with the birth of modernism (and the roots of modern fascism). The production opened with the recruitment-poster image of Kitchener projected upstage, the amplified voices of women singing a First World War recruitment song, and the lurking physical presence of the Pope behind the upstage muslin. The Pope appeared at intervals throughout, always behind the scrim, and always seeming to appear from nowhere to control the action as a personification of hierarchical authority. At the end of the play, the full company assembled (including characters long dead), and as the Bastard spoke his final lines, the audience's eyes were drawn inexorably toward the white rotundity of Rome.

The stage itself was flanked by facing rows of Victorian side chairs, furnished with modern modular pine-and-metal set pieces familiar to Phillips aficionados, and backed upstage by gauze/scrim draping extending from floor to grid. It was, for the most part, brightly lit with clean, white light, and decorated sparsely. Blocking was tightly controlled, battle scenes were mimed with expressionist clarity, and visual imagery was consistently stunning, underscoring the aestheticism at the roots of modernism.

Phillips and his actors paid the play the complement of taking it seriously, and avoiding the bluster that often besets what few contemporary productions *King John* receives. The result was a production no less about lies and expediency than is traditional, but one in which the characters convinced themselves, at least, of their sincerity, and one in which the roles of the play's powerful women came to the fore. Janet Wright's Eleanor was very much the power behind the English throne, and contributed to one of the production's most effective moments by ushering young Arthur upstage centre, where she stood condor-like, in silhouette and dressed in black, with her arm enveloping the boy, while downstage, across the full expanse of the thrust, Nicholas Pennell's John insinuated the idea of Arthur's murder into the mind of Hubert, his whispers chillingly amplified throughout the theatre. This was the last scene before the interval, and as the lights faded we saw Eleanor, still in silhouette, facing as through the looking glass the contrasting white and unscripted figure of the Pope behind the gauze.

Goldie Semple's Constance was equally strong, and for once her grief was given its due, in a performance that rendered the men's impatience with her odious rather than sympathetic, as it often is. Her great scene in Act II, scene 3, in particular, was deeply moving, as she managed to hold the stage and our engaged sympathies while concluding the speech collapsed on the floor and partially obscured upstage and off-centre. Phillips's and Semple's unconventionally effective control of focus here was brilliantly unsettling, as a scene that is often embarrassing in performance became a centerpiece of the production.

If the strength of the production's women was refreshing (and of course helpful in explaining the collapse of John and of the entire structure of the play world after their deaths), the serious playing of these and other roles also caused some problems for Stephen Ouimette, the actor playing Phillip of Faulconbridge. Usually the touchstone to productions of *King John*, since he can undercut the bluster of the others, the role of the Bastard of Faulconbridge was difficult to place in this production, given the already understated playing of the rest of the cast. I saw the show three times: in preview, half-way through, and late in the run; and what early on was a struggle for Ouimette eventually became one of the show's strengths. Ouimette's Bastard first entered wearing a kilt, the only character in the play to do so, and though he eschewed the Scottish accent that might have been expected to accompany the costume, it was enough to set him apart from both the militant French and the somewhat effete English. (Among the production's brilliant strokes were the English camp's tea-party picnic before Angiers, and the comfit-munching image of Nicholas Pennell's archetypally British King John during Constance's quarrel with Phillip of France in Act III, scene 1.) This Bastard's natural affiliations were with Eleanor and Hubert, and he, more than anyone else, made the audience aware of the cost of politics to those such as Arthur, or, notably here, the soldiers so pointlessly lost in the Lincoln Washes. His ironies here were harsher, less amusing than they often are, and the production consequently concerned itself more directly with the social cost of playing politics.

Interestingly, the almost naturalistic focus of the actors on character and motivation, placed in this highly stylized context, resulted somewhat unexpectedly in a withdrawal of sympathies from individual characters. It created for the audience a sense that to focus on the psychological motivations of individuals is to ignore the theatre of politics as a social arena. The action was played out on what was for the most part a brightly-lit stage, and the arrangement of the flanking and rarely-used rows of chairs seemed (in Canada) parliamentary, placed as they were before an audience that was itself brightly lit for much of the production and lined up like back-benchers behind them. The public forum that was the play, then, resonated evocatively during a run that encompassed a leadership convention and election campaign in Canada, in which personality eclipsed the discussion of issues, in spite of the alarming fact that the country's social programs were on the block.

This was not, however, Sinfield's "Shakespeare-plus-relevance," at least not as it is usually understood. The production made no effort to address contemporary issues, or to point up its connections with contemporary Canada. Like most high modernist works, this *King John* was essentially self-referential, existing self-sufficiently in its own and fully realized world, and referring outward only through metaphoric connections made in the minds of audiences. There were no post-structuralist fissures here, none of the *Dream*'s erotic metonymy, and little that could be constructed as subversive, but the production made brilliant and self-conscious use of its own *means* of production, and it exposed and probed within its own form the modes and mechanisms of power. It succeeded on its own terms in a way that no other production did at Stratford in 1993, and it did so by taking fully into account its theatrical context and means of production.

***

No production of Shakespeare can be assessed outside of the material context within and through which it is produced, any more than can the production of the scripts themselves. At Stratford, Ontario in 1993, where even more than at most theatres the institutional context tended to function with remarkable directness as an Ideological State Apparatus,[5] funded by government and corporate grants and catering to an audience it constructed as monolithic, the production of Shakespeare is necessarily the reproduction of a complex and shifting but nevertheless conservative, affirmative culture, endorsed by the appropriated, high-cultural image of a universalist "bard of Avon." It is important that directors, designers, actors, and technicians acknowledge and even confront the material conditions within which they work, particularly if they wish to achieve any kind of intervention into the circulation of cultural values – if they wish for their work to be culturally productive rather than simply reproductive. It is equally important for reviewers and critics to resist the universalist urge to treat all theatrical production as taking place in a material vacuum, to treat all productions of Shakespeare as somehow comparable theatrical realizations or interpretations of what is "in" the scripts. It is important, then, that reviewers and critics of Shakespearean production, at the Stratford Festival and elsewhere, learn not simply to interpret and analyze production texts *as* texts, but also analytically to read the material theatre itself, and the conditions that shape theatrical production.

---

[5]   "Ideological State Apparatus" is a term used by the Algerian philosopher Louis Althusser to refer, in contradistinction to Repressive State Apparatuses (the army, the police, the prison sustem, and so on), to institutions such as the church, the family, the school system, the political system, and the media, through which dominant ideology is disseminated and reproduced. See Althusser.

# PART II

## SHAKESPEARE AND QUÉBEC

CHAPTER 3

# Focus, Faithfulness, Shakespeare, and *The Shrew*: Directing as Translation as Resistance

*It was found highly dangerous to employ the natives as inter-
preters, upon whose fidelity they could not depend.*

William Jones, *A Grammar of the Persian Language*[1]

It is my project in this chapter, writing as a Canadian and drawing
upon feminist, postcolonial, and post-structuralist theories of translation, to initiate a retheorizing of the theatrical directing of classical
scripts, particularly Shakespeare, and particularly as performed in
postcolonial contexts, as resistance.[2] The attempt derives from a frustration at the fact that the ways available to me of theorizing my own
work as a director – the ways that I have learned to discuss, apply, and
teach directorial technique – are no longer adequate to the task I want
to undertake.

Why theories of translation? It struck me in reading contemporary
translation theory that translators have for many years faced characteri-

---

[1]   Quoted in Niranjana (1992: 47).

[2]   Both "postcolonial" and "resistance" as used here may require some clarification.
Postcoloniality in settler/invader colonies, particularly Canada, and even more particularly Québec, is extraordinarily complex, involving as it does the colonizing of
indigenous peoples by French and English settler cultures, the colonial relationship
between those settler cultures and their European source cultures, the colonial relationship between English Canada and Québec and between both of those and other
francophone cultures within Canada, the economic colonization of Canada by the
United States, and the complex neo-colonial relationships between the two founding cultures and various "others," "immigrant cultures," and "resident aliens" in one
of the world's most (problematically) "multicultural" societies.
The resistance that I'll be discussing here is in part a first-level resistance against
the authority of colonial textuality. It is also an enabling resistant *tactic* that attempts, by examining the ideological structural unconscious of directorial practice,
to resist the structural containment of thematically oppositional productions and
make effective social and political resistance in the theatre possible.

zations and criticisms of their work analogous to those faced by directors,[3] and have similarly suffered from the denigration of that work as
secondary, reproductive, or subordinate "service". Translating, unlike
directing, has been gendered female (an issue to which I will return),
but like directing it has been evaluated by its degree of "faithfulness"
to (or betrayal of) a (masculinist, colonialist, "authorized," or originary) text. "The issues do not change," as Tejaswini Niranjana says:
"[S]hould a translator be literal or licentious, faithful or unfaithful?"
(1992: 53-54). But what is at the root of this "preoccupation with
textual fidelity," in James C. Bulman's phrase (1996: 8)? Or, as
W.B. Worthen puts it, "what can 'fidelity' to 'Shakespeare' mean?"
(1996: 13). And, as Susanne de Lotbinière-Harwood asks, "who are
you going to be faithful to?" (1991: 101).[4]

Currently dominant modes of directing classical texts have been
rooted in the traditions of dramatic naturalism, and the relentlessly
naturaliz*ing* understanding of human identity and dramatic character
that underlies "building a character" or "creating a role."[5] They have,
by and large, failed to take into account the split that is effected in
Saussurian linguistics and Lacanian psychoanalysis between signifier
and signified, and between the self that speaks and the subject represented in that speech, as they have remained innocent of feminist
analyses of women as self-alienated subjects, or accounts of the con-
flicted "ironic compromise" of postcolonial subjectivity (Bhabha,
1984/1989: 235).

---

[3]    In fact, directing has been explicitly discussed on many occasions as a form of
translation, particularly by those who see the script as a kind of (literary) source
text, and the performance as (theatrical) target text. In this construction the performance attempts to say in the language of the stage what the script already says in
words. See Pavis, 1982, 147; Scolnicov; Vitez; and Zuber-Skerritt. Some translators, on the other hand, see their work explicitly as performative, as when Susanne
de Lotbinière-Harwood discusses feminist translation in the context of performance
art (1991:159-62).

[4]    In addition to the passages cited, see Barbara Johnson's evocation, not only of
fidelity, but also of love, marriage, and the family, adultery, reproduction, dissemination, impotence, castration, and incest in her discussion of "Taking Fidelity Philosophically." See also Marco Micone's English translator, Jill MacDougall, who
argues that "translation is the most intimate form of reading. The relationship between the text and its translator is like that of a seasoned couple: full of familiar and
uncanny signs, affectionate gestures and frustrating barriers, encounters and separa-
tions" (1995: back cover).

[5]    *Building a Character* and *Creating a Role*, of course, are titles of two of Stanislavski's major works as translated by Elizabeth Reynolds Hapgood in 1949 and 1969
respectively, and reissued in paperback in Routledge's "Theatre Art Books" series
in 1989.

Clearly, traditional translation studies and traditional theories of directing are alike deeply implicated in a metaphysics of presence, a primary concern with the translation of *meaning* (see Johnson, 1985: 145), and an understanding of mimesis that effaces the materiality of language and of the stage, both of which become mere and immaterial transmitters of essential, stable, and universal meaning. Like the traditional theory and practice of translation, the largely untheorized contemporary practice of directing classical texts, particularly in "the colonies," is conceptually grounded in a familiar universalist humanism that refuses to acknowledge what Niranjana, following Derrida, calls "the heterogeneity that contaminates 'pure meaning' from the start" (1992: 55).

What I have been calling "traditional translation studies" refers to discussions of translation, often confined to translator's notes or methodological guides, that precede poststructuralist interventions, particularly as evidenced in the work of Derrida and the renewed interest, largely initiated by Derrida, in Walter Benjamin.[6] Recent work in the emergent discipline of translation studies begins from the poststructuralist recognition that "the operation of language already includes translation, just as it requires difference" (Graham, 1985: 8),[7] that the transfer of meaning in translation can never be total, and that the site of translation must therefore always be an arena of struggle. In feminist and postcolonial areas, in particular, this work has begun to re-theorize "translation as disruption" or resistance (Niranjana: 163 ff), as the "belles infidèles" (unfaithful beauties), as mistranslation was

---

[6]   For analyses of the contributions of Derrida and Benjamin to translation theory, see Graham, Niranjana, and Robinson.

[7]   According to Susan Bassnett-McGuire, the term "translation studies" was proposed by André Lefevere in 1978 to describe the emergence of the systematic study of translation as a discipline. Bassnett-McGuire's 1980 book *Translation Studies* brought the term into wide circulation. Elin Diamond, in her application of Brecht to the construction of "a gestic feminist criticism," provides an admirably concise and useful summary of Derridean difference that is applicable to both translation and theatre:

> Derridean deconstruction posits the disturbance of the signifier within the linguistic sign or word. The seemingly stable word is inhabited by a signifier that bears the trace of another signifier and another, so that contained within the meaning of any given word is the trace of the word it is not. Thus the word is always different from itself, or, as Barbara Johnson patiently teases out its connotations, "difference" is not a difference between [...] independent units [...] but a difference within." Texts, she argues, are not different from other texts, but different from themselves. Deconstruction thus wreaks havoc on identity, with its connotations of wholeness and coherence: if an identity is always different from itself it can no longer *be* an identity. (1988: 85)

(Diamond is quoting Barbara Johnson [1980: 4].)

denigrated in 17th-century France, are reconfigured positively for contemporary feminist Québec, for example, as "*re*-belles et infidèles:" "translation as rewriting in the feminine" (Lotbinière-Harwood, 1991: 98-99); and as "the *founding objects* of the Western world," as Homi Bhabha describes canonical texts, "become [in (mis)translation] the erratic, eccentric, accidental *objets trouvés* of the colonial discourse – the part objects of presence" (1994: 92).[8]

Directing, however, particularly the directing of classical drama, remains for the most part mired – at lease in its theory, if not always in practice – in a "traditional" phase. Its theory is still for the most part embedded in director's notes, interviews, and collections such as *Directors on Directing* (Cole and Chinoy) and its 1996 successor, *In Contact with the Gods?* (Delgado and Heritage), prescriptive textbooks on method, and academic studies of individual directors such as those in the Cambridge "Directors in Perspective" series. Its essentialist humanism is, for the most part, innocent of poststructuralist questionings.[9] It might be useful, then, to draw upon recent translation theorists' formulations of "affirmative deconstruction" and "enabling discursive failure" (Niranjana, 1992: 42) to construct a theory of directing-as-resistance that makes available a more dynamic and less simply reproductive relationship between what translators might call the theatrical target text and its dramatic source text. In doing so, it will be important to remember that directing, like all translation, involves more than a movement between languages: it involves a productively problematic process of translation into an entire cultural discourse, which in the case of the theatre includes the discourses of contemporary theatrical practice, training, and tradition. In the case of works carrying the cultural capital and originary authority of theatrical classics, as Denis Salter warns, "unless a text has been radically disarticulated, interrogated, and *denied*, it will inevitably invoke [...] traditional narrative (en)closure; the interpretative freedom enabled by the tran-

---

8    Bhabha goes on to quote a letter from a missionary in Bengal, published in *The Missionary Register* in May 1817, 186, about *the* canonical text:

     Still everyone would gladly receive a Bible. And why? – that he may lay it up as a curiosity for a few pice; or use it for waste paper. Such it is well known has been the common fate of these copies of the Bible.... Some have been bartered in the markets, others have been thrown in snuff shops and used as wrapping paper. (1994, 92)

9    Perhaps the most disappointing recent publication is Jon Whitmore's *Directing Postmodern Theatre*, which presents a very conservative primer in semiotics for directors, with no interrogation of the *role* of the director or the *process* of directing in a postmodern theatre. The Directing Program at the annual Association for Theatre in Higher Education conference in the United States tends to be equally unsophisticated and unhelpful in addressing poststructuralist or feminist questionings of process and practice (rather than product and message).

sience of performance hasn't a chance against the permanence of the written literary text" (1993: 67). Salter goes on to argue that postcolonial strategies of resistance such as mimicry, "parentheses," and cross-grained performance "seem destined for assimilation within the conventions they were meant to supplant." This is so in part, he argues, (perhaps too vehemently in his reifying construction of the inevitability of text-as-problem), because directors of such interventions are "frustrated not only by Shakespear[ean Textuality] but, even more urgently, by the limitations of theatre itself." It is this last problem – the hegemony of theatrical training, tradition, traditional wisdom, and theatrical reviewing – the discursive space that constitutes contemporary theatre – that I would like to try to address.

Not surprisingly, many of translation studies' debts to Derrida are eventually traceable to the theatre, and specifically, not surprisingly, to Brecht. Much resistant theorizing of translation recovers as an advantage the traditionally demonized doubleness of translation, focusing on *choice*, and on a Derridean double inscription in which every choice is shadowed by and points towards the choice not made. "Not this," Brecht would say, "but that." The translator's "deux mots pour chaque chose" (Lotbinière-Harwood, 1991: 74), in this construction, becomes an opportunity, in which the challenge of translation, and by extension directing, becomes less one of bridging inevitable cultural, linguistic, and discursive gaps on the way to recovering lost essences, than one of recognizing in the acts of translation and directing a *hybridity* that deforms, displaces, and subverts essentialist models of reading, viewing, and interpreting.[10] At its best, as Susanne de Lotbinière-Harwood suggests ("read my... lèvres," 76), this doublespeak involves gendered *jouissance* as much as it does subaltern resistance, even as it involves the *construction* rather than the reproduction of "text."

There are two specific areas for exploration of the application of recent translation theory to the theory and practice of directing Shake-

---

[10]  See Homi Bhabha: "Hybridity is the revaluation of the assumption of colonial identity through the repetition of discriminatory identity effects. It displays the necessary deformation and displacement of all sites of discrimination and domination" (112). In the context of my argument, and its focus on contemporary Québec, the postcolonial context is as relevant as the feminist one. I would argue, however, that, like Québec and Canada, the United States also remains culturally if no longer economically colonized by the English, as is evidenced by the rampant anglophilia of American royal watchers, ye-olde Shakespeare festivals, and Royal Shakespeare Company pilgrims. Even (especially?) among Shakespearean performance critics at the Shakespeare Association of America, and in *Shakespeare Quarterly* policy and coverage, the RSC retains an almost exclusive privilege that can only be explained by its culturally colonizing relationship to the Shakespeare of the Americas and elsewhere.

speare. The first, which will be the subject of the middle section of this chapter, has to do with what is usually considered to be the pre- or extra-rehearsal work of the director in developing "a concept," working alone or with a dramaturge on the "source text," working with the designers on a production's visual dimension (including blocking), and so on. The second, work with actors in rehearsal, is the subject of another part of this project, and will only be touched on here.[11] Both, however, begin and concern themselves primarily with the role and authority of the director, with the question of choice, and with the achievement of focus.

A significant impetus (if a theoretically problematic one because of its *own* claim to independent author-ity) behind the new "translation studies" has been the insistence of translators on their right to be regarded independently as authors or co-authors (or for feminist translators, in the words of Lotbinière-Harwood, "co-authers"), to have their work protected by copyright legislation, acknowledged on title pages, and considered thoroughly and seriously by reviewers.[12] Interestingly, directors to a significant degree won these battles early in their history – which is to say at the time of the emergence of directing as an independent theatrical function in the late 19th century. As I indicated above, however, the role of the director has not tended to be gendered female to the same degree as that of the translator, partly, one suspects,

---

[11] Of course these are not entirely separable from one another even in the most conservative of productions. Their separability is precisely part of the discourse of traditional theatrical production that needs to be reconsidered. Versions of the developing second part of this project were delivered at the ATHE conference in New York in the summer of 1996, and at the Association for Canadian Theatre Research in St. John's in the Spring of 1997, as "Show Me: Directing as Translation as Resistance, II: The Director in Rehearsal."

[12] See Lotbinière-Harwood on the (limited) gains that have been made in these areas in Canada:

> In Canada, the copyright in the translated work often remains the property of the translator. Since 1988, translations are expressly included as literary works for copyright purposes. As an instance of the fact that translators are indeed co-authers, the Trade Book Contract for Translation drawn up by the Literary Translators' Association (1991) specifies, among other things, that the translator's name must appear on the book's title pages and jacket of every copy of the translated work, in all advertising, press releases, review slips, etc. However publishers are not obliged to use this contract. In addition, provided work meets certain criteria, the Public Lending Rights Commission will pay the translator an amount established according to her or his contribution to the translated work... There are also programs of compensation for reprography (photocopy) rights... Depending on the contract signed, royalties may also be paid after a percentage of sales, but this is the exception. (1991: 156)

The situation with reviewers is less rosy, as is indicated by Lotbinière-Harwood's subsection entitled "On (Not) Reviewing Translation" (1991: 162-63).

because of the hierarchical nature of the theatrical workplace, in which the function of the director has always been in part managerial and patriarchal. This component of directing, which leads textbooks over-whelmingly to characterize the director as "missionary," "ship's cap-tain," "benevolent dictator" and the like,[13] has nevertheless not entirely dispelled directorial anxieties about the gendering of their role, anxie-ties that have played themselves out as claims for privileged access to the authority of the classical text, or for creative privilege as *auteurs* in a "director's theatre." Thus, on the one hand, as Richard Schechner notes, "perhaps unconsciously but nevertheless powerfully the [earli-est] directors drew on the tradition of [biblical] exegesis," claiming the priestly function of privileged interpreter (1994: 237). On the other hand, anxiety about the gendering of their interpretative (or service) role led, I suggest, to the cultivation of the cult of the director in which all theatrical activity revolves around the informing, generative concept of the director as *auteur* and source.

In theorizing the role of the director as neither exegete nor *auteur* but (resistant) translator – "co-auther" –, and in formulating a practice of directing that is "speculative, provisional, and interventionist" (Niranjana, 1992: 173), the feminist or postcolonial theorist will, I suggest, consider the process of directing not as one of building unities around a central and exclusionary concept which must be illustrated and reinforced by decisions about design, acting style, and the cutting and rearranging of the text, and not as one that places the director in the priestly position of mediator between the authority of the Author/ God and actor/human, explaining, guiding, judging, forgiving, and leading the company towards the "discovery" of pre-existing meanings (as opposed to the *construction* of contestable gests and positionali-ties); rather she will implement a collaborative practice that is rooted in history, in the agency of the actors, in the meticulous uncovering of the instability of the "source text," the deconstruction of originary myths of textual purity or unified subjectivity, and the inscription of hetero-geneous and contradictory traces of choice – of the Brechtian/Derrid-ean not/but. Directing, that is, might usefully be reconfigured, not as a containing, unifying, and disciplinary force, but a disruptive, dissemi-nating, and *contaminating* one that trails dialogic traces of the hetero-geneous discourses, cultures, and practices of which theatre is neces-sarily constituted. The role of the director might also usefully be reconfigured less as exegete or *auteur*, than as director/de*flect*or, a

---

[13]   These examples are all drawn from one popular directing text, Louis E. Catron's *The Director's Vision*, 1989: 25, but they are representative of handbooks on directing.

centrifugal force that decentres author-ity and insists on the necessity and necessary provisionality of choice.

In a brief discussion of directorial choice, I want to focus here on the question of theatrical focus, and to tease out of this issue some more general applications. The director's process is traditionally seen to be one of making a series of choices, each of which narrows the options available for the next, and the sum of which determines the character of the production. Thus conceptual choices (or uni-linear constructions of throughlines – rising actions, climaxes, and falling actions) become delimiting contexts within which set- and costume-design choices are made, which in turn restrict the range of options available to the actors, whose movement patterns and acting decisions frame the work of the lighting designer, and so on. Much of this process centres around the achievement of focus – narrative, thematic, stylistic, or visual – as the director attempts to guide the audience toward an understanding of what "the play" is essentially about. In the process "he" (accepting for the moment the currently dominant gendering) cuts off options for the audience – what to think about, what storyline to follow, what to look at, and so on – that he has decided are extraneous, potentially confusing, or needlessly diffuse. Thus set design (often employing the techniques of depth perspective in which spatial and psychological conceptions of "depth" are conflated), costuming (in which the most eye-catching colors and styles are reserved for those actors who have been designated the primary objects of the gaze), lighting (singling out or highlighting "centres" of attention), blocking patterns (traditional wisdom and practice about which all have to do with "the achievement of focus" on stages that are, or that directors have learned to treat as, proscenia, with single vanishing points and their attendant strong positions and "centres" of focus).

But why is there so pathological a need for the achievement of focus in contemporary productions of Shakespeare? Why do directors, even oppositional directors, consistently undercut their potentially resistant thematic interventions by adopting positions in the theatrical hierarchy and employing theatrical practices that function hegemonically to reinforce and reinscribe currently dominant values? Why do directors need to reserve choice for themselves, and work with modernist obsessiveness to repress the (return of the) choice not taken? Is it possible to reconceive of directing as a project of multiplication, one that presents as broad a range of choices, of focal points, and of interpretative nodes as possible to an audience empowered as a heterogeneity of potential viewpoints? And finally, is it possible to reconceive the job of the director as one that foregrounds, rather than mystifies, the ideologies of choice and the productive tension and discursive *stakes* involved in the confrontation of the historicized dramatic source text, the (also historicized) theatrical target text, and the interpretative production of meaning by a heterogeneous audience?

I want briefly to examine the production and the critical reception – or reconstruction – of a *Taming of the Shrew* performed in Montreal in March-April, 1995. *La Mégère apprivoisée*, at Le Théâtre du Nouveau Monde (Montreal's leading classical theatre company, under artistic director Lorraine Pintal), was a production by director Martine Beaulne of trilingual Italian-Canadian Marco Micone's *La Mégère de Padova*, a translation, or "tradaptation"[14] into French of the Shakespearean source text – itself, of course, in part a tradaptation of Gascoigne's *Supposes*, itself in turn a "prose version" of Ariosto's *Suppositi* (translated from the Italian).[15]

Productions of the classics at TNM since Lorraine Pintal was appointed to the position of artistic director in 1992 have been marked by careful attention to historical research and detail, together with an unwillingness to present merely the unruffled veneer of accurate historical reproduction.[16] Martine Beaulne's *La Mégère apprivoisée* was no exception: in the details of its costuming and in the care taken in the program as well as the production, Shakespeare's work was precisely located within its own social, historical, and cultural (including theatrical) contexts – a contextualization that included, among other things, information about the Copernican revolution relevant to the production's playing with the trajectories of the sun and moon.[17]

---

[14]     The term, as far as I know, was coined by Michel Garneau to describe his Québécois version of *Macbeth* in the late 1970s, and later of *Coriolanus* and *The Tempest*, all three of which in turn were later staged together by Robert Lepage in 1992-93 as "The Shakespeare Cycle:"

> Garneau's twofold project of translation *and* adaptation is a sustained exercise in linguistic preservation of a kind peculiar to minority cultures struggling for autonomy on many different front(ier)s at once. Tradaptation is close to being oxymoronic, as it discloses the kind of prodigious doubling to which the translator's identity (personal and public) is necessarily subjected. Shakespeare supposedly represents timeless and universal values; but to accept this as true, even for a moment, is an act of surrender – a qualified or perhaps even an absolute denial of your own time, your own space. (Salter 1993: 63)

[15]     "Prose version" is Ann Thompson's phrase from the introduction to her New Cambridge edition of *The Taming of the Shrew* (1984: 10) which I am using throughout.

[16]     These productions, many of which have been notably women-centred, have included *Andromaque* and *Les Troyennes* (Euripides), *La Locandiera* (Goldoni, translated by Marco Micone and directed by Martine Beaulne), *En pièces détachées* (Tremblay), and *Jeanne Dark* (Brecht).

[17]     One reviewer, picking up on this, began his account of the production by questioning, "Est-ce la terre qui tourne autour du soleil ou la mégère qui tourne autour de l'homme? On sait que la terre tourne autour de soleil, mais quatre cents ans après la

But at same time, in the interventions of the translation, the employment of an onstage and visible contemporary musician,[18] and the
intrusion of contemporary (feminist) issues, the production took equal
care to problematize historical difference through the carefully disjunc-
tive and denaturalizing juxtapositioning of the historical past with the
(thereby) historicized present. The program, the translation, and the
*mise en scène* resisted the universalizing tendency to comment on the
present from the point of view of an authoritative past and originary
author – the "Shakespeare-really-did-know-just-about-everything"
school of Shakespearean production; rather they emphasized an historical not/but, and, through acknowledging historical difference and
the fact that times *have* changed,[19] inscribed social change as both
possible and desirable. Shakespeare, the director and translator were
determined to make clear, is decidedly *not* "our contemporary" (David,
1995).

The use of translation, of course, already displaces the Shakespearean "original," invokes (or makes relevant) the translation theories
discussed above, and, as Dennis Kennedy has shown, provides the
director with a freedom that is less easily achieved for English-
language productions. As James Bulman remarks, "the very act of
translation subverts the authority of Shakespeare's text" (1996: 7). The
potential for directorial subversion of classical unitary purities and
authorities is significantly increased when a translation of *The Taming
of the Shrew* is commissioned by the artistic director and director –
both Québec women – to be written by an Italian-Québecker to "serve"
the production rather than the originary text, when that translation is
itself consciously subversive, and when the translator explicitly and
with considerable sophistication defends his work by citing Brecht,
Shakespeare's transcultural tradapting of Ariosto, and Québécoise
feminist translator Sherry Simon's transgressive theories of contesta-

---

création de *La mégère apprivoisée* on ne sait toujours pas qui tourne autour de quoi
dans les rapports amoureux" (Beaunoyer).

[18]  Luc Boulanger's extravagantly negative review of the play accurately if disparag-
ingly described what I felt to be the very effective deployment of the musician: "ce
qui m'a davantage agacé, c'est l'omniprésence de la chanteuse et musicienne, Silvy
Grenier, au balcon de ce décor [élizabéthain]. On se demande ce qu'elle fait là,
jouer de son 'tubuphone' entre les scènes. Sa musique, grave et dramatique, ne colle
pas du tout avec l'esprit loufouque [*sic*] de la pièce."

[19]  The program note cited, for example, the current information technology revolution, including such things as interactive CD-ROMs, as contemporary perceptual
dislocations comparable to but historically and culturally *different* from that of the
Copernican revolution.

tory translation (Micone, 1995b).[20] But it is important to note that the translation as commissioned does not in this configuration become the (masculinist) playtext – counterhegemonic and resistant though it may be considered to be – to which the production is then "faithful" in traditional ways. Rather the translation functions here as one of the many and multiple strategies *deployed* by the director, and set in productive tension with other strategies and techniques in a collaborative process.

I want to begin by looking briefly at two scenes in Micone's translation, and to suggest that he is knowingly playing against audience expectations, that he is self-consciously serving as a collaborator on the production rather than as servant of the author, and that he is consciously foregrounding the not/but of choice. I suggest, that is, that he is both evoking and playing *against* the classical text rather than replacing it with his own unities, which the production might then be obliged to serve.[21] In the first of these scenes, 4.2, Micone opens with the sun/moon argument in what might be called the spirit of the source text, as Petruccio asserts his right as his mother's only son to name the planets:

PETRUCCIO. Je dis que c'est la lune.

CATERINA. Moi, je sais que c'est le soleil.

PETRUCCIO. Par le fils unique de ma mère, ce sera ce que je déciderai: la lune, une étoile, n'importe quoi... sinon notre voyage s'arrête ici. (1995a: 95)

The translation moves quickly, however, to incorporate many of the insights and arguments of feminist criticism of the play, going beyond most of them in giving Caterina not only control of the game that she and Petruccio are playing, and initiative in the address to Vincenzo (she rather than Petruccio first addresses him as "amiable dame," and she later upbraids Petruccio for going along with her: "voyons, cher époux! Vous n'êtes pas aveugle, j'espère. C'est un homme ridé, flétri,

---

[20] In his defense of the TNM production against the attacks of Robert Lévesque, Micone cites Brecht's "leçon... qui nous met en garde contre l'idolâtrie des classiques et nous exhorte à nous servir d'eux," together with Sherry Simon's reference to "le pouvoir transgressif du texte plurilingue et comment celui-ci conteste la pureté et l'unicité culturelles."

[21] I am discussing the translation itself, in a chapter on directing, because the parallels in strategy between the two in this instance are particularly instructive, and more importantly because of the ways in which the review discourse surrounding the production deflected reviewers' (gendered) anxieties about faithfulness and authority to the level of text and translation rather than directorial choice.

fané"), but also (erotic) power over her husband, as the scene becomes the turning point in the play:

PETRUCCIO. Donne-moi un baiser, Catie.

CATERINA. Quand vous serez devenu plus doux. (1995a: 96)

Who is taming whom here?

What is interesting about this scene beyond the feminist revisionism, however, is its evocation of audience recognition of that revisionism – particularly interestingly in the early underlining of the intertext with another adaptation, *Kiss Me Kate* ("donne-moi un baiser, Catie," a line which in the source text doesn't occur until the end of 5.1). The sun/moon, budding virgin/old man debates, as reconstructed by Micone, like the Brechtian not/but, are primarily about what the characters agree to NOT say. Kate's entry into the game, which precipitates Petruccio's request for a kiss, is far from a surrender; rather it is the beginning of a negotiation:

CATERINA. Je vous en prie: que vous disiez soleil, lune ou même torche de paille, je vous jure que désormais je ne vais plus vous contredire.

PETRUCCIO. Je dis donc que c'est la lune.

CATERINA. J'ai bien entendu: Vous dites que c'est la lune. (1995a: 95)

The scene establishes a game of choice that prepares the audience for yet more radical revisioning in the final scene (5.2), involving the wager and Kate's famous final speech. But before reaching that scene, Micone again significantly modifies the source text's "Kiss-me-Kate" exchange at the end of 5.1, drawing attention as he does so to his earlier addition, all of which serves to increase the stakes and the tension both here and at the end of the production:

CATERINA. Suivons-les. Je veux voir comment cela va se terminer.

PETRUCCIO. Oui, mais d'abord un baiser.

CATERINA. Encore?

PETRUCCIO. Comment encore?

CATERINA. Vous m'en avez déjà demandé un.

PETRUCCIO. Que tu ne m'as pas donné.

CATERINA. Je vous le donnerai lorsque vous le mériterez.

PETRUCCIO. Alors, nous rentrons. Grumio, nous repartons.

CATERINA. Repartez, si vous voulez; moi, je reste.

GRUMIO. Allons, mon seigneur, suivez-la si vous voulez qu'elle vous embrasse.

(*Ils entrent chez Battista*) (1995a: 104)

The audience approaches the final scene, then, with a considerably different set of expectations than they might in any merely "faithful" staging of the source text. By the end of 5.1, in fact, as I have suggested, considerable doubt is possible about which is the tamer here and which the shrew. As reconstructed by Micone, the wager omits the explicit test of obedience (line 67 in the source text), Petruccio – whom Micone's stage directions indicate is drunk – proposes only that the winner will be "celui dont la femme viendra dès qu'il la demandera" (1995a: 106). When his turn comes – in the wake of a debate about to whom a woman owes obedience that concludes with Ortensio's "plus qu'à son père et à son mari, la femme obéit à l'homme" (1995a: 107) – Petruccio sends to Caterina as follows: "Va dire à Catie que je l'aime tendrement et que j'aimerais être auprès d'elle, mais un rhumatisme m'empêche de marcher. (*il boit*) Ne l'implore pas, reste digne quand tu lui demanderas de ne pas venir" (1995a: 108). Between this request and Caterina's arrival, moreover, Micone replaces the source text's exchange with Ortensio with a more general exchange about disobedience and desire:

> (*Petruccio chuchote quelques mots à l'oreille de Grumio*)
>
> LUCENZIO. Qu'avez-vous susurré à l'oreille de Grumio?
>
> PETRUCCIO. Que Catie doit me désobéir.
>
> ORTENSIO. Elle viendra, ou elle ne viendra pas?
>
> PETRUCCIO. Elle me désobéira.
>
> LUCENZIO. Vous voulez, ou vous ne voulez pas qu'elle vienne?
>
> PETRUCCIO. Les femmes serviles émoussent mon désir. (1995a: 109)

When Caterina appears ("Imprévisible comme sa mère," according to Battista), she rewrites the submissive speech of her source-text counterpart as follows:

> Je suis venue pour vous désobéir, car l'obéissance ternit la beauté comme la gelée brunit les prés. Une femme servile est comme l'eau troublée d'une source fangeuse et répugnante qu'on ne devrait pas daigner boire, ni même toucher des lèvres. Rendons parole pour parole, menace pour menace, mais aussi baiser pour baiser et caresse pour caresse. (1995a: 109)[22]

---

[22] The rest of the play in Micone's translation is worth quoting in full, supplemented by the information that the actor playing Petruccio doubled as Christopher Sly in the Prologue, where there had been an extended debate between Sly and the Page, as Sly's wife, about when s/he would "viens au lit." The scene resonates with both that prologue and the two kiss-me-Kate scenes described above, particularly Kate's resistant "encore?" in 5.1:

ORTENSIO (*étonné*). Mais elles ont toutes désobéi!
LUCENZIO. Quel sombre dessein cela cache-t-il?

Martine Beaulne's deployment of this script – which diverged somewhat even from the text as I have quoted it, most notably by extending Kate's speech in ways that made explicit those to whom a woman did *not* owe obedience – was designed, in the words of a program note, to show "le désir d'une femme de créer un ordre nouveau à l'intérieur du couple" (Program, 1995: 10). It did so, moreover,

---

BATTISTA. Mon Dieu, vers quel gouffre allons-nous?
PETRUCCIO. Donne-moi un baiser, ma douce Catie.
CATERINA. Devant tous ces gens?
PETRUCCIO. Sortez, sortez tous! Nous devons rester seuls.
ORTENSIO et LUCENZIO. Où est ma femme?
CATERINA. Elles sont au salon en train de bavarder au coin du feu.
(*Tous sortent sauf PETRUCCIO et CATERINA*)
PETRUCCIO. Et maintenant, viens au lit, Catie.
CATERINA (et Le PAGE du prologue). Encore?
PETRUCCIO. Comment encore?
CATERINA. Ne vous souvenez-vous pas qu'un serviteur nous a surpris dans le lit de Lucenzio? Le vin vous a-t-il déjà fait tout oublier? Ne me disiez-vous pas que jamais vous n'aviez vécu un tel enivrement? Vous m'avez donc menti!
PETRUCCIO. Je me souviens maintenant... du lit à baldaquin, des draps soyeux, du serviteur stupéfait...
CATERINA. De tout, sauf de moi.
PETRUCCIO. De toi aussi, Catie. C'est parce que je me souviens de ces moments d'extrême volupté que je veux y retourner.
CATERINA. Vous mentez encore! Comment osez-vous penser que j'aie pu aller au lit avec un menteur, un emporté, un tyran...?
PETRUCCIO (*légèrement moqueur*): Toi, tu n'es pas tyrannique: tu ne fais que t'affirmer; tu ne t'emportes pas: tu donnes libre cours à ta spontanéité; et si tu cries, c'est à cause de ma surdité. (*affectueux*) Cesse de mentir Catie, et viens au lit avec moi.
CATERINA et le PAGE. Lorsque vous serez devenu aussi doux qu'un agneau. Pas avant.
PETRUCCIO (*redevient SLY*). Ne le suis-je pas aussi peu que toi?
CATERINA et le PAGE. Quittons cette ville. Retournons à la campagne.
PETRUCCIO-SLY. Tous les chemins sont pleins de boue.
Le PAGE. Sauf les sentiers interdits.
PETRUCCIO-SLY. Les chevaux sont fourbus.
CATERINA. Nous irons à pied.
PETRUCCIO-SLY. Il ne reste qu'un seul serviteur.
Le PAGE. Nous remercierons celui-là aussi. Venez. (*courte pause*) Qu'il est resplendissant le soleil!
PETRUCCIO-SLY. Mais il sera bientôt minuit!
CATERINA. Peut-on vivre toute une vie à deux, si on ne voit pas le soleil en pleine nuit?
(*On entendra à plusieurs reprises PETRUCCIO répéter "c'est la lune" et CATERINA répondre "c'est le soleil."*)

within the context of the attempts of two women – Martine Beaulne and Lorraine Pintal – to create a new order, insofar as one can, within the constraints of the appropriative interior spaces of a leading metro/cosmopolitan classical theatre, the theatre profession, the Montreal theatre scene, and the fraught relationship between the patriarchal canonical English text and the Québécoise (female) director.[23]

Beaulne's work as a classical director emerges less from standard North-American directorial training and tradition than from a background in *commedia*, in Japanese theatre, and in improvisation.[24] The program for *La Mégère apprivoisée*, interestingly, characterizes her working method as privileging fidelity, but here fidelity is not the traditional translator's or director's fidelity to an authoritative (masculinist) text – Shakespeare's *or* Micone's; rather it is fidelity to a theatrical "troupe" and a non-authoritarian ensemble process.[25] Beaulne is widely known as a generous director, one who respects her co-workers, and who constructs a supportive context within which others are given creative freedom. Even her selection of repertoire, according to the program, testifies to the director's "volonté de travailler en collégialité, dans l'esprit d'une troupe" (Program, 1995: 16).

Beaulne's working process, in the case of *La Mégère apprivoisée*, resulted in a production whose *mise en scène* (including a Brechtian, demonstrative acting style rooted in *commedia*) worked to establish the instability of the (theatrical) sign, by selectively deploying split focus and foregrounding, or – Brecht again – *demonstrating* performative and directorial choice. The set, designed by Claude Goyette, extended

---

[23]  At TNM this relationship is particularly fraught, not only because of the colonizing relationship between English and French within Canada, and not only because of the colonizing cultural role that Shakespeare has played in English Canada (particularly surrounding and since the founding of the Stratford Festival), but also because of the curious relationship that TNM has had with Stratford, as artistic directors such as Michael Langham have used TNM actors to play the (defeated) French in productions of *Henry V*, and as the late Jean Gascon moved from TNM to direct Molière, and eventually to serve as the first Canadian Artistic Director, at Stratford. See Chapter One.

[24]  For information about the background and training of Martine Beaulne (and Lorraine Pintal), see Beauchamp. I am grateful to Professor Beauchamp for showing me an early draft of this essay in advance of its publication.

[25]  "Martine est une femme fidèle" (Program, 1995: 16). But the fidelity is directed toward her co-workers – composers, designers, actors, and others who together constitute for her a "troupe." I recognize, of course, the public relations role of theatre programs, which nevertheless do function to frame audiences' horizons of expectation – in this case productively creating the expectation of an ensemble (democratizing?) effort. The program's account of Beaulne's way of working is confirmed, moreover, by her reputation in the world of Montreal theatre, and by Gilbert David's account of her working methods in *Le Devoir*.

the architecture of the auditorium, including its wooden facade, to create a pillared circle around a central arena, unbroken except for the musician's platform stage balcony right. Within this neo-Elizabethan architectural frame, where, in Gilbert David's phrase, "la scène de-vient... une place publique," the focus was strong on the centre of the arena, but that centre was configured as a social, performative space – a *platea*, in Robert Wiemann's politicized sense[26] – with a centrifugal pull outwards, as the ensemble (including the omnipresent musician) watched and reacted from the balcony and the peripheries as the audience did.

The set provided, then, a strong central point of focus, but eschewed depth perspective (even as the acting style eschewed psychological depth). The centre of focus was often multiplied, moreover, and complicated by blocking patterns that pulled against it, naturalizing the peripheries: because the circle's centre was configured as performative, the peripheries seemed to be more naturalistic, in the way that in *Hamlet* blank verse can be heard as natural speech in the wake of what is often considered to be the relatively archaic or artificial verse of the players. In a sense, then, the peripheral areas claimed a complicating kind of off-centre focus and agency. Beaulne also frequently made use of split focus (usually between Caterina and Petruccio), and staged byplay at the peripheries that pulled (and problematized) focus, providing commentary on the (universal) centrality of any action when seen from the points of view of the servants and women that the source text pushes to the edges. Early in 5.1, the (drunken) revelry of the men's sports, for example, was effectively upstaged by Caterina's stage-right hailing of a serving man, diagonally across the space, and her subsequent devouring of "kates" from his tray. If there *was* a consistently recurring centre of focus achieved through blocking, particularly as the production moved towards its close, it was, unusually, Caterina, whose abrupt diagonal crosses and sweeping gestural movements most frequently drew the eye *away* from stage centre, except in the final scene, when she purposefully assumed that position to deliver her performatively revisionist final speech.

This use of space and blocking to reconfigure theatrical focus was reinforced by a lighting plot that for the most part eschewed specials, that refused to establish naturalistic time schemes (refusing, for example, naturalistically to take sides in the sun/moon debates), establishing

---

[26]   See also Michel de Certeau's related discussion of "place" as a fixed site of power, (associated with the "strategies" of dominance), as opposed to "space" as "practised place" (associated with the shifting "tactics" of the disempowered), in *The Practice of Everyday Life*, 117-18.

only the performative interior of a theatre, and employing intensities and textures that reviewer Gaëtan Charlebois described as "industrial and harsh." Costumes were dominated by Caterina's strikingly bright red dress, complete with hip-pieces seemingly inspired by Elizabethan drum farthingales, on which she habitually rested her hands, elbows out, in a posture of determined self-assertion. But all of the costumes were rich and resonant, if "[ils] renvoient," in the director's words, "au caractère ludique du théâtre et, en même temps, aux incertitudes concernant l'identité réelle des êtres" (Beaulne, qtd in David, 1995).

All of this worked, like the sun/moon debate that featured so prominently in the production, to destabilize signification itself, to insist on the multiple interpretability of the theatrical sign, the multiplicity of theatrical focus, and the malleability of the text.

To return to the play's final scenes as tradapted by Micone and staged by Beaulne, it is worth noting the degree to which 4.5 and the concluding sequence of 5.1 prepared the audience, in theatrical terms, for the production's final sequence. Both scenes used general area lighting across the stage, into which Caterina moved at the opening of 4.2 to "take" the space, insisting on interrupting the journey to Padua by wresting a trunk to stage centre and ostentatiously seating herself upon it. Petruccio's entrance followed hers, and he never quite caught up: Caterina controlled the space as she did the argument, striding diagonally across its breadth while Petruccio remained in an off-centre position that configured his emotional confusion. At the end, Caterina engineered the exit by performatively proffering her arm to a Vincenzo who had been unresponsive to Petruccio.

Also interestingly, the final sequence of 5.1, after the stage had cleared, saw Petruccio and Caterina sharing the focus on either side of the stage, balanced in opposition, with Grumio between them upstage centre, before Caterina strode purposefully off left, leaving a bemused Petruccio inhabiting an awkward space stage right, conspicuously off-balance and out of place for the first time in the production.

After Petruccio's exit in pursuit of Caterina, the lights dimmed and servants entered to encircle the arena with torches for the final scene, closing down the space to that of a domestic interior and obscuring the extreme left and right (though not centre) balcony. Kate entered conspicuously from up centre with the others, but was made prominent by her red dress and her belligerent, arms-crossed stance. The early stages of the scene established two simultaneous *ways* of achieving focus: eye-catching movement, through the boisterous and ribald laughter of the drunken men, and a stillness on the part of the three women which competed equally for the eyes and attention of the audience. As the scene proceeded, the women found themselves thrust forward to stage centre, objects of the gaze of an encircling on- and offstage audience. In the wake of the men's "vas-y Catie!" and "Vas-y, ma femme," the women refused to fight for the sport of their consorts. Caterina responded to Bianca's resistance with Micone's invented "Bianca a raison. Partons madame," as she took the widow's arm (here played by the male actor who also played the Page in the framing scenes) to march off upstage centre accompanied by the disappointed groans of the men.

It was this same centre-stage space, where the three women had found themselves on display, that Caterina reclaimed at her re-entrance and in her revisionist/feminist speech. She was again, of course, encircled by an audience configured male, but on her own terms now. The lights did pick her out, powerfully, but they also and equally pulled focus to the centre balcony above and behind her, where Bianca conspicuously watched and listened to her speech, leaning casually on a pillar. Once again, Beaulne and her lighting designer, Michel Beaulieu, had created two *kinds* of focus for two kinds – genders – of audience, resisting any homogenizing "rightness" of viewpoint.

What followed effectively and retroactively destabilized any confident understanding to which we might have come about what we had seen. In the wake of Caterina's speech, she and Petruccio did kiss, passionately, for the first time in the play, establishing what felt like the satisfying narrative closure of conventional heteromance. On Petruccio's line, "et maintenant, viens au lit, Catie," however, Caterina abruptly broke from him (in a resistant circular sweep that, accompanied by a stage-right cross, recurred as a gesture throughout), and spoke a challenging "encore?" in unison with the Page of the Prologue, who had entered up centre dressed identically to Caterina, and who moved to stage left to mirror her position. The rest of the scene, as Petruccio devolved into a disoriented Christopher Sly, saw Caterina and the Page mirroring one another across the stage, baiting Petruccio at stage centre, and reconfiguring that position as the site, not of power (as it usually is in proscenium stagecraft), but of interrogation. After the Page's "Venez," and as s/he, Caterina, and Petruccio revisited and reverberated "c'est la lune" and "c'est le soleil" (his lunacy and her sense, still split between wor[l]ds), the cast entered, bowed to the collapsing Sly, and left the space."[27]

---

[27]   Gaëtan Charlebois, writing in *Mirror*, the city's English-language weekly, saw the ending somewhat differently, his review containing the production's radical resistance within a welcoming but somewhat stiflingly universalist embrace:

   Micone's ending... is downbeat but ultimately more engaging. You leave this production not all a-giggle and tepidly discussing the status of women. You leave

The critical reception was almost as interesting as the production itself, and for many of the same reasons. Not surprisingly, moreover, it was divided on gender lines, the Québécoise (women) reviewers for *Le Journal de Montréal* and CITÉ-FM radio alone giving the production rave reviews.[28] The critical *fraternity*, however, particularly in the French-language press, which has been consistently critical of TNM since its artistic directorship was awarded to a woman, and which has been particularly critical of women-directed productions of the classics, was unanimously outraged by what seems to have been a conflation of the production's lack of faithfulness to Shakespeare and Caterina's lack of obedience to Petruccio.[29] Establishing Shakespeare as a universal genius speaking across the centuries,[30] these reviewers

---

thinking about disguise; the play within the play, the masks, fake beards and drag worn by all, the shrew who is a strong, vivacious woman and the sweet sister who is a spoiled brat. Micone [*sic*: not Beaulne?] has made *Mégère* about identity, and that, it seems to me, is the source of the war between men and women. In changing the play so drastically, Micone has found a truer meaning for it – a meaning for our times. (1995)

My reconstruction of these scenes is based on my own viewing of the production, and on my reviewing of the TNM archival video.

28    See Montessuit and Lessard. The only woman who reviewed the play in the English press was Pat Donnelly, in *The Gazette*, who praised the production for revising "that which Stratford is hesitant to doctor in the slightest," and for being "a charming, crowd-pleasing thing, not the least bit difficult to sit through" (1995). She nevertheless also found it to be "palatably PC at the cost of poetic nuance and plot logic." There was a certain schizophrenia in this response, which emerged not least clearly in Donnelly's presumably cynical comment that, "as David Mamet proved with Oleanna, backlash is in. Gender war is hot box office."

29    The partial exception to this rule was the mixed, English-language review of Charlebois.

30    For example:

Pourquoi monter encore des pièces de cet auteur aujourd'hui? Parce que Shakespeare avait du génie. Parce que son oeuvre est un richissime et complexe composé de poésie d'une sophistication suave, d'intelligence à l'état pur mise au service de la grandeur d'âme, de sens de la dignité humaine qui confondit toutes les classes sociales sans nier les injustices dont elles étaient la source, de flirt constant avec la dimension métaphysique de l'Amour, et d'un sens déroutant du subtil, du risible, de la noblesse du sentiment, et de la beauté... des femmes. (Bélisle, 1995)

On peut avoir bien des raisons pour jouer une oeuvre de répertoire. Toutefois, une raison demeure essentielle: la conviction qu'une pièce, ayant traversé les siècles et les guerres, put encore éclairer l'existence de nos contemporains. Bien sûr, le théâtre est un art vivant. On peut adapter un classique aux réalités du jour, lui apporter une lecture actuelle. Mais cela ne doit pas aller à l'encontre de la vision de l'auteur. (Boulanger, 1995)

Finally, Marie Labrecque, in her (generally balanced) article about the "controversy" over the production, quotes a number of prominent (male) Québécois playwrights who agree that "la seule chose qui reste pareille, c'est le texte." Michel

attacked the production for lack of purity, for "ideological transvestism," for sabotage and treason, and, perhaps most interestingly, for
emasculating both Petruccio and the text.[31] After all, as Luc Boulanger
argued, "Shakespeare a écrit une comédie misogyne, machiste et
teintée de grivoiserie" (1995) and clearly it should be presented that
way. Arguments against simple (ideological) reproduction of Shakespeare's misogyny "ne sont qu'interprétations de théoriciens," and are
therefore dismissible.

Among the most interesting features of this attack, given that the
typical reviewing practice is to ignore translators or acknowledge them
only in passing, is that it was directed less at Martine Beaulne or
Lorraine Pintal than at Marco Micone. An anonymous notice in *Le
Devoir*, which lists the entire creative team assembled "pour servir
Shakespeare," goes on to lament that "*Micone* a jugé Shakespeare
maladroit et a voulu le corriger. Hélas" ("La Mégère," 1995, my
emphasis). Others attack "la gentille Mégère de monsieur Micone"
(Lévesque, 1995) with barely a mention of Pintal or Beaulne, while
still others, noting that the production "a transgressé une règle d'or: il
faut respecter la parole d'un auteur," construct a hierarchy of conspira-
tors: "Marco Micone – avec l'aval de la metteure en scène, Martine
Beaulne, et de la directrice du TNM, Lorraine Pintal – fait de Caterina
une héroïne féministe qui prône l'égalité des sexes" (Boulanger, 1995).
The strategy is a fascinating one, allowing as it does these reviewers to
avoid charges that their attacks are themselves misogynist criticisms of
Beaulne and Pintal, while at once relegating both women to service
positions in relationship to a text – now configured as Micone's – over
which they have no authority. Cumulatively the reviews deployed a
culturally hegemonic strategy of containing the potential opened up by
resistant directing and translation: they denied the possibility of a
poststructuralist, postcolonialist, or feminist theorizing of the role of
the director, allowing only for Beaulne-as-director's faithful reproduc-

---

Tremblay (himself a prominent translator as well as Québec's most respected playwright), talks of faithfulness, of the text's role in authorizing translation and production decisions, and of "le respect essentiel dû à l'auteur." He points to Micone's
rewriting of Catherine's monologue as "une grande trahison." Interestingly, as one
of the few accounts of the production or the controversy written by a woman, Labrecque's article is alone in giving its last word to Lorraine Pintal.

[31]   These are taken, respectively, from Bélisle, Boulanger, Robichaud, and Lévesque.
Pat Donnelly, in *The Gazette*, interestingly talks about the production's "taming" of
the play, while Robichaud criticises Micone's "soumission à la rectitude," by which
he means political correctness, rather than what would be a more appropriate submission to "Shakespeare." Shortly thereafter in his review, without apparent awareness of the parallel, Robichaud notes that in the source text "Caterina fait profession
du soumission à son mari" (1995).

tion of a masculinist translation-as-text; and they denied the same possibility for the role of the translator, which was itself theorized within the traditionalist discourse of translation, in which a translation is either good (faithful service), or bad (duplicitous betrayal[32]). Neither director nor translator, in this formulation, was allowed the option of a positively formulated, multi- rather than du-plicitous, productive, or poststructuralist resistance. In the process, moreover, the review discourse successfully effaced the fact that Pintal and Beaulne had provided the (originary?) opportunity for the production of the translation by commissioning and staging it. By focusing their attacks on Micone's script, the reviewers denied agency to a female director whose techniques and effects they virtually ignored.

Martine Beaulne's *La Mégère apprivoisée* was produced, and produced its meanings, through the discourses, practices, traditions, and institutional structures of a major classical theatre, employing theatre workers trained and experienced in essentially reproductive techniques and processes, performing before a theatre-going public positioned by the discourses of publicity and reviewing, as well as by their own theatre-going experience, to read classical theatre as a transparent window on the transcendent insights of great writers. Clearly its potential to function as significant disruption or resistance of the kind envisioned by the new translation theorists was limited and, to some extent, contained by these constraints. Nevertheless, the critical reception of the production, its gender and linguistic divisions, and particularly the intensity or even ferocity of the attacks of the male critics, suggest that its differences were recognized and resisted with considerable protectionist anxiety. This is particularly true in a Québec in which the prominence of theatre and theatre criticism early in the contemporary postcolonial nationalist movement has been superseded, as the *indépendance* movement is increasingly closely aligned with Québec's corporate and conservative élite. Resistance, in this context, is increasingly configured less as counterhegemonic Québec nationalism than as antihegemonic and multiple (including as it does native, feminist, and

---

[32] Barbara Godard, in a review of Lotbinière-Harwood, and George Woodcock, quote the Italian proverb, *"traduttore, traditore."* Godard calls this "a venerable adage... A gendered one," and translates it (ironically) as "to translate is to betray" (1995: 71). Woodcock, on the other hand, renders it as "translators are traitors" (1988: 72). I'm indebted to Godard's review article and the book by Lotbinière-Harwood that she is reviewing for the inception of the idea that became this paper. My discussion of translation is also indebted, in ways that are not immediately apparent, to Graham, Niranjana, Robinson, Bassnett-McGuire, Bassnett and Lefevere, Lefevere, Hermans, Homel and Simon, Brisset, and the 1989 special "Translation" issue of *Canadian Literature.*

"ethnic" – such as Italian[33]) – opposition to Québec's separation from Canada.

It is not surprising, moreover, that these critical attacks on *La Mégère* consistently represented the production as unproblematically delivering the overly simplified, but still unitary, revisionist "message" of Marco Micone rather than the disruptive "re-belles et infidèles" multiplicities of Martine Beaulne working within Lorraine Pintal's TNM to develop new, resistant, and more multiple theatrical ways of meaning. After all, it has been a time-honored strategy of those who like their translations, their classical theatre, and their women faithful, their politics right and naturalized, and their focus clear, to attack unauthorized tamperings with textual, sexual, and other authorities, accusing the opening of social and political fissures of psychological and poetic reductionism – or aesthetic incompetence because of un-clear focus. Either way you lose. But the reviews also consistently deflected attention, not only away from the female director to the male translator, and not only consistently away from the production's real textual, processual, and sexual complexities – no reviewer, for exam-ple, mentioned Petruccio's crowd-pleasing line, "les femmes serviles émoussent mon désir" (1995a: 109) – but also away from its genuinely multiplicitous experiments with promiscuous focus, towards compara-tively less significant but more easily targeted textual infidelities. These deflections, and the anxieties revealed by the vehemence with which they were articulated, suggest that Beaulne's *La Mégère* went at least some distance towards reconfiguring the role and process of the director – and reconfiguring the not/but of theatrical choice and focus – along lines theorized by resistant feminist, postcolonial, and poststruc-turalist students of translation. Perhaps it's time that the resistant theorists of directing caught up with the most sophisticated of its practitioners.

---

[33]  Micone's Italian-Canadian heritage may not be insignificant in this regard. The then-Premiere of Québec, Jaques Parizeau, in his concession speech after the 1995 referendum on separation, (in)famously blamed the narrow loss of the "yes" side on what he called "money and the ethnic vote."

# CHAPTER 4

# From Dream to Machine: Peter Brook, Robert Lepage, and the Contemporary Shakespearean Director as (Post)Modernist

This chapter considers the cultural work done by the role of the Shakespearean director, locates the discourses and practices of contemporary Shakespearean directing within the appropriative discourses and practices of high modernist formalism, and traces continuities between modernist and postmodernist manifestations of the directing of Shakespeare, focusing on Peter Brook and his 1970 production of *A Midsummer Night's Dream*, and on two Shakespearean productions by Québec's Robert Lepage. It begins with a story.

In the weeks leading up to the last referendum on Québec sovereignty (30 October 1995) there was a campaign across Canada (or "Rest of Canada," as Canada outside Québec is called) involving bumper stickers that read, in French or English, "My Canada includes Quebec." In the French version, "include" was rendered "comprend" – which of course also means "understands." The campaign was mounted by well-meaning, liberal-minded Canadians who wished to distance themselves from the anti-Québec sentiments of many Anglophone Canadians. Few among the Anglophone federalists, it seems, considered the implied positionings of one group's claims to "include" and "understand" another, particularly an "other" within the differential power relationships that obtain historically and currently within the Canadian confederation.

I tell this story not only because it locates my essay within contemporary Canada and Québec, framing an argument that culminates in a discussion of the work of a Québec director who is at the same time positioned among the internationalist avant-garde, but also in order to clarify the ways in which I understand the workings of modernist and postmodernist appropriations of various kinds of otherness. These appropriations circulate, I suggest, not merely around audience reading, as has been argued, or around a supposedly communicative and enfranchising postmodern globalism.[1] Rather they involve a number of related strategies of assimilation, of "understanding," and of inclusion: my west includes your east; my masculine includes your feminine; my high culture your mass culture; my psychological and individualist your social; my capital your labor; my civilization your primitivism; my imperial centre your colonial margin; my modern your Early Modern. Ultimately, my formalist, inscrutable, unchanging work of art includes – *comprend* – your messy, fluid, corporal, feminized, social, and otherwise threatening life: my shaping understanding kills you into art.[2]

And that art involves a particularly modernist form of closure, in which form is not considered to be a social or public forum, but a structuralist end in itself. It is not accidental that Russian formalism developed in the context of constructivism in the arts, or that structuralist criticism, including the Canadian variety best represented by Northrop Frye, developed within the (internationalist) context of modernist movements in the visual arts, fiction, poetry, and criticism (notably, here, the poetry and criticism of T. S. Eliot[3]).

For the high modernist artist and critic art is non-referential, functioning within its own separate realm and satisfying internal standards of clarity, integrity and autonomy. Frye has famously asserted, of course, that Shakespeare, as transhistorical and transcultural exemplar of the artist, "has no values, no philosophy, no principles of anything except dramatic form" (1965: 39). The modernist work of art, then, exists and must be read as a product, a kind of "in-itself," that creates a realm of experience either indifferent to life, or a substitute for it, but in either case self-contained and, by external standards, inscrutable.

---

[1]   For the former, see Erika Fisher-Lichte, "Staging the Foreign as Cultural Transformation;" for the latter see the introduction, and the introductions to various sections of Patrice Pavis, ed., *The Intercultural Performance Reader*; and Brian Singleton's guest editor's introduction, "The Pursuit of Otherness for the Investigation of Self," in *Theatre Research International*'s special issue on "Theatre and Interculturalism." "Intercultural" appropriation, which I will discuss below, is often defended in theatre and performance criticism as cultural exchange by critics who ignore power differentials and compare, for example, Peter Brook's *Mahabharata* with a production in India of *Peer Gynt* by Brook's critic and "other," Rustum Bharucha (see *Theatre and the World*) – ignoring the fact that India is not now nor has ever been in a colonizing relationship with Norwegian culture. See Maria Shevstova, "Interculturalism, Aestheticism, Orientalism: Starting from Peter Brook's *Mahabharata*."

[2]   The phrase "killing into art" was brought into circulation by Sandra M. Gilbert and Susan Gubar, *The Madwoman in the Attic: The Woman Writer and the Nineteenth-Century Literary Imagination*.

[3]   I am thinking, in particular, of the Eliot of "Tradition and the Individual Talent" in *The Sacred Wood* (47-59); of *Elizabethan Essays* and *Elizabethan Dramatists*; and of "The Wasteland." I am thinking, that is, primarily of the Eliot of the 1920s.

The modernist *artist*, in turn, is constructed as visionary individual who creates by imposing the coherence of form on the chaos of recalcitrant, "unruly" existence, producing bright, jewel-like kernels of inscrutable truth from the garbage heap of the natural, threatening, uncivilized, collective, and feminine world. In this formulation the modernist struggles to achieve and maintain oedipal resolutions that are *constitutive* of unified dramatic form (not to mention masculinity) by containing the threat, sweat, subjectivity and du- or multi-plicities of a slippery pre- or a-symbolic "other," typically gendered female, or an unruly and disruptively upstart mob, within the unchanging realm of pure (spatial, and therefore timeless) form.[4] But, as Leonard Cohen reminds us, "there is a crack in everything" (1993: 373) – or in Terry Eagleton's version, "the body can never be fully present in discourse" (1986: 97) – including, I suggest the embodied discourses of the theatre. And there, for the modernist, is the rub. If, as Lacan claimed, the symbol is the death of the thing, then the living, leaking, and sweating bodily "thing," corporal and social, is the dis-ease that threatens the symbol(ic).

In terms of the cultural work it performs, the retreat from application and social reference – together with the retreat from theatre as *collaborative* work, in the social and historical realms, into the individualist/universalist realm of the director as *auteur* and controlling consciousness – can be seen as a retreat from artistic responsibility into the realm of "pure" aesthetics, where the work is potentially dehumanized and left open to appropriation by other ideologies of purity and social control, including, in their extreme form, fascism.[5] In this sense,

---

[4]   In *Culture and Society* in 1958 Raymond Williams provided a useful analysis of Eliot's *The Idea of a Christian Society* and *Notes Towards the Definition of Culture*, including Eliot's anxieties about the ways in which "industrialism, when it is unregulated, tends to create not a society but a mob." Eliot's answer to the problem is vaguely to propose kind of privileged, "patronage" class to protect "the best that is made and written" (Williams, 1958/1990: 229-30).

[5]   There has been, of course, considerable interest in the complicity between modernist artists and fascism in the Europe of the 1930s and 40s, most notably Frederic Jameson, *Fables of Aggression: Wyndham Lewis, the Modernist as Fascist* and Frank Kermode, *The Sense of an Ending* (93-124). Kermode notes the links between modernist formal and aesthetic closure and "the formal elegance of fascism" (1967: 114), and between "the spatial order of the modern critic [and] the closed authoritarian society" (111). I am also indebted to the essays in Malcolm Bradbury and James McFarlane, ed., *Modernism, 1890-1930* and to Astrudur Eysteinsson, *The Concept of Modernism.* Raymond Williams, in *The Politics of Modernism: Against the New Conformists* provides a careful historical account of modernism that traces the loss of "its anti-bourgeois stance" and its "comfortable integration into the new international capitalism," culminating in a discussion of advertising as modernism's final form (1989: 35). In Canada, the subject has been most power-

the modernist artist, including the director of Shakespeare, can be seen to be doing cultural work potentially complicit with the politics of nationalism, industrial capitalism, colonialism, and culturally appropriative western orientalisms.

*** 

The emergence of directing as an independent function in theatre in the late 19th and early 20th centuries coincides, not accidentally, with the consolidation of the nation state and of industrial capitalism, as well as with the birth of various forms of modernism in the arts. Its discourses and practices remain, for the most part, under-theorized, and their ideological implications uninterrogated. Indeed, theories of directing are still for the most part embedded in directors notes, interviews, prescriptive textbooks on method, and academic studies of the work of individual directors, where they continue to naturalize the early tendency of directors to draw, as Richard Schechner notes, "on the tradition of [biblical] exegesis" in constructing their role as priestly interpreter, mediator between the authority of the Author/God and actor/human, explaining, guiding, judging, forgiving, and leading the company towards its "discoveries" (of pre-existing meanings) (1994: 237). The trope of the director as exegete, I suggest, has worked together with anxieties about the gendering of the interpretative, or "service" function of the director as feminine, and together with the professional/managerial functioning of the (individual) director in relation to actors-as-workers in the capitalist entertainment industry (not to mention anxieties about theatre as a collective enterprise within an individualist/ownership economy), to support the cultivation of a cult of the director as guiding genius, *auteur*, and source.[6]

It is perhaps worth looking briefly, then, at the discourses of directing (and Shakespeare is always at the centre of these discourses), as represented by such books as *Directors on Directing* (1963) and its 1996 successor, *In Contact with the Gods? Directors Talk Theatre* (which takes its title from its interview with Robert Lepage), in the context of high-modernist critical strategies, in order to contextualize the discourses and practices of Brook, Lepage, and their modernist and

---

fully explored by Timothy Findley in his novel *Famous Last Words*, by playwright John Krizanc in his environmental-theatre hit, *Tamara*, and by Margaret Hollingsworth in her provocative one-act play, "Poppycock."

[6]    See Chapter Three. An interesting gloss on directorial anxiety about theatre as a collective enterprise is provided by Iris L. Smith in an article on "The 'Intercultural' Work of Lee Breuer" (46). Smith notes that Breuer's anxiety about collective identity effacing individual identities within "his" theatre company, Mabou Mines, led to his own sense of "vanishing." "This anxiety," she says, "has haunted all his work."

postmodernist contemporaries. In "The Emergence of the Director," the introductory essay to *Directors on Directing*, Helen Krich Chinoy, without mentioning modernism as such (and therefore naturalizing, or mystifying the relationship), traces the ways in which what she calls

the animators of the modern theatre – Antoine, Stanislavsky, Appia, Craig, Reinhardt, Meyerhold, Copeau – [...] insisted that if theater was to retrieve its unique, primitive, communal power, a director would have to impose a point of view that would integrate play, production, and spectators. By his interpretation a director would weld a harmonious art and a cohesive audience out of the disturbing diversity increasingly apparent in our urban, industrial, mass society. By his multifarious activities the director would restore the artistic and social unity that has always been the central demand of the collective art of theater. (1963: 3-4)

Given that it was not Chinoy's intention to do so, this passage articulates with remarkable clarity many of the central features of the modernist project, particularly modernist angst about urban industrial alienation and mass culture,[7] and about the potentially disturbing diversity and slipperiness of an essentially collaborative art form – together with the resolution of this angst through appropriative artistic visions of renewal, harmony, and unity through the shoring up of cultural fragments against "our" ruin. It also articulates the role of the director as artist/*auteur*, the individual creator who must be responsible for work in any genuine (that is, "pure" and therefore also individualist) art form as it achieves its "ideal condition" (Chinoy, 1963: 14).[8]

The achievement of this ideal condition, throughout Chinoy's introduction and much of the book itself, is imagined as arriving through such things as "rediscovering the [essential] wellsprings of theatre" (Chinoy, 1963, 39). The director, Chinoy says (in a number of hauntingly precise anticipations of the Peter Brook of *The Empty Space* that are scattered throughout her essay), who "must capture the spirit of the primitive unity of drama" (46), is constructed as "visionary" (42) and "creative genius" (54) who through an "exacting sense of form" (53) "distils" "the impalpable essence of things" in a theatre understood as existing "almost in the domain of religion" (69). And as Jacques Copeau constructs it, the "creative director is the god of this religion:"

---

[7]   As Michael Bristol points out, "high modernism was a form of resistance to the encroachment of a commercial mass culture of pulp fiction, film, and recorded music" (1996: 89).

[8]   Steven Connor, in "Postmodern Performance," provides a useful summary of high modernism's posited ideal, "an art committed absolutely to the realization of its own principles" – "a condition of absorption, of autonomy, or self-sufficiency which is threatened or diffused by any awareness of the contexts of its reception, or other form of impurity" (1996: 111-12).

"It is I who will absorb it, who will direct it, who will clarify it and who will transmit it to you little by little, all fresh, all new, pell-mell with the personal godsend of my unpublished science. No substitution. A creation. Life" (quoted in Chinoy, 1963: 46). Chinoy concludes her introduction, quoting from an early manifesto of the Group Theater, by describing the director as "a single creative force" whose formalist job it is to "organize the conditions necessary for "theatre in its truest form" (77).

Since the 1960s, when the second edition of *Directors on Directing* appeared, the director's role has established itself even more clearly along these fundamentally modernist lines, evincing many of the most basic characteristics of the modernist artist, and relying, in theory as in practice, on the director's relationship with the classics, and in particular with Shakespeare and the Elizabethans, for the necessary establishment of credentials. In the introduction to *In Contact with the Gods?*, editors Maria M. Delgado and Paul Heritage attempt to explain what they call "the continuing fascination with Shakespeare for modern directors eager to prove their value (and power) in the contemporary theatrical market:"

> It is hardly surprising that texts which emerged from the fiercely competitive Elizabethan theatre industry should attract directors today. The potent mix of nascent capitalism and monarchical government that characterized the time in which Shakespeare's plays were first performed certainly finds echoes in many of the societies that are performing them today. (1996: 7)

Such echoes are precisely those which most of the directors interviewed in the book – indeed most contemporary directors of Shakespeare – have sought to achieve in their productions. It is interesting that this deployment of the Elizabethans is remarkably like that of Eliot as modernist critic, for whom Shakespeare and his contemporaries were both, in Richard Halpern's phrase, "native informants"[9] from a

---

9  For Eliot as for other modernist artists, as Halpern notes, "the 'primitive' was an aboriginal, timeless realm reproduced or represented through the apparently transparent medium of ethnography, and available for comparison with, or enrichment of, European culture," and Shakespeare in this model "occupies a kind of third position, at once conduit and datum of historical information," a native informant, translator, and guide who mediates the process of colonialist ethnography. See Halpern on "Shakespeare as Native Informant" in his *Shakespeare Among the Moderns*, 42-50. Directing has often similarly been constructed ethnographically, particularly in the theatre anthropology of Richard Schechner and Eugenio Barba. Barba is quoted by Shomit Mitter, in a discussion of Jerzy Grotowski's influence on Peter Brook in *Systems of Rehearsal: Stanislavsky, Brecht, Grotowski and Brook*, as linking gendered, primitivist, and imperialist discourses in a comparison of the former's work to "an anthropological expedition. It goes beyond civilized territories into virgin forest" (Mitter, 1992: 105).

primitive past, and at the same time sources of historical information and cultural authority.

For the Eliot of "Tradition and the Individual Talent," the modernist poet is a kind of medium in which "not only the best, but the most individual parts" of his [*sic*] own work are "those in which the dead poets, his ancestors, assert their immortality most vigorously" (1960: 48). The theatre – particularly the traditions and practices of directing Shakespeare – may be the last outpost of this position, in which theatrical traditions and the directorial practices of one's predecessors are notoriously grist for the individualist mill of the contemporary director-as-*auteur*. Eliot combines with his views on tradition and the individual talent, of course, an understanding of Early Modern English culture as itself somehow essentially modern, an historically allegorical understanding, as Halpern says, "which allowed him to read in that period's 'anarchism, dissolution, and decay' a reflection of his own times" (1997: 44),[10] and one which connects him closely with the currently dominant and culturally affirmative school of Shakespearean directing that Alan Sinfield has called "Shakespeare-plus-relevance" (1985: 176).

I would suggest, then, that the complicated relationship between Shakespeare and the modernist artist and critic as represented by Eliot continues to apply with considerable precision to the relationship between "Shakespeare" and contemporary Shakespearean directors, who tend to function, and to position themselves, as mediums and artists both of pastiche and of unity, shoring up fragments of culture against our modern ruin by rendering them coherent, unified, and therefore manageable; who regard Early Modern culture as at once usefully primitive and essentially modern, its anarchy and dissolution reflecting our own time and serving us as valuable metaphoric ground for the resolution of our own anxieties; and who play the role of colonialist ethnographers in relation to the primitive Elizabethan age as well as other "othered" cultures, constructing Shakespeare very much as "third-position" cultural translator and native informant about our "primitive," essential selves.

The canonical catalogue of contemporary Shakespearean directors, of course, extends from Brook through figures such as, for example, Ariane Mnouchkine, Giorgio Strehler, and Peter Stein, and it draws upon a variety of theatrical and cultural forms. In Mnouchkine's case these range from Meyerhold's biomechanics to Japanese cinema, employing Indian imagery, Japanese iconography, and Chinese ritual forms in what is frequently called a "pervasive orientalism" that treats

---

[10]   Halpern is quoting from Eliot, *Elizabethan Essays*, 18.

Asiatic forms and Shakespeare alike, together with certain "carnivalesque popular forms," as both primitive and exotic fodder – constructed as "mysterious" – for productions of Shakespeare that in their formalist ahistoricism are archetypally modernist.[11] Giorgio Strehler and Peter Stein are also positioned as masters of the European modernist avant garde, *auteurs* whose individualist geniuses contain and curtail the fragmentation, vulgarity, and decline that are variously associated with the popular, the collective, the foreign, or the feminine. Strehler, for example, shares with Eliot and other high modernists a profound anxiety about contemporary mass culture – he is said by the editors of *In Contact with the Gods?* to have "pitched the length and profundity of this classic of European humanistic literature [in this instance Goethe's *Faust*] against what he sees as the deplorable wasteland of contemporary mass-media culture" (Delgado and Heritage, 1996: 263).[12] And Peter Stein similarly voices a typically modernist nostalgia for primitive communal unities in asserting the importance for directors of remembering that "the director came into the business of theatre at a time of and as a sign of decline" (Delgado and Heritage, 1996: 253).

But the tradition that I am tracing is nowhere more powerful than in England, where echoes of both Eliot and Brook are pervasive still in the contemporary discourses of Shakespearean directing, particularly at the Royal Shakespeare Company. As Christopher J. McCullough and Alan Sinfield have demonstrated, the so-called political radicalism of the RSC in the 1970s and 80s masked a fundamentally conservative, *metaphoric* modernism that can be traced from the company's Cambridge connections – Leavis and the like – directly to Eliot (McCullough, 1988; Sinfield, 1985).[13] But even in a young and

---

[11]   See "Ariane Mnouchkine," Delgado and Heritage, 175-190, particularly Delgado and Heritage's introduction to Mnouchkine, 176-78, where they refer to her having "drawn on numerous ritualistic traditions and carnivalesque popular forms" (1996: 176), compare her "pervasive orientalism" with that of Peter Brook's *Mahabharata* (178), and point out the range of sources I have cited here. They provide a selection from "critics on her work," where the variety of Asian theatre forms upon which she draws is cited and the common comparison with Brook is reiterated, and they quote Mnouchkine's own comment that "Shakespeare's such a mystery" (180).

[12]   See also the editors' quotation from Michael Coveny, "An Island Free from Arnie's Grip:" "[Strehler's work] represents the humanitarian, humanist strain in the European enlightenment and culture, and it defies absolutely the local critical trend, which defines art as Schwarzenegger and TV sitcom" (1996: 264).

[13]   Again, Iris Smith on Lee Breuer is helpful here in identifying the metaphoric approach as appropriative and "unabashedly totalizing" (1997: 44). Smith cites Peggy Phelan, who points out in *Unmarked: The Politics of Performance* that "metaphor works to secure a vertical hierarchy of value and is reproductive; it works by erasing dissimilarity and negating difference; it turns two into one" (1993: 150).

"experimental" director such as Declan Donnellan, of London's Cheek by Jowl Theatre, the discourses of high modernist formalism in combination with colonizing brands of essentialist humanism are deep-seated. Thus within the context of a search for "the essence of theatre" as a form, "the absolute essential of the theatrical experience" – one that involves Brook-like "paring down to essentials" that are at once pure theatrical form and universal common humanity – Donnellan can assert that "it's the superficial things that tend to change from country to country; the essence stays the same."[14]

Donnellan here might be quoting Brook's well-known position that "Each culture expresses a different portion of the inner atlas: the complete human truth is global and the theatre is the place in which the jigsaw can be pieced together" (Brook, 1989: 129). (Brook crucially fails to address the problematics of who does the piecing together, and from what position). As a director, Brook typically deploys "pastiche as a medium of wholeness," believing that "the purpose of theatre is... making an event in which a group of fragments are suddenly brought together... At certain moments this fragmented world comes together and for a certain time it can rediscover the marvel of organic life. The marvel of being one" (Mitter, 1992: 139; Brook, quoted in Mitter, 1992: 78).[15]

---

One of the ways in which this functions, I suggest, is as an essentially metaphoric construction of directing itself that is related to its contemporary roots in Stanislavski, and in particular his concept of the "magic if," which, as Mitter notes, "by denying the claims of actuality... denies it grounds on which to disturb the still waters of imagined truths" (1992: 8). This, together with "the ability of the 'if' to rid the imagination of the claims to actuality" is analogous to Frye's modernist attempt to remove literature from the realm of representation. As Mitter notes, in a passage that resonates with Frye on many levels, "the impulse to realism in Stanislavski... seems not entirely to have been based on a desire to imitate reality. Rather, it seems to be borne of an overwhelming urge to *engender* nature, to *beget* an order of reality which we cannot possess in life, a reality which we desire precisely because it is 'other'." "The subject," Mitter says, "is not life but its transcendence" (1992: 9-10).

[14] I am quoting from "Declan Donnellan and Nick Ormerod," interviewed together in Delgado and Heritage, 79-92. References to "the essence of theatre" and "paring down to the essentials" are pervasive, but are cited here from Ormerod's contribution to the conversation, 86; "the absolute essential of the theatrical experience" is from the editors' introduction to the interview, 80; and the final quotation is from Donnellan, 84.

[15] In a suggestive observation that once again resonates with Frye's modernist structuralism, Mitter elsewhere describes Brook's work as providing "an alternative system of ethics in which 'good' and 'bad' are replaced by 'whole' and 'incomplete'" (1992: 111). In other words, Brook, like Frye, replaces ethics in art with a parallel system of *form*.

Brook, in turn, might here be quoting Eliot, as elsewhere he exemplifies Eliot's arguments in "Tradition and the Individual Talent" in operating as what Shomit Mitter, in his book *Systems of Rehearsal*, calls "an admirably astute assimilator, a singularly canny user of other people's ideas and techniques" (1992: 3). Finally, Brook's work in making Shakespeare our "contemporary"[16] – treating Shakespeare as raw material in much the way he treats mass or "other" cultural forms (and in much the way the logging industry treats trees) – exemplifies what Halpern calls "Eliot's allegorical mode of reading [which] allowed the past to be reconfigured in conformity with current needs and preoccupations" (1997: 3). Indeed, Brook's concluding chapter to *The Empty Space*, and in particular his advocacy of theatre as "representation" ("when something is re-*present*ed," with an emphasis on the "present" and which activity Brook argues "denies time"), may usefully be understood as a theatrical application of Eliot, who argued that reading and understanding the Elizabethans "does not so much require the power of putting ourselves into 17th-century London as it requires the power of setting Jonson in our London," or, in Halpern's suggestive phrase again, using "Shakespeare as native informant" (Brook, 1972: 155; Eliot, 1964: 67; Halpern, 1997: 42).

*** 

Brook's 1970 production of *Midsummer Night's Dream* is perhaps canonically iconic of modernist Shakespearean production, much as Beckett's *Waiting for Godot* is canonically iconic of modernist dramaturgy – and of course Brook famously invoked Beckett, by way of Jan Kott, in his 1962 production of *King Lear*. Indeed, Brook's description of the self-contained "central images," the "kernel[s] engraved on [the] memory" by Beckett's works might equally apply to the imagistic residue of his own white-box *Dream*, with its actors on trapezes and its clown-nosed Bottom in Titania's bower. "Beckett's plays are symbols," Brook writes, "in the exact sense of the word" (1972: 152):

> [A] true symbol [he says] is *hard* and *clear*. [...]The two men waiting by a stunted tree, the man recording himself on tape, the two men marooned in a tower [...]: these are pure inventions [...] and *they stand on the stage as objects. [...] We get nowhere if we expect to be told what they mean.* (1972: 64-65, my emphases)

Brook's *Dream* also shares with Beckett's drama, of course, a peculiarly modernist deployment of popular culture forms, notably drawn

---

16  For Jan Kott's influence on Brook see, for example, J.L. Styan, *The Shakespeare Revolution*, 231. See also Brook's tribute to Kott, "It Happened in Poland," in *The Shifting Point*, 43-45.

from circus and vaudeville, as well as an "icily but fatally beautiful" orientalism, that, as Barbara Hodgdon has noted, anticipates Brook's later "intercultural" work (1996: 84, 83).[17]

The formal coherence of Brook's *Dream* in fact exemplifies the ways in which modernist formalism can conspire with industrial capitalism in its self-construction as *product*, and it is not accidental that the production has been discussed as a "technically brilliant" "director-shaped *commodity*" (Styan, 1977: 230, my emphases).[18] Finally, Brook's *Dream*, for all his focus on actors' physicality and the freeing of bodily responses *en route* to transcultural understanding, participated in a tradition that ranges from Meyerhold's "biomechanics" and Craig's "*ubermarionettes*" through to Robert Wilson's manipulation of his actors as puppets, as part of a proliferation of Hamlet- and other machines, to which I will return: John Russell Brown described Brook's white box as "a machine for acting in," to which J.L. Styan added, "the actors acting in it were the visible puppets of the machine" (1977: 225).

***

To turn from Brook's *Dream* to the work of Lepage is to turn from modernist Shakespeare to the theatre of the post-industrial, post-national age; from a concentration on the body to the realm of technology; and from the imperial centre to the colonial margins. Indeed, Shakespeare is native informant for Lepage, as a Québecker, in a rather different sense than for Brook, and at first glance it would seem that Lepage's 1992 *Dream* at the National Theatre in London was quite literally throwing postmodern mud all over Brook's pristinely modernist white box, together with Shakespeare and the entire British theatrical tradition. And as Barbara Hodgdon has demonstrated, it was widely received in precisely this way: British reviewers were appalled by the production's mud-bath set and its appropriations, by colonials, of the King's English and Shakespeare's verse. It is possible, then, to see Lepage as a Québecker "talking back," within the walls of the British National theatre itself, to the imperial Centre. But as Hodgdon has also shown, in an essay suggestively subtitled "Robert Lepage's Intercultural *Dream* Machine," Lepage can also be seen to have taken the *Dream* "in a direction Brook had mapped out" (Hodgdon, 1996: 84).

---

[17]    "Icily but fatally beautiful" Hodgdon is quoting from Patrice Pavis (1992: 211). The most sustained critique of Brook's later work, as represented by *Mahabharata*, is in Bharucha. See also David Williams, ed., *Peter Brook and the Mahabharata: Critical Perspectives*; Gautam Dasgupta, "*The Mahabharata*: Peter Brook's 'Orientalism';" and, for a different perspective, Maria Shevstova (1997: 98-101).

[18]    Styan is quoting David Selbourne, in *Culture and Agitation* (13-28).

It is perhaps worth pausing briefly to notice some of the continuities and distinctions between the two productions, most notably, among
the continuities, the crisp, inscrutable, and totalizing symbols, worthy
of Beckett. Indeed, Lepage is an imagist in the best modernist tradition,
and his *Dream*, like his other works, leaves after-images as sharp as
does Brook's or as do the Beckett plays Brook cites: Angela Laurier's
Puck scuttling crab-like across the stage, or attached to Bottom's back
like a growth, her feet his ass's ears; Sally Dexter's bat-like and (literally) ravishing Titania; the mud, pool, and light-bulb set itself. Lepage
followed Brook, too, in his Kottian treatment of sexuality, and in his
now conventional rejections of the Mendelssohn-and-muslin staging
traditions of the play.

Lepage's *Dream* is also and perhaps most clearly continuous with
Brook's, however, in its appropriations of popular culture and "eastern" – in this case primarily Indonesian – theatrical and cultural traditions, and with the later Brook in its "multicultural" casting and its
determined but unlocalized and ahistorical selective interculturalism.[19]
In fact, as Hodgdon says, Lepage's "multicultural" production "seemed
the theatrical equivalent of... *The Wasteland* – a modernist otherness-
machine for essentializing cultures" (Hodgdon, 1996: 83-85).[20]

Where Lepage's production *differed* from Brook's most significantly, I think – and this may account for some of the quality of the
reviewers' responses that Hodgdon's article surveys – is that it was
messier in more than the obvious ways, and in particular that, in contrast to Brook's ethereal and adept display of virtuosity in circus tricks
and verse speaking alike, its efforts showed: critics policing traditionally British modernist aesthetic standards, explicitly invoking Brook's
*Dream*, complained of physical grotesqueries, of actors' difficulties
with language, of movement and imagery upstaging text, of frustrated
linear narratives and rational logics, and above all, again, of cultural
sacrilege, as England's National poet was mud-spattered at its National

---

[19]    Hodgdon provides a catalogue of Indonesian cultural factors that "trouble Lepage's
       'orientalism' (if it can be called that), [and] expose the contradictions in his desire
       to adopt a culture's mythology but without its attendant historical materiality, turn-
       ing it into an abstraction which can be evoked in the name of transcultural unifica-
       tion and universal harmony" (83). Hodgdon's comments on Lepage's use of Indo-
       nesia echo Una Chaudhuri's critique of Brook's *Mahabharata* in "The Future of the
       Hyphen: Interculturalism, Textuality, and the Difference Within," as a collusion
       with cultural imperialism "in which the West helps itself to the forms and images of
       other without taking the full measure of the cultural fabric from which these are
       torn" (Chaudhuri, 1991: 193).

[20]    Hodgdon credits Sarah Suleri, *Meatless Days*, and Kwame Anthony Appiah, *In My
       Father's House: Africa in the Philosophy of Culture* for the coinage of "otherness
       machine."

Theatre, and Olivier parodied on the stage that bears his name.[21] Indeed, it may be that the productively interventionist work performed by the Lepage *Dream* was the thoroughly site-specific deconstruction of the remaining high-cultural traces of post-imperial British nationalism – a role that Lepage's work has arguably played in comparable ways at national theatres in Ottawa and Stockholm.

But in spite of reviewers' anxieties it is doubtful that the cultural work performed by his *Dream* was a resistant "talking back" in any larger sense. It may, in fact, be possible to read the production less as a postcolonial rupture with modernism, or even as the playing out of Lepage's anxieties of influence, than as a playing out of anxieties that are *continuous* with those of Brook, multiplied and complicated in a post-modern world of late capitalism that, according to Philip Auslander, began in the 1970s (1994: 5-8)[22] – the decade ushered in by Brook's *Dream*.

***

But the *Dream* does not appear to be Lepage's play of choice. He has tended, when directing Shakespeare, to work, usually in translation or "tradaptation," on such problematic plays as *Macbeth*, *Coriolanus*, the postcolonial *Tempest*,[23] or, most obsessively and appropriatively, *Hamlet*, Shakespeare's most famously imperfect play and the one that troubled Eliot so deeply (Eliot, 1960: 95-103). It is not surprising that the archetypal modernist production of Shakespeare was of the *Dream*, traditionally understood to be Shakespeare's most perfectly structured play,[24] or that for Lepage, as for many other postmodern directors, *Hamlet* is the play of choice.

To move from the *Dream* to *Hamlet* can be seen as a move from the obsessions of modernism and its achievements of Oedipal resolution to the anxieties of postmodernism and its never fully successful struggle to *maintain* those resolutions. In an essay on Eliot's reading of *Hamlet*, Jacqueline Rose argues that critical and creative demands for integrity – or structural "perfection" – "merely repeat that moment of repression when language and sexuality were first ordered into place, putting

---

21 See Hodgdon, 1996: 76-79.

22 It is perhaps more accurate to say the Auslander locates postmodernism as a "post-1960s" phenomenon.

23 For a valuable discussion of Lepage's productions of *Coriolanus*, *Macbeth*, and *The Tempest* in Michel Garneau's "tradaptations" (a discussion that includes consideration of the implications of "tradaptation"), see Denis Salter, "Between Wor(l)ds: Lepage's Shakespeare Cycle."

24 Brook himself indicates that the *Dream* "seemed to me to be a perfect play. [...] I don't think you can change a word without losing something" (1989: 38).

down the unconscious processes which threaten the resolution of the
Oedipal drama and of narrative [or dramatic] form [...]." (1985: 102).
In such work, then, particularly when grappling with the perceived
imperfections of a text such as *Hamlet*, the Oedipal drama, agonizingly
for the modernist, can never be fully resolved. It is perhaps significant
that Lepage's productions are always presented as works-in-progress,
always changing, never satisfyingly complete, fixed, or finished.[25]
    Lepage's obsession with *Hamlet* is long-standing, and it interest-
ingly exceeds the boundaries of his own work as auteur or director, as
it exceeds his work on *Hamlet* itself (and as *Hamlet* itself may be
considered, as it was by Eliot, to be excessive). In Denys Arcand's
1989 film, *Jesus of Montreal*, Lepage plays René, the character who, in
a Québec theatre in-joke that relies on the viewer recognizing Lepage
in the role, at first refuses to take part in the staging of the pageant
around which the film revolves because it is to be based on a collec-
tively-written script: "I like being able to read the text before deciding.
That's why I don't work very much" (quoted in Arcand, 1992: 357).[26]
Later, however, he returns and asks if it would be possible for him to
deliver Hamlet's "to be or not to be" soliloquy as part of the play,
which he ultimately and incongruously does.
    It doesn't end there. In each of the three extant versions of *Poly-
graph*, which Lepage co-wrote with Marie Brassard, and which might
best, if inadequately, be described as an extended theatrical meditation,
in the form of a postmodern murder mystery, on the instability of truth,
one character or another delivers the same soliloquy, in French – and in
one version at least holding an iconic skull.[27] It is arguable, too, that

---

[25]   Lepage has employed variations on the "RSVP" cycles that he developed with
      Jaques Lessard at Québec City's Théâtre Repère in the 1980s out of Lessard's ex-
      perience working at the San Francisco Dancer's Workshop. This involves working
      with a *R*esource (usually an image or object rather than a theme), towards a *S*core
      (an arrangement of performance elements built on the resource), towards a "*V*aluac-
      tion" (suggesting an improvisational evaluation through the acting out of the score),
      resulting in a *P*erformance (which becomes the *R*esource for the beginning of the
      next cycle). I am indebted to Harry Lane for this summary account of Lepage's
      process, in a lecture prepared for my Canadian Drama class at the University of
      Guelph, Winter 1997. For Lepage's own, and somewhat different account of the
      RSVP cycles, see his interview with Alison McAlpine in Delgado and Heritage,
      133-35.
[26]   The joke here, of course, is that Lepage at that time was best known for his work in
      collective creations. His early productions all entered rehearsal without a script.
[27]   The one first published in *Canadian Theatre Review* and reissued in *The CTR
      Anthology*. Another version is published in the second volume of the 1994 and sub-
      sequent editions of Jerry Wasserman, ed., *Modern Canadian Plays*. Finally, there is
      a feature film version, *Le Polygraph*, directed by Lepage. The focus on the "to be or
      not to be" soliloquy in combination with the skull (which of course Shakespeare's

both *Vinci* and *Needles and Opium*, Lepage's virtuoso one-man shows about artists, can usefully be read as variations, or improvisations, on the theme of the same speech. What is it about *Hamlet*, Hamlet, or this particular speech – one dreaded by most actors because of its over-familiarity – that makes Lepage return to it so obsessively?

Partly, I suggest, it has to do with anxieties of control, anxieties about seas of troubles and the thousand natural shocks that flesh and text are heir to, and the exigencies, as the play says elsewhere, of this too, too solid/sullied – *living* – flesh (and too unstable text) – anxieties, that is, that are characteristically modernist in origin, but that perhaps refuse – particularly for a Québecker from the provincial/national capital, Québec City, with a vexed relationship to the cosmopolitan cultural capital, Montreal, who positions himself in his interviews as a citizen of the world – to resolve themselves quite so easily into the *Dream*'s complete, transcendent, textually stable, and internally coherent "great constancy."

\*\*\*

Richard Halpern concludes his excellent book, *Shakespeare Among the Moderns*, in which he traces (among other things) continuities between the (modernist) Early Modern drama criticism of Eliot and Frye, on the one hand, and the (postmodern) New Historicism of Stephen Greenblatt, on the other, with a brief chapter about various modernist and postmodernist "Hamletmachines" from high, popular, and mass culture, ranging from Gilbert and Sullivan through Gordon Craig, Jean Cocteau,[28] Jacques Lacan, and Heiner Müller, to Arnold Schwarzenegger. In a section entitled "William Shakespeare/Sigmund Freud," Halpern ends by asking what it is about *Hamlet* that causes modern readers and interpreters to treat him as a machine, what "nurtures" these intimations of the mechanical (1997: 279). He answers, in part, with a suggestion that may illuminate Lepage's and others' obsessive rewritings of the play, and may serve as a starting point for

---

Hamlet holds in another scene entirely) suggests that Lepage is interested less in *Hamlet*, the play, than in "Hamlet" as the cultural icon, or symbol, at least as clear and powerful as the iconic Beckett cited by Brook. It is interesting in this regard that Lepage uses, in both *Le Polygraph* and the French-language version of *Elsinore*, the Victor Hugo translation of the play rather than any more vibrant but less culturally iconic Québécois or even 20th-century translation.

28   Interestingly, Cocteau is one of three central character's in Lepage's technically stunning *Needles and Opium*, in which Lepage is suspended above the stage, representing Cocteau suspended in an aeroplane above the Atlantic. *Needles and Opium*, in fact, might itself usefully be read as an intercultural Hamletmachine (or an extended meditation on the "to be or not to be" soliloquy). The other characters are the modernist jazz trumpeter, Miles Davis, himself a kind of Hamlet figure, and a contemporary Québecker clearly representing Lepage himself.

understanding the cultural work they perform: "[t]he Oedipus can never fully 'take' on Hamlet," Halpern argues, "because the maternal flesh on which it is written keeps deleting it. ... Hamlet's 'problem' is not that he is *too* Oedipal but that he isn't Oedipal enough" (1997: 283-84).

***

Lepage's most extended meditation on Hamlet's soliloquy, and on *Hamlet* itself, in fact, occurs in and as *Elsinore*, his one-man Hamlet-machine, which I use here as a representative site for the interrogation of postmodern Shakespearean directing that has often been considered, because of its strategies of decentring and fragmentation, to be politically interventionist.[29]

After an opening "ghost-over," as it were (the ghost in the machine?) – a voice-over of Hamlet Senior's account of his murder – *Elsinore* in its Fall 1997 manifestation opened its "embodied" text with "to be or not to be," and thereby framed what followed as an extended meditation upon the soliloquy.[30] What followed was an astonishing appropriation of the *Hamlet* text itself, in which one actor – in the first versions in both English and French this was Lepage himself, who also directed and designed the production – played all the roles, male and female, and spoke all the lines, subjugating them to his own radical selection and rearrangement. *Elsinore*, then, "contained" all the language and all the roles, artistic as well as dramatic, within one (male) body, one voice, one performance.

An example of how this functioned, and of how powerful the production was at its best, was the treatment of Ophelia's death: the actor entered as Gertrude, stage right, in a stiff, gilded dress, and delivered Gertrude's IV.iv speech "straight," and effectively, in front of the curtain. At the end of the speech, the dress broke away from the actor like the encrustation from a pupa, and Ophelia emerged embryonic in a

---

[29]   These include not only the intercultural Shakespearean productions of directors of the European avant garde such Mnouchkine, or the "signature" pieces of directors such as Strehler or Stein, but also the *Hamletmachine*s written by Heiner Müller and directed by the American Robert Wilson working in Germany or Gilles Maheu working in Québec.

[30]   My descriptions of the Fall 1997 production, directed and designed by Lepage and performed by English actor Peter Darling, are based on the performance at the National Arts Centre, Ottawa, September 13th, 1997. The production then toured to Stanford, New York, Dublin, and Madrid. The English-language performances by Lepage himself at the DuMaurier World Stage in Spring 1996 opened with the ghost's voice-over followed by Claudius and Gertrude's greeting of Rosencrantz and Guildenstern, framing the play quite differently as an investigation into Hamlet's state of mind.

flimsy white undergown, partially open at the chest to reveal the male body beneath, evoking an effective androgyny that was reinforced by the falsetto singing of a medley of the standard early-modern settings of Ophelia's songs from IV.v. At this point the actor-as-Ophelia crossed to centre stage – the curtain had risen – and lay down on a vast blue cloth, his/her arms crossed, as the stage mechanism rose – all but a rectangular, coffin-shaped opening at its centre, into which the body seemed to sink, engulfed by the drapery that slid into the grave-like opening to enshroud her. As the machinery lifted, however, the same actor, as Hamlet, emerged from beneath it, completing a breathtaking – and economical – series of metamorphoses.

The stage imagery *was* breathtaking, and in its own modernist way definitive of a powerfully individualist artistic vision: complete, self-contained, and (socially) inscrutable. And the appropriations, cuts, and radical rearrangements of Shakespeare were, of course, entirely continuous with the history of Shakespearean production, including the Brook and Lepage *Dreams* (not to mention Lepage's and others' appropriations elsewhere). What was different, perhaps, from the modernist tradition was that, like the Walker Evans photograph reprinted, framed, *signed,* and exhibited by postmodern feminist artist Sherrie Levine (see Kaplan, 1996: 87), the production was renamed, reframed, and signed by Lepage: the program announced *"Elsinore,* written and directed by Robert Lepage." *Elsinore*'s appropriations of Shakespeare, like its virtuoso pulling together of all the dramatic and artistic roles into one controlling (male) subjectivity, were not mystified as interpretations, justified or authorized by "Shakespeare," or "the text," but flaunted.[31] The revelation late in the show that the apparently solo actor was supplemented by a silent double – a simulacrum? – reinforced the effect: what kind of one-man show has two men? But as Lepage joked in his program note, "you can't make a Hamlet without breaking a few eggs" – at least not at this particular historical moment. And of course the appropriation, not of mass-cultural forms, but of *Shakespeare,* as opposed to rhetorical or real deferral to his genius as in the modernist tradition, is potentially legible, particularly in the postcolonial context of Canada and Québec, as resistance rather than

---

[31] It is interesting to note, in relation to the open rather than naturalized appropriation of female characters by male directorial visions, that, in spite of the fact that because of a childhood illness Lepage is hairless, he performed *Elsinore,* including the female roles, with a beard. Similarly Peter Darling, in the revival, did not wear a wig to disguise the fact that he is balding and therefore to facilitate the transvestism. For an extended and detailed analysis of the discourses of authorship and authority in Shakespearean performance and performance criticism, discourses that centre around "Shakespeare" and "the text," see W. B. Worthen's important book, *Shakespeare and the Authority of Performance.*

modernist containment or allegorical appropriation.[32] For Lepage, commenting on the instability of text and authorship in Shakespeare, however much the plays provide "an avalanche of resources, a box of toys to be taken out," "there's something about these texts that [is] doubtful [...] there's something doubtful about the property and the invention" – even as there is something "doubtful," excessive, and unstable about his own play, as both property and invention (Lepage, 1996: 243).

I have argued that the production "contained" all the roles, artistic and dramatic, within one body, but it most *notably* contained them within one immense and complex multi-media stage *machine*. The set for *Elsinore* consisted of modular flats manipulated by a computer-controlled hydraulic system. All of the flats could be performed or projected upon, using slides, video, and a complex lighting plot, and the central flat housed a large circular section that could spin or tilt independently, within which a cut-out rectangle could open or close, serving as doorway (occasionally with a step unit), window, ship's hatch, or grave.

The use of machinery, of course, might also be seen to be continuous with the modernist tradition: even Brook's white box was described as "a machine for acting in," his actors as puppets. Puppets, in fact, *uber-* or other, are central to modernism in the theatre, and even the combination of actor and machine is prefigured in Brook, whose "culture of links," as he describes it, includes links not only "between man and society, between one race and another, between microcosm and macrocosm... between the visible and invisible, between categories, languages, genres," but also "between humanity and machinery" (1989: 239).

In Lepage, however, the binaries of linking, which in Brook as elsewhere tend to perpetuate and police borders, become the instabilities of blending. He talks, on the one hand, about the "freedom" provided him by technology in ways that echo Brook on the "natural" freedom to be discovered through the transcendent body of the actor.[33] But on the other hand, sounding very much like another director of Hamletmachines, Robert Wilson, Lepage describes actors as themselves machines: "I tell stories with machines. The actor is him/herself

---

[32]   As it is in such work as Robert Gurik's *Hamlet, Prince du Québec* (1968), or Paula de Vasconcelles *Le Making of/de Macbeth* (1995). I am grateful to Leanore Lieblein and Denis Salter for information about these productions, and am indebted to their papers at, respectively, the Waterloo International Conference on Elizabethan Theatre, University of Waterloo, July, 1997, and the Performance Text conference at the Graduate Centre for the Study of Drama, University of Toronto, April 1997.

[33]   See Richard Ouzounian, "Lepage's Struggle to Stay Free."

a machine" (Lepage, 1995).[34] For Lepage, then, as for many postmodern artists, technology is not part of the problem to be repressed, as for the modernist, but part of the solution – part of the mechanics of repression. Unlike the modernist director, for whom the actor embodies nostalgia for the verities and unities of the "natural," the postmodernist director is likely to treat the body as part of the *technology* of theatre.[35]

Shannon Steen and Margaret Werry have argued that in *Elsinore* the use of technology disrupts the economy of the modernist delivery system of meaning from author through director and actor to audience, using Derrida to suggest that technologies are *opposed* to "the logocentric order which attempts to fix meaning by reference to the 'natural,' 'self-evident,' 'inner truth' of the order of the body" (1998: 142). Indeed, reviewers have regularly lamented what Christopher Winsor called "a kind of techno-anarchy" in the design, and what Benedict Nightingale called, perhaps in unconscious tribute to Lepage's egg joke, a "scrambled" quality in the acting (Winsor, 1996; Nightingale, quoted in "Critics," 1997). Steen and Werry suggest that "[i]n his technological manipulation, Lepage was seen to occlude the conditions for the exploration of subjectivity" (1998: 144) and therefore to open the way for the proliferation of meanings: "In *Elsinore*, the avowed and visible presence of technology highlighted the process and production of simulacra, of proliferation of image and sign… and prompted in the critical community a resort to that all purpose rhetorical prophylaxis, 'authority'" (1998: 146).

Clearly, then, it is possible to read the production, particularly from the position of doctoral candidates at an American University (as were Steen and Werry at the time of writing), as politically effective, transformative postmodernism, as opposed to the "postpolitical," "ludic postmodernism" so often lamented by the left.[36] And Lepage's refusal

---

[34]  "Je raconte des histoires avec des machines. L'acteur en soi est une machine. Je sais que plusiers acteurs n'aiment pas qu'on parle d'eux comme étant des machines mais lorsque tu fais du théâtre, c'est un peu ça." Clearly the silent double performing in *Elsinore* functions very much as part, or even agent, of the machinery, as does the operator of the technology, who in the Ottawa performances, at least, was fully visible to the audience.

[35]  See Kaplan, 87, for an illuminating discussion of romantic modernist nostalgia for the real, the original, the natural, and the (creatively) detached as opposed to postmodern acceptance of a fragmented and decentred world of simulacra – and therefore of technology.

[36]  I take the terms and concepts of "postpolitical" and "ludic postmodernism" from Teresa Ebert, "The 'Difference' of Postmodern Feminism" (1991: 887; also quoted in Hodgdon, 1996: 81). For other critical efforts to come to terms with a political postmodernism in performance see Baz Kershaw, "The Politics of Performance in a Postmodern Age" and Auslander. It is important to note here that I do not wish to

to present the show as finished "product," together with its sheer *excess* (of ambition as well as actorly and technological display), reinforces the argument that its multiplication of significations works to disassemble cultural and theatrical practices that restrict and stabilize meaning: that it resists containments, authoritative artistic or social visions – indeed authorities and hierarchies of all kinds. But of course this argument, like the touring production itself, tends towards decontextualization: *are* there hierarchies "of all kinds"? Authorities, hierarchies, and containments tend to function in specific social and material ways, and to universalize hierarchies can work to perpetuate them, by effacing their material causes and consequences.

It is interesting to note that Lepage claims to have been attracted to *Hamlet* – as a Québecker living and working in what he calls the incestuous world of Québec theatre and culture – by its exploration of the incest theme (see Charest, 1995: 202).[37] But no reviewer has noticed this theme in *Elsinore*, its connection with Québec, or indeed *any* immediate social or cultural signification. We have seen that what political effect was achieved by Lepage's *Dream* seemed to derive directly from the site of its intervention, emerging through the modernist and nationalist anxieties of British reviewers (who have consistently praised Lepage *except* when he has directed Shakespeare in English). Since the production of his *Dream*, however, Lepage has retreated from National Theatres in London, Ottawa, and elsewhere, and has established a multi-media, mixed-genre production machine, "Ex Machina," in his home town, Québec City, geographically decentred in global terms, if not those of Québec nationalism. Again, the geographical decentring and the explorations in interdisciplinarity, the turning away from cosmopolitan Montreal and from English and English-Canadian centrist Nationalisms, and the relocation within the political heart of his own local culture, would all seem to open the door for destabilizing, site-specific political work. But Ex Machina does not have a full-scale performance space in Québec City, and its productions, including *Elsinore*, have their official openings elsewhere and tour internationally (as do most postmodern performances), most often to the placelessness of international festivals – multinational "free-

---

condescend to Steen & Werry, from whose paper I have benefited a great deal, but to place their insights, like those of the reviewers, in their historical, cultural, and national context. As doctoral candidates at the time, in an American university, they were required to demonstrate competence in certain kinds of discourse, including, in this case, the new historicist and cultural materialist discourses of resistance and containment.

[37] Lepage elsewhere is quoted as saying that "Quebec is a closed, insular, incestuous society that I'm very proud to be part of" (Ouzounian, 1997).

trade" marketplaces for *cultural* capital, where shows from different countries "represent," but do not speak to, their respective national cultures, and generate decontextualized and formalist interest among audiences that are communities only by virtue of their shared interest in theatre as a form. Any potential social referents, I suggest, are lost in this global politics of decontextualization,[38] where the local or culturally specific is of value only in the service of a fuzzy universalism: "If you discuss what goes on in your back yard," Lepage has argued, trotting out the cliché, "then you are universal" (Ouzounian, 1997). In this context – or lack of context – the ways in which productions such as *Elsinore* can be interventionist are unclear, or into what, beyond the evolution of theatre as an art form, they might intervene. Indeed, the reviews of *Elsinore* in England were more dismissive than wrought with the protectionist anxieties surrounding Lepage's *Dream*, and assessments elsewhere, particularly in English Canada and Québec, suggest fascinated indifference rather than threat. Writing as an expatriate Englishman and former theatre critic for *The Observer*, Robert Cushman ended his review in *The Globe and Mail* (which presents itself as "Canada's national newspaper") by saying, "I don't know that it signifies much beyond itself, but it takes the breath" (1996).[39]

\*\*\*

It is not entirely clear, then, that the shift from modernist containments to postmodern multiplicities, or from the modernist body to the postmodern machine, was anything more in *Elsinore* than a shift from complicity with the ideologies of industrial capital and the nation state to complicity with the ideologies and technologies of late-capitalist, multinational globalization and its assaults on cultural diversity in a post-national world. As far as contemporary discourses and practices of Shakespearean directing are concerned, "our" world still "includes"

---

[38] Kate Taylor, in her review of the French-language production in Montreal, ("Dancing Exuberantly on Hamlet's Grave"), points towards another radical kind of decontextualizing practised in *Elsinore*, one which also reinforces our sense of Lepage's work as directly continuous with modernist humanism. Noting that Hamlet's "what a piece of work is man" speech "is staged with large projections of Eadward Muybridge's serial photograph of a naked man running and Leonardo da Vinci's drawing of the human body inside a circle and a square," she comments that "evoking these famed anatomical images, Lepage delivers the speech not in its dramatic context... but rather its historical one: It is one of Western civilization's great monuments of rational humanism."

[39] Cushman is curiously positioned in Canada. His writings about the (culturally colonialist) Stratford and Shaw Festivals and about international touring productions have been consistently sympathetic, detailed, and illuminating, but he has tended to be dismissive of new Canadian work, for which he seems not to have acquired cultural reference points.

(*comprend*) all others, or, in the public discourse of Coke, IBM and the Internet, "*we are* [still] the *world*." It is perhaps worth asking of the politics of postmodern Shakespearean directing, in relation to those of its modernist predecessors, precisely "what, and where, is the difference?"

# PART III

## SHAKESPEARE AND ADAPTATION

# CHAPTER 5

# "The real of it would be awful:" Representing The Real Ophelia in Canada

> *"I'm thinking next season, I'm thinking of doing Hamlet."*
> *"Whatever for?"*
> *"Because I have an Ophelia."*
> *"Who?"*
> *"Guess."*
> *"Me? Oh no."*
> But she is trying not to smile.
> *"You'd be better off having a Hamlet,"* she says. *"Ophelia has a short shelf life."*
>
> (Carole Corbeil, 1997: 45-6)

> *She went down singing*
> *So they say*
> *Ophelia*
> *Ophelia*
> *Ophelia –*
>
> (Elizabeth Burns, 1991: 43)

> *Being weak is not one of my strengths.*
>
> (Frances Barber, on preparing to play Ophelia at the Royal Shakespeare Company, 1988: 138)

Judith Thompson's 1992 "relay" play, *Lion in the Streets*, opens with an address to the audience by the young Portuguese girl Isobel who provides the through-line and a bridge among the play's linked scenes. Her speech frames the play by introducing, among other things, issues of representation. "Doan be scare," she says pointing to her downtown Toronto neighborhood. "Doan be scare of this pickshur! This pickshur is niiiice, nice! I looove this pickshur, this pickshur is mine!" (1992:15). In a later scene, a neighborhood woman, Joanne, tells her friend Rhonda that she has cancer of the bone, and asks for her help:

> You know that picture? That picture I had in my bedroom growing up? [...] My aunt and uncle sent me that from England, the poster it's OPHELIA, from this play by Shakespeare, right? And she she – got all these flowers, tropical flowers, wild flowers, white roses, violets and buttercups, everything she loved and she kinda weaved them all together. Then she got the heaviest dress she could find... you know how dresses in the olden days were so long and heavy, with petticoats and that? And she got this heavy blue dress, real... blue and then she wrapped all these pretty pretty flowers round and round her body, round her head, and her hair, she had this golden, wavy hair, long, and then she steps down the bank, and she lies, on her back, in the stream. (1992: 34-5)

Joanne provides a lengthy reading of Ophelia's death-by-drowning as represented by John Everett Millais, concluding that "she dies... good. She dies good." "I want to die like that," she says. "But... I don't... want to do it all alone" (35). She proceeds to ask Rhonda's help, not only in arranging for her death and funeral, but also in controlling her own passage into representation:

> I want you to help me, with the flowers, and with the dress, and my hair, I want you to make sure the willow branch is there, and the stream is right, and maybe... maybe that... Frank... sees I... wouldn't mind him seein... me in that stream, with the flowers, and the heavy blue dress... I wouldn't mind if you took maybe some pictures of me like that and then you could have them printed and given out at the funeral, something like that... just, you know, two by four, colour, whatever, it's the one thing that would make it alright – it's the one thing... (1992: 35)

Rhonda, not surprisingly, is reluctant:

> [I]t's all very lovely and that, your picture, in your room, but that's a picture, you dimwit! The real of it would be awful, the stalks of the flowers would be chokin you, and the smells of them would make you sick, all those smells comin at you when you're feelin so sick to begin with, and the stream, well if you're talking about the Humber River or any stream in this country you're talkin filth, in the Humber River you're even talkin sewage, Jo, you're talkin cigarette packages and used condoms and old tampons floating by you're talkin freezin, you'd start shakin from head to toe you're talkin rocks gashin your head you're talkin a bunch of longhairs and goofs on the banks yellin at you callin you whorebag sayin what they'd like to do to you, you're talkin... and where would you get dress like that, eh? You'd never find the one in the picture, Jo, it'd be too tight at the neck and the waist, it'd be a kind of material that itches your skin, even worse wet, drives you nut-crazy, the blue would be off, wouldn't look right your shoes

wouldn't match you could never find the same colour, Joanne. You can't become a picture, do you know what I mean? I mean you can't... BE... a picture, okay? (1992: 36)[1]

I am quoting this play and this passage at length to introduce a discussion of the cultural role played by a range of representations – "pictures" – of Ophelia in Canada in the 1990s, and in Canadian drama in particular. These representations, in their very different ways, often explicitly raise, as this one does, the question of who controls women's passage into representation. They also often set an image that makes implicit claims to "reality" against a romanticized version of Ophelia that is implicitly or explicitly associated with 19th-century Romantic or pre-Raphaelite images of Ophelia-as-victim and, in particular, with reproductions of the Millais painting invoked from the childhood of Thompson's Joanne.

Elaine Showalter's analysis of French and English representations of Ophelia, including the Millais painting (which is of course a touchstone for more than Canadians), notes that "Millais's Ophelia is sensuous siren as well as victim," and also notes that "the [male] artist rather than the subject dominates the scene (1985: 85):"

> The division of space between Ophelia and the natural details Millais had so painstakingly pursued reduces her to one more visual object; and the painting has such a hard surface, strangely flattened perspective, and brilliant light that it seems cruelly indifferent to the woman's death. (1985: 85)

Showalter includes in her discussion of the Millais work a brief survey of romantic Ophelias, which evince a fascination with, and eroticisation of, female madness and construct her as "the girl who *feels* too much" (1985: 83).[2] It is this pervasive and naturalized image, and the culturally reproductive construction of gender that it hegemonically effects and reinforces, with which contemporary Canadian Ophelias must continue to negotiate.

---

[1]   Needless to say, Rhonda's "real of it" is also an artfully constructed and far from disinterested representation.

[2]   Rebecca West, in *The Court and the Castle: Some Treatments of a Recurrent Theme* (New Haven: Yale UP, 1957), 18, argued that Ophelia as a "correct and timid virgin of exquisite sensibilities" who dies of a broken heart is "a misreading [that] would not have lasted so long in England had it not been for the popularity of the pre-Raphaelite picture by Sir John Millais which represents Ophelia as she floated down the glassy stream, the weeping brook; for his model was his friend Rossetti's bride, the correct, timid, sensitive, virginal, and tubercular Miss Siddal." I am indebted for this reference, and throughout my discussion of Margaret Clarke's play, to Burnett, 1997.

Judith Thompson's use of Ophelia, and her evocation of the specificities of a contemporary Canadian landscape – the Humber River and
its attendant "filth," together with the speech rhythms of the characters,
the (mis)reading of the "tropical" flowers and other iconography from
the Millais painting, and the source of the print as a gift sent from
England, all contribute to the perverse humor of the passage and
communicate through a kind of grotesque realism some of the characteristics of a postcolonial critique.[3] Canadians familiar with Christmas-
card robins, Gainsborough prints on the bedroom wall, and Shake-
speare-at-Stratford will recognize the dislocation articulated by Rhonda
in her search for "the real of it," if some might also recognize the
comforts of a childlike, colonialist submission to the fantasy authorities
of cultural certainty, however absurd, at a time of stress. The invoca-
tion of Shakespeare, of "olden days," and of an English pastoral landscape is not unique to Canada, of course, but it plays a particular, and
in the context of recent postcolonial critiques, familiar role in the
cultural life of former English colonies. It is this comforting role that
Joanne imagines being replayed in funeral rituals and in the circulation
of photos of her own romantic drowning to "Frank" and her other
survivors and mourners, though there is also something refreshingly
self-assertive, however comically naive in this context, in her desire to
orchestrate her own passage into representation.

Thompson is not alone in evoking the high-culture, colonialist comforts of submission to romantic and dehistoricized imagery from
Shakespeare, and from Ophelia in particular, though not all such
representations constitute critiques. One thinks, for example, of the
stunningly beautiful representation of Ophelia's suicide in Robert
Lepage's one-man *Hamlet, Elsinore*, described in Chapter Four, in
which the (re)emergence of the actor as Hamlet contained the representation within a closed narrative, a closed semiotic system, and single
(male) body. The audience was left moved and perhaps comforted by

---

[3]    It is the specificities of place and localized language that set Thompson's Canadian
      confrontation of the romantic image with "the real of it" apart from a comparable
      moment in Scottish poet Elizabeth Burns's poem, "Ophelia:"

> This is not the beautiful floating death by water
> She will not have her skirts drawn out around her
> billowed along by the current
> her hair floating like some golden weed
> and a cloak of wildflowers scattered round her
>
> This death by water
> will be sticky with mud
> Her wet clothes will drag her down
> and the stones in her pockets
> sink her quickly. (1991: 41-2)

the aesthetic beauty of the sequence, but also functioning at some comfortable remove from any "real of it."

Ophelia plays a similar, if more oblique because more radically de- and re-contextualized role in "Never Doubt I Love," Ted Dykstra's setting and recontextualization of Hamlet's letter to her as recorded by pop singer Melanie Doane on her album, *Shakespearean Fish* (Doane and Dykstra, 1996). Hamlet's lines, "doubt that the stars are fire/doubt that the earth doth move/doubt truth to be a liar/but never doubt I love," read in II.ii by Polonius to Claudius and Gertrude (satirically, in most productions) as evidence of the source of Hamlet's distraction, are here beautifully sung in the lyrical female voice of Melanie Doane, and framed as chorus to a song that plays variations on the theme established by the first verse:

in an age of troubles

in an age of uncertainty

in an age of dwindling hope

you still have me

The song ends with an astonishing shift in context, appropriating lines from the marriage negotiations of Beatrice and Benedick from V.ii of *Much Ado About Nothing*, and effectively invoking closure, effacing Ophelia, and invoking conventional, and conventionally gendered comforts: "I know your pain I won't pretend/Serve God, love me, and mend." The song also, of course, without taking on any serious revisioning of *Hamlet* – in fact without explicitly invoking Ophelia, Hamlet, or the play at all – stakes an implicit claim to a particular kind of "high-culture" seriousness within the pop music pantheon through its use of "olden-time" Shakespearean language and through its placement on an album which invokes both Shakespeare and Yeats.[4] In doing so, of course, it also allows listeners the dubious

---

[4] The lyrics for the album's title song, "Shakespearean Fish," were adapted from Yeats by Melanie Doane. For a discussion of female pop vocalists, including Canadian Jane Siberry, in relation to high and popular culture, see Lucy O'Brien, "'Sexing the Cherry': High or Low Art? Distinctions in Performance." The use of Shakespeare by pop musicians in Canada to position themselves culturally is similar to that elsewhere, ranging as it does from Loreena McKennit's high-culture Celtic settings of Shakespearean songs and speeches (together with others by Blake, Tennyson, and Yeats), to the entirely gratuitous title, *Shakespeare My Butt*, of the debut album of the rock group, The Lowest of the Low – gratuitous in that the album contains no other Shakespearean references. Both of these types, of course, serve to reinforce the high/low-culture binary, and police its borders. Somewhat more complex is the song "Cordelia" by the Tragically Hip, with its reference to stage superstitions, "Treading the boards, screaming out Macbeth/Just to see how much bad

and self-congratulatory pleasures of intertextual recognition, or at the very least of sophisticated taste that unlike Thompson's intertextual references are fully congruent with continuing colonialist submission to British cultural imperialism.

It seems curmudgeonly – "that's a picture, you dimwit" – to suggest that the artful and aesthetically beautiful appropriations of Ophelia by Lepage and Doane play essentially affirmative, reproductive, or colonizing cultural roles, particularly given Thompson's representation of the comforts they can provide to those in particular kinds of need. But the larger cultural work performed by them is not without significance, aligning as they do the "high"-cultural authority of Shakespeare and of old-world culture with romanticized validations of feminine passivity, victimization, and service to masculinist artistic, cultural, and social goals.

Other Canadian productions, revisionings and recontextualizations of *Hamlet*, however, tell different stories of their Ophelias, attempt to redress historical imbalances in order to recover or represent "the real of it" in their various ways, and play a range of different cultural roles. These include productions of the play featuring the now conventionally strong-willed Ophelias of such actors as Marti Maraden at Stratford in 1976, who played her truly frightening mad scenes strapped to a yoke which she wielded with considerable danger to those around her; of Sheila McCarthy at Toronto Free Theatre in 1986, whose Ophelia's steely will was reflected in her determinedly expressionless countenance, particularly in the wake of a II.ii scene in which she was exhibited to the Court by her father as a virtual prop in support of his argument to the King and Queen concerning Hamlet's madness; or of Linda Griffiths in *The Passe Muraille Hamlet* in 1983, in which the character lingered throughout, even after her death, in dark corners of the theatre, as a kind of "imagistic enlargement" of Ophelia's significant presence, which had been pointed up in II.ii by her strategic use of remembrances – a mirror or a Pierrot doll, at the actor's discretion.[5] Finally these include Peter Eliot Weiss's 1986 *Haunted House Hamlet*, a revision and expansion (!), environmentally-staged by Tamanhous Theatre in an old Vancouver house, haunted, as is much of Canada's cultural landscape, by the ghosts of Shakespeare's characters, where the audience followed actors of their choice between rooms where the

---

luck you really get," and its revisionist refrain, "It takes all your power/To prove that you don't care/I'm not Cordelia, I will not be there" (1991).

5    Although I saw both the Passe Muraille and Toronto Free Theatre *Hamlets*, I am indebted for my accounts of the productions to G. B. Shand, who worked on both productions, for lending me archival videos of the productions and for his article "Two Toronto *Hamlets*."

action was simultaneously being played out. This production/rewriting/revision saw a somewhat inconsistent Ophelia. She was, for the most part, weak, the "object" of Horatio's affection[6] and, in a pattern that will become familiar below, the victim of Gertrude's machinations, who nevertheless appropriated the "to be or not to be" soliloquy and its attendant assertion of independent subjectivity, and successfully fought off an attempted rape by Hamlet. Her suicide was falsely reported by Gertrude as a romanticized drowning: in fact she died singing "It was a lover and his lass" (interpolated from *As You Like It*), covering her face with a piece of lace, and lowering herself with some deliberation into a coffin. These inconsistencies in what seems to be an attempt to represent a strong and independent Ophelia in *The Haunted House Hamlet* are typical of attempts to revisit the character in contemporary versions of the Hamlet story. They perhaps point to the difficulties associated with attempting to portray a strong character whose role in the received text is nevertheless a minor one, in the face of so resilient a residue of the Millais archetype.

But "strong" Ophelias have become the rule rather than the exception, even in mainstream productions of *Hamlet* since the 1980s, even at the Royal Shakespeare Company, as my third epigraph indicates. In the Canada of the 1990s, however, there was a shift in direction, as the Judith Thompson intertext with which I began might suggest. And of course in the 1990s, in the wake of post-structuralist destabilizations within Canada as elsewhere, the question of "the real of it" shifts its ground.

Showalter's history of the representation of Ophelia in England and France, which neither begins nor ends in the romantic period, of course, historicizing her objects of analysis as well as her own method, takes this cultural turn into account. Focusing on "the representational bonds between female insanity and female sexuality" and beginning with Elizabethan stage conventions and the representation of Ophelia's madness as "erotomania," Showalter moves through Augustan, romantic, Victorian, and Freudian representations to contemporary "postmodern" depictions of the character as schizophrenic – post-Laing, and post-Deleuze and Guattari. Showalter carefully distinguishes between contemporary male and female representations, the former tending to focus on schizophrenic fragmentation, complete with "head banging, twitching, wincing, grimacing, and drooling," the latter on protest and

---

[6]  Horatio/Reynaldo was metatheatrically performed by a new character, Jimmy "Spider" McKuen, who initiated the action by breaking in through a broken basement window and "activating" the ghostly cast. Although not commercially published, the script of the *Haunted House Hamlet* that I have consulted is available in copyscript form from Playwrights Canada Press, Toronto.

rebellion, including representations of "the madwoman as heroine" (1985: 91).[7]

Canadian and Québécois representations of Ophelia in this decade are also gendered, but if the stuttering Ophelia of Ken Gass's play, *Claudius*, would seem to echo the thumb-sucking and twitching characterizations in Jonathan Miller's productions,[8] the gender divide is perhaps not so clear on this side of the Atlantic – at least in Canada – where postcolonial menfolk are perhaps more likely to identify with the character, and women more like to distance themselves from her apparent passivity (not to mention the text's cultural authority). E.D. Blodgett, problematically, in his construction of women as metaphor, and in his swallowing of feminist practice in the interests of an essentializing – "natural" – Canadian alterity, may nevertheless have a point that accounts in part for Canadian fascination with revisionist, and revisionist feminist representations of Gertrude, Ophelia, and other Shakespearean women: he argues that

> A Canadian is, it would seem, by nature of but not in, and thus endowed with attributes similar to those of a woman in a patriarchal world. To accept these conditions is to become, by definition, a heretic, refusing the official version, whose text consequently becomes the articulation of such a state, such a country. Life and history, as [Janice Kulyk] Keefer has remarked, happen to Canadians elsewhere. (1990: 5)[9]

Gender-conscious representations of Ophelia in contemporary Canada and Québec include, in 1990, Carbone 14's astonishing production of Heiner Müller's *Hamletmachine*, directed by Gilles Maheu, with its Ophelia (in one of her four guises) as Marilyn Monroe (as victim – in this case victim-as-simulacrum) who could nevertheless on occasion be found in the erotic costume of the Monroe of *The Seven Year Itch* slapping her Hamlet senseless. The effect, although undoubtedly eroticized, was that, in the words of the production's reviewer in *TDR (The Drama Review)*, "some in the audience, like Ophelia, have seen through the veils of representation" (MacDougall, 1988: 18) – whether to infinite postmodern reproducibility or to some (other?) form

---

[7]     On schizophrenia Showalter cites and discusses R. D. Laing's *The Divided Self*, but might also have made reference to Gilles Deleuze and Felix Guattari's *Anti-Oedipus: Capitalism and Schizophrenia*. Her descriptions, respectively, are of Jonathan Miller's 1981 production at the Warehouse, London, and Melissa Murray's agit-prop play, *Ophelia*, written for Hormone Imbalance in 1979, in which "Ophelia becomes a lesbian and runs of with a woman servant to join a guerrilla commune."

[8]     Ken Gass, *Claudius*, first performed by Canadian Rep Theatre, Toronto, September 1993, and published in 1995 in Toronto by Playwrights Canada.

[9]     Blodgett is quoting Janice Kulyk Keefer (1986: 289).

of "the real of it" was unclear. There is little doubt, however, that the Carbone 14 *Hamletmachine* worked to destabilize and denaturalize conventional gender roles, together with the cultural authority of canonical texts and the simple binary division between high and popular culture.

*** 

Both Ophelia and "the real of it" in Canadian Hamlet plays of the 1990s has been variously represented. The remainder of this chapter will focus on three quite different approaches to *Hamlet* as source text for dramatists: feminist "revisionist mythmaking;" politico-personal meditation on morality, sexuality, politics, and survival; and revisionist re-source-making in the guise of a "Viking Hamlet Saga."[10]

In her three-person version of the story, *Gertrude and Ophelia* – the only contemporary Canadian dramatic revisioning of *Hamlet* by a woman that I know of – Margaret Clarke dramatizes two versions of the "real:" she incorporates the female subject and the action involving the play's women that Shakespeare's *Hamlet* leaves unrepresented, and, in a metatheatrical frame, attempts to represent the "real" situation of women like herself working in the theatre in Canada and attempting to provide alternative theatrical views of canonical texts. The frame-work consists primarily of a debate between the Playwright, who plays Gertrude, and the Actor playing Horatio, who insists on offering rewrites "to represent the men who are missing from the action." After all, he argues, "You're a feminist. You believe in all this process stuff" (1993: S2). This frame allows Clarke to give voice to her own frustrations about the "real" patriarchal nature of the professional theatre in Canada, including a workshop process for new play development which often serves to bully playwrights into rewrites that betray their politics in the interests of what "we all agree" is "better" dramaturgy. It also allows her to voice critiques of her Shakespearean source texts, and thereby to justify her own revisioning. As she tells the Actor/ Horatio early on,

> [W]hat you don't understand is that as "The Mother," Gertrude is like an ideological sponge. The crap and piss left over from shaping the play is sucked up into the Gertrude character, where we can safely feel all the disgust and contempt we want. Then we're supposed to identify like crazy with Hamlet and his pals, feeling our ever-so-neat fear and pity, because all the nasty bits have been displaced into her. Well, I'm here to tell you it's a crock. I identify with Gertrude and I don't like the bad press she's been getting. (1993: S2-S3)

---

[10] "Viking Hamlet Saga" is Michael O'Brien's characterization of his play, *Mad Boy Chronicle*, in his foreword (1995: 9).

The main plot, the play-within, is essentially that of Shakespeare's version, although neither Hamlet nor Claudius appears on stage, a point of some concern to the only male in the cast: the Actor argues to the Playwright that "Everyone agrees. Your play needs a Hamlet," and later asserts that "no play can stand on its feet just on the strength of two women talking" (1993: S3, S10). But this is more or less what we get, as the traditional "action" takes place offstage and is recounted by Ophelia to Gertrude, who gives advice and is portrayed as a skilled political manipulator.

Linda Burnett has argued that what *Gertrude and Ophelia* does is amplify what Stephen Greenblatt calls (in reference to Caliban) "the voice of the displaced and oppressed" (Greenblatt, 1990: 232) in Shakespeare so that it can be registered clearly. Acknowledging that the play does more to criticize existing structures than to counter them, she argues that it "does function to permanently change the way we view Shakespeare's tragedy" (Burnett, 1997: 26), to operate as "revisionist mythmaking," and to work "to change our notion of the masculine canon and [...] make cultural change possible" (26).[11] The play's placement of its women at centre stage, and its treatment of Gertrude as strong, astute, and unscrupulous – a complex and coherent central character – can certainly be cited in support of Burnett's attractive feminist argument, which is also strongly supported by the arguments of the Playwright in the metatheatrical frame.

The play's treatment of Ophelia and "the girl" (Clarke, 1993: S3) who plays her, as Burnett acknowledges, is somewhat less encouraging. Noting that "unlike her Gertrude, Clarke's Ophelia is not a coherent character," Burnett finds "at least four possible Ophelias in *Gertrude and Ophelia*" (Burnett, 1997: 21): the delicate, virginal, and naive figure of the Millais archetype; the innocent victim of the court's machinations, robbed of her honesty, driven to insanity and suicide; the not-so-innocent accomplice with the court who spies on her lover, aborts herself with little regret, and loses her integrity, referring to herself before her suicide as "a very great sinner" (Clarke, 1993: S12); and finally "the madwoman of recent feminist criticism" (Burnett, 1997: 22), who gains insight and strength from her "madness" (understood as any deviation from societal norms) and spurns the status quo that Gertrude survives by embracing. Burnett argues that this "problematic melange of types" (22), which she suggests is not so much a reading of Ophelia as a reading of what the critics have had to say about her, serves some of the same purpose as Elaine Showalter's

---

[11]    Burnett takes the term "revisionist mythmaking" from Alicia Ostriker, "The Thieves of Language: Women Poets and Revisionist Mythmaking."

history of Ophelia in representation, but it also ultimately reproduces the problematics of *Hamlet* itself. It is impossible, it seems, to employ the plot of Shakespeare's play essentially unaltered – to be, in a curious way, "faithful" to the (masculinist) authority of the source story – and at the same time avoid its gendered pitfalls: the story, after all, is by, for, and about men.[12]

But I wonder if this is the only problem to take into account in analyzing the cultural work done by Clarke's play. Presenting itself explicitly as feminist revisionism, the play nevertheless represents the victimization of women *by* women in an empathetic if not positive light, moving towards a kind of neo-cathartic understanding, and therefore acceptance, of such collaboration with patriarchal oppression. And precisely *because* this is presented as feminist it is perhaps all the more problematic. *Gertrude and Ophelia*'s Playwright argues that "Ophelia may be dead, she may even have to die offstage, but I will not have it passed over with some bracketed phrase – 'She should have died hereafter'. … Women are always dying in asides" (S13). But in spite of these intentions, "the girl" playing Ophelia is left during the play's framework debates, as the stage directions indicate, "*carrying a basket of flowers. She waits for their exchange to end and rehearsal to begin*" (1993: S3). And Ophelia herself doesn't really fare much better in the "play proper," where her victimization includes her rape by Hamlet and betrayal by a Gertrude who, forced to choose between her child, Hamlet, and her allegiance to Ophelia as a woman, is serving the interests of her son. Ophelia's madness is a direct result of Gertrude's abandonment of her, as is her suicide. But the play-within ends with Gertrude rocking Ophelia's bridal veil-as-shroud in her arms, and laying it out on her bed:

> Ophelia, if you hear me, if such a place exists where you can hear me, forgive me. You knew that all I did was for him. It was never for you. I could not play your mother, although we would both wish it so. In being true to him, I wronged you. I was as true and as wrong as any woman can ever be. (1993: S15)

All that follows this speech is a very brief closing of the metatheatrical frame after "the guys have all gone," in which the Ophelia actor

---

12  By way of contrast, Scottish playwright Joan Ure, in "Something in it for Ophelia," written for the entirely site-specific purpose of production at the Edinburgh fringe opposite a mainstage Festival production of *Hamlet*, avoids the *Hamlet* plot altogether by staging a debate at Waverley Station between a young girl, Hannah, and a middle-aged male professor, Martin, following the Festival's *Hamlet* that they have both just seen. Hannah is shocked by the play's representation of Ophelia ("a simple, perhaps rather stupid girl"), and engages Martin in a debate about the cultural role played by the performance.

thanks the Playwright for some unidentified rewrites, and they leave
together, thinking and hoping, respectively, that "everything will be
fine" (1993: S15).

If *Gertrude and Ophelia* represents "the real of it" as, on the one
hand, the actual professional situation facing women attempting to do
feminist work in the theatre in Canada, and on the other as the internal-
ized, hegemonic operation of gender-based oppression *through* women
such as Clarke's Gertrude, two Canadian *Hamlet* plays written and
produced by men have reconceived the "real" Ophelia in quite different ways. The closer of these plays to both *Hamlet* and *Gertrude and
Ophelia* is Ken Gass's *Claudius*, which is more about Gertrude than
Claudius in its explorations of sex and power, but which acknowledges
in its title the centrality to Gertrude and to the play of what its author
calls "the Claudius factor" (1995: 7).

Gass's Gertrude is an astute political manipulator and realist. Discussing with Emilia (imported into the play from *Othello*) the proposed
marriage between Hamlet and Ophelia, she notes that "people who are
in love sleep together, but marriage is always political" (1995: 120).
She controls much of the play's action, puts Hamlet up to killing
Polonius, and ends the play alive and in power, having decided in the
best Elizabethan tradition (and after two marriages and a birth) that
"it'll be safer, much safer, if I remain celibate" (121). In fact, Gass's
Gertrude is not dissimilar to that of Margaret Clarke, though she has
more power and fewer regrets, and her view of Ophelia echoes that of
Clarke's version of the character: "Ophelia isn't fit to be queen. She's
vague, stupid, neurotic, not useful at all" (Gass, 1995: 121).[13] Or, in
Clarke's somewhat softer version, "She could not have been a Queen.
Too delicate for the strain of it" (1993: S13).

But the Ophelia we actually see in the play is no wilting flower. She
exists as an independent subjectivity and exercises what control she
can within a plot that isn't of her own devising. Early in the action,
although she knows that Hamlet wants to marry her for political reasons, and knows of his mistress, Genevieve, she is nevertheless seen to
be capable of relatively unbridled sexual/textual/conceptual fantasies
undreamed of in the imaginary of Clarke's, or Shakespeare's version of
the character:

> With him, I am chaste only in deed. My body is still, not even twitching,
> but my mind is racing, galloping over lips, cheeks, lips again, again. I love

---

[13]   Hamlet's mistress, Genevieve (with whom he spends a good deal of the play in bed)
       echoes Gertrude's judgement, though with a proto-feminist slant: "Did it ever occur
       to you Ophelia might have thoughts of her own," she asks him, "even if she is a
       fucked-up, fucked-over moron?" (1995: 67).

Hamlet. I love the idea of Hamlet, the notion of Hamlet stirring my body into liquified madness. Nothing is dry any more. I'm an ocean of desires. Mad, watery desires. Wet, delirious, excruciating, blazoning, disgusting, delicious wet, wet, wet, wet, wet, wet Hamlet desires... (Gass, 1995: 52)

At this point in the action, Ophelia's fantasies are essentially passive: her body is imagined as being still, as she is acted upon by Hamlet (which may, of course, simply reflect the male authorship of the play). But her fantasies also evince a concentration on the conceptual rather than the material – it is "the idea of Hamlet" that she loves, "the notion" of his sexual stirring – and this perhaps prepares the way for what later emerges as a fantasy fascination with the textual. It is unclear, however, whether the idea of Hamlet that she loves is the one inherited from Shakespeare – the scripted Hamlet, as it were – or from the character's own experience in the represented world of Gass's play – a point to which I will return.

In any case, it is clear that over the course of the action Ophelia as represented by Gass develops quite a different relationship to language, words, and text than Clarke's version of the character evinces. The weakness of Clarke's Ophelia is signalled in *Gertrude and Ophelia* by her lack of access to or power over (patriarchal) language, and the onset of her madness is marked by what is seen to be a regression into the pre-symbolic, or what Julia Kristeva calls the "semiotic" realm (see Kristeva, 1986).[14] She says to an imagined Hamlet, "I will make words, like you, and be the victor...," but, as the stage directions indicate, she then "*mouths words which have no sound. Finally giving in to the pain, sound does come from her in the form of a long howl [...].*" The passage ends with her complaint that "the devil has all the words" (1993: S11). Gass's Ophelia, by contrast, seems to have been reading (or writing) Barthes, evincing as the action proceeds a well-developed understanding of the pleasures of the text and the determined materiality (as opposed to the meanings) of language, which figures as itself pre- or a-symbolic. "I love books," she tells Hamlet, in a scene in the middle of the play in which she insists that he "keep asking" her to marry him:

There's something about the printed word that conjures up a spiralling imagination. Books are my passion. I eat words, I devour syllables, I suck, chop, chew into vowels with a violence that language itself is powerless to describe. I love archaic words, words that defy meaning, words whose meanings are obscure, hidden in time, suggestive only in the traces of their lettering. I feed on etymology and symbiotics. I fantasize on the power of

---

[14] Kristeva of course also associates madness, creativity, and resistance with the semiotic realm, particularly in *Powers of Horror: An Essay on Abjection*.

alliteration, assonance, onomatopoeia, rhythm, symbolism, allusion. I fuck myself with foreign alphabets, syllogisms, structural grammar. I breathe linguistic paradox. There's no need for marriage. My life *is* language. (1995: 70-71)

When Hamlet tries to interrupt and ask again, as it were, for her hand, she protests, "don't say any more. Especially pale words like sweet and love and queen. If you must talk, use brave talk with compound nouns and a lack of adverbs." By this point, then, Gass's Ophelia has abandoned the passivity of her earlier sexual fantasies, and both within her fantasy life and beyond seems quite capable of seizing the first person singular.

Indeed, her actions through most of the play are anything but weak or passive. She has to leave the funeral of her father because she can't contain her laughter, and she is capable of telling Hamlet that his mad games are "b-b-boring," (she stutters when she's nervous), that he's transparent, "like a pale glass of water," and that, "even if you ask a hundred times. I'll kill myself before I m-marry you" (32-33). Which she does, though not in the canonical manner. This Ophelia is last seen naked in a bathtub with Hamlet, sharing vows, a ring, and a double suicide: "Till death do us part," asks Hamlet? "Till death do make us one," she replies, and dies (109).

The "real of it" as represented by Gass's Ophelia, then – her ultimate response to her brother's early plea, "get real" (30) – is quite complex. On the level of dramatic fiction she remains, I think, the sacrifice that validates (yet again) Gertrude's "plotting" and signals, like *The Haunted House Hamlet* and *Gertrude and Ophelia*, the difficulty involved in evoking the Hamlet story without a more radical disarticulation while attempting to shift the cultural ground. But on another level of representation this Ophelia might be seen to choose and seize a world of meta-discourse that exists outside the represented fiction, a realm of the material text that in its focus on words as things rather than signs, and on eating, fucking, and other bodily functions, textually embodies a "reality" that the play's represented world, with its ghosts, mysteries, and lies, denies. Her mad scene directly invokes her earlier sexual and textual fantasies, completes a shift from passive sexual fantasies about Hamlet through textual auto-eroticism ("I fuck myself with foreign alphabets") to embodied subjectivity, and represents her own willed ingestion and embodiment of the play's action and the Hamlet story. She is discovered sitting on the floor "in a semi-catatonic state," "putting bunches of her hair into her mouth, and chewing on them:"

I – Eat – I – Eat – Eat my life I – I – I eat – words – I eat – lies – eat people – eat persons – eat eat eat – eat politics – eat violence – eat murders – eat

Ophelia eat G-G-G-Genevieve eat father – eat eat eat happiness – eat my Hamlet – eat wedding bells – I eat – I eat mouth eat eat eyes eat hair – eat hair – eat myself – eat my cunt eat my body – Eat my love fuck – eat – I eat I eat I eat I eat – Eat – eatEat – Eat – Eat – Eat – (1995: 99-100)

In a sense, Ophelia's choice of madness and death, considered *as* a choice, and seen in the context of her otherwise inexplicable discourse on words, can be seen to be, however self-consuming, an exit from the symbolic and an entry *in* to the prediscursive, presymbolic *materiality* of language. In this sense, then, she can be seen as the only character in the play who understands the sheer, material *real* of *Hamlet* and of *Claudius* (which *is* "awful"). The speech begins, after all, with the ingestion of words, and of lies, proceeds through plot fragments from the play, and arrives at her own textual body and subjectivity – her own "I."

Even so, in terms of the represented world of the play and the persistent shape of the Hamlet myth itself, this Ophelia's seizing of subjectivity has little impact on the action, and doesn't get her very far. Gass's play, like that of Margaret Clarke, suggests that it's easier by far to rewrite Gertrude than Ophelia.[15]

In the Forward to *Claudius* Gass responds to the question, "why the Hamlet story?" by referring to Shakespeare's own borrowings: "it wasn't original with Shakespeare, and anyway, this has nothing (almost) to do with Shakespeare. But, like many great legends, it rests firmly in our consciousness and allows me, the writer, to tinker around, to do my mischief with a minimum of explanation" (1995: 7). Michael O'Brien, in *Mad Boy Chronicle*, goes one step further than Gass, and perhaps does more mischief. Drawing on the so-called "bad quarto" and on the *Gesta Danorum* of Saxo Grammaticus, a primary source for the Hamlet legend, he shifts the historical ground to that of Shakespeare's own source material, locates the action at the historical moment of Christian contact with the Viking world represented in Saxo, and uses the opportunity to deal with the currently topical issues in North America of Christianity, hypocrisy, and power.[16]

---

[15] Other Canadian considerations of Gertrude, in which Ophelia does not figure very prominently, include Carole Corbeil's novel, *In the Wings*, from which my first epigraph is taken, and G. B. Shand's article "Realizing Gertrude: The Suicide Option."

[16] In addition to the play's roots in the Hamlet story, it's conclusion seems to echo another early modern revenge play, Marlowe's *The Jew of Malta*, in its representation of opportunistic Christian hypocrisy: king Fengo, newly "converted" to Christianity for political reasons, responds to the vicious murder of the Mad Boy, impaled by a monk on a wooden cross, with "Well done, my Christian soldiers" (1995: 149).

O'Brien's play is the most radical deconstruction of Shakespeare's *Hamlet* of the three plays under consideration, deconstruction seen as a re-source-ing of the play – a returning to the play's sources in search of another kind of anarchic, multiple, and textually unstable author-ity. In a sense, O'Brien begins his work having come to the point at which Ann-Marie MacDonald's Constance arrives toward the end of *Goodnight Desdemona (Good Morning Juliet)* (discussed in Chapter Six, below), when in her search for the original manuscript and author of Shakespeare's plays she comes to understand that "it's not the man you seek, [but] the Manuscript" (that is, 'the man you script'), yourself, as reader and therefore author of the plays' meanings (1990a: 73). As O'Brien describes his writing process, he began with "scissors and glue" and "a pile of mangled scripts" that included the "Bad Quarto" of *Hamlet* and the *Gesta Danorum* and set about "trying to debase the greatest play of all time." "Eventually I began tossing in a line or two of my own. Soon more lines appeared, the setting and scenes began to change, and so too did the names of all the characters" (1995: 8). The result was a "Viking Hamlet Saga" set in a mythical "Helsingor" and featuring (in addition to a disreputable pair of Christian Brothers, two old women who may have been inspired by *Macbeth*'s witches, various "Vikings, monks, wolves, spirits," and "the ghost of Jesus Christ"): Fengo (the Claudius character), Gerutha (Gertrude), Horvendal, or "the Mad Boy" (Hamlet), Matthius (Polonius), Ragnar (Laertes), and last, but by no means least, Lilja, O'Brien's version of Ophelia.[17]

While the Ophelias of Clarke and Gass both remain recognizably within the representational record as (re)constructed by Showalter and Burnett, as they remain determinedly in margins of the story, O'Brien's Lilja may be seen to break with, or at least to stretch that record. For one thing, she is a spirited thirteen-year-old "who'd rather lop off her father's head than quietly drown in a river," as reviewer Martin Morrow noted (1995: 153). She is first seen as the object of Fengo's lust and public abuse in a carousing court scene where she slaps the king across the face in the presence of her father and calls him "a fukkin animal" (1995: 18). The "advice scene" with Ragnar/ Laertes and Matthius/Polonius sees her making an obscene gesture at both of them, and ends with an exchange that sets the gendered tone interrogated by the play:

---

[17]   The names come from a variety of sources, and some seem to be pure invention. "Fengo" and "Horvendal" are from Saxo, though the latter is an adaptation of what is there the name of Hamlet's ("Amleth"'s) father. "Gerutha" also derives from Saxo.

MATTHIUS. I know it's hard to be the girl, my dear. I know it's hard, me lovin him more than you. But ye gots to accept yer lot in life. It's the godds' will.

LILJA. Aye, I do accept it. At least I'm not a horse.

MATTHIUS. That's the spirit. That's the feminine spirit. Oh Lilja, Lilja, me sweet sweet pride and joy. A fine woman yer turnin out to be.

LILJA. You too, father. (33)

These scenes establish the background for her converting to Christianity-as-resistance (though Christ is established by Lilja as "the god of being... Crucified! Crucified! I think – I'd like to be Crucified!" [45-6]); getting stigmata and wearing a crown of thorns – appropriating for herself the role of Christ; converting Horvendal/Hamlet to her brand of Christianity, in the course of which conversion – a revision of the eavesdropping scene – he bites off her ear; considering suicide (though she is advised by her father that "suicide's for men... It's an honourable death" [75]); rejecting an arranged political marriage with Fengo ("Say somethin sweet to old Fengo. Say somethin all girlie and sweet," he asks, to which she replies, "Bugger your dog" [95]); killing her abusive father and brandishing his severed head at the Court; and urging Horvendal (both in her own voice and that of his father's ghost) to take "VENGEANCE" (123). She is finally murdered in action by her own brother, who mistakes her for "the Mad Boy" after she has, in the interests of getting something accomplished, exchanged clothes with the weak-willed Horvendal/Hamlet. (The latter, in a role and gender reversal from *Hamlet*, attempts to drown himself in a hole in the ice while roaming the landscape dressed in Lilja's clothes, but he characteristically botches the job). Even after she is dead, however, this Lilja/Ophelia remains a presence – she is heard singing to mark the murder of Gertrude – and even seems to retain agency: she appears to effect her own revenge, for example, when Horvendal emerges from her coffin and shroud, imbued with her spirit, to impale her brother Ragnar/Laertes on "Skull-Byter," Ragnar's own petard, as it were.[18] O'Brien's Lilja, then, may be the most consistently and disruptively revisionist of the Canadian Ophelias under consideration here, resisting the romantic comforts of victimization or virgin martyrdom, the pleasures of guilty complicity, and the early feminist comforts of resistant "madness," in favor of an active seizing of agency and assertion of female subjectivity, in the context of however masculinist a script (or

---

[18] This moment might be seen as a reversal of the appropriation of Ophelia within a male actor's and character's body in Lepage's *Elsinore*, described above, in that here the ineffectual male body of Horvendal is appropriated and transformed by Lilja's active female spirit.

scripts). But Lilja nevertheless finally passes into (mis)representation in *Mad Boy Chronicle* even as Ophelia has done in critical discourse, through a eulogy delivered by the murderous and hypocritical Fengo before her funeral pyre:

> Hold off your torches just a little while;
> Gots to allow for any tardie guests.
> Let's remember this girl, the example she set.
> A good and gentle angel, inspirin to us all [...]
> At times like this, we often do reflect,
> Does life, does death, harbour any hope?
> Or is we haccidents, toss'd upon this earth,
> Doomed to fight and hack each others bones?
> I tell ye verily, look upon this girl,
> And try to say to mee, there's no hope for this world. (145)

The eulogy ends with a breezy and delightfully undercutting couplet that, in a manner that I would argue is characteristic of drama, theatre, and artistic representation in general in Canada, is rich with the type of irony that invites a critical revisiting of the play's action, and perhaps also of critical considerations of Ophelia and her sisters:

> All a man can say is – God is Love;
> Let's torch this child and praise the Lord above. (146)

The cultural work performed by O'Brien's representation of Ophelia might be seen as emerging from the contrast that is made visible (and risible) between this speech and its masculinist appropriation of representation – its seizing of control of the ways in which women pass into representation – and the wildly vibrant character we have witnessed in the course of the action. The speech is part of a pattern in the play that echoes a pattern in critical discourse about Shakespeare's women, in which men insist on the fragility, sweetness, or appropriate femininity of "their" women in spite of all evidence or protestation to the contrary.[19]

---

[19]   In addition to Matthius's speech to Lilja, quoted above, and Fengo's eulogy, such passages in the play include the following exchange between Fengo and Gertrude:
FENGO. Oh straind Gerutha, paragon of womanhood.
What a rack this plight of yours must be!
Faithful wife, loving mother, honourable, brave:
Sometimes woman, I think yer too good for this world.
GERUTHA. No I ain't.
FENGO. Course you is! (60)

*** 

In his Playwright's Foreword to *Mad Boy Chronicle* Michael O'Brien suggests, without expanding on the idea, that "only in Canada could such a play get writ" (9). I don't know if this is true; other cultures have produced irreverent and culturally productive revisionings of canonical texts. But it *is* true that Shakespeare has played a very particular and crucial cultural role in a postcolonial Canada for whom British cultural imperialism, as represented by institutions such as Ontario's Stratford Festival, remains alive and well. It is true, too, that intertextual, parodic, and ironic revisionings of canonical, and particularly Shakespearean texts, proliferate in a country known for its sophisticated production of incisive and politically satiric work that ranges from television's "Codco," "Kids in the Hall," and "This Hour Has Twenty-Two Minutes" to the early days and greatest successes of Second City – not to mention scholarly workers in the field of parody, irony, and intertextuality such as, most notably, Linda Hutcheon.[20] Parody, in Hutcheon's definition as "repetition with a critical difference" (1985: 6; if also in Canada a respectful if double-edged critical *deference* in the case of Shakespeare), may itself be seen to be characteristically, if schizophrenically Canadian, as Hutcheon suggests in *Splitting Images*, her book on contemporary Canadian ironies. Hutcheon there indicates that ironic intertextuality is a mode peculiarly amenable to Canadian sensibilities, an argument made in a different but compatible mode by E.D. Blodgett when he argues that "our history [...] is a matter of ambiguous and multiple positionings between the desireds of culture, the subject, and discourse that finish the text with its inevitable ephemerality" (1993: 16).[21]

It seems in any case to be true that Canada, with its extraordinarily complex postcolonial matrix as a settler/invader colony founded on displacements, is well positioned to engage in intertextual ironies, parodic "tributes," and complex revisionings.[22] Finally, it is true that

---

[20] See Linda Hutcheon, *Narcissistic Fiction: The Metafictional Paradox*; *A Theory of Parody: The Teachings of Twentieth Century Artforms*; *Irony's Edge: The Theory and Politics of Irony*; and, especially, *Splitting Images: Contemporary Canadian Ironies*.

[21] See also "Canadians Can't Spell; or, the Virtues of Indeterminacy," in Richard Paul Knowles, "Representing Canada: Teaching Canadian Studies in the United States."

[22] As I have indicated in the Introduction to this volume, Canada may be seen to have been founded on displacements of First Nations peoples by European settlers, of course, but also by settlers who were themselves displaced in the Highland clearances, the "potato famine," the expulsion or escape of United Empire Loyalists during the American revolution, the expulsion and return of the Acadians, and more recently in various immigrations from a wide variety of countries suffering from economic or political repression. Colonial and postcolonial relationships exist

Canadian postcolonial and feminist revisionings of Shakespeare, including those considered in this survey, for all of these reasons and more, often have at once a harder edge and a more pronounced and politicized seriousness than do many attempts to "poke fun at the Bard" that emerge from British or American sources, or that are regularly performed "in good fun" at venues such as the Edinburgh Festival. Shakespeare, it seems, has come to serve Canadians in complex ways as a site for the serious negotiation of social and cultural identities, gendered and otherwise.

Showalter's history of Ophelia in representation concludes that "there is no 'true' Ophelia for whom feminist criticism must unambiguously speak, but perhaps only a Cubist Ophelia of multiple perspectives, more than the sum of all her parts" (1985: 92). What this survey of Canadian Ophelias may do, beyond asserting that some of her parts reside in Canada and providing another plane face of the cube, is to locate some problematically gendered revisionings of Shakespeare within a postcolonial settler-colony culture founded in the 19th century, where the contemporary push against Shakespeare as symbol of high-cultural, imperialist oppression registers directly against the continuing pull of Shakespeare as authority and source. It is not surprising, if it is also somewhat discouraging, that Ophelia, a minor character in *Hamlet*, plays a central and determinate role in none of the representations under consideration here, and this, again, may mark the difficulty and complexity of attempting to write revisionist cultures and do politically productive cultural work by evoking, however critically or irreverently, canonical texts. But perhaps the cumulative effect of such revisionings is to remind us, sometimes forcefully, that, however "niiiice" the dominant representation of Ophelia-as-woman-as-victim may be, like other representations, "that's a picture, you dimwit!" "You can't... BE... a picture, okay?

---

within Canada between the two "founding cultures" themselves, as the English, historically and currently, play a colonizing role in relation to the French, and both these groups act as colonizers in relation to First Nations peoples within Canada and Québec as they do in relation to various "ethnic" groups. In addition, of course, Canada has continued to experience culturally colonial relationships to France, England, and other "homeland" cultures, and to function as an economic and political colony of the United States.

CHAPTER 6

# Othello in Three Times

*[T]he Shakespeare's mine, but you can have it.*
(Sears, 1996: 52)

Among Shakespeare's best-known plays, *Othello* has been of relatively little interest to Canadian directors, translators, or theatre companies in the last half of the 20<sup>th</sup> century, and when the play has been
staged here it has not been notably successful.[1] This is so, perhaps,
because as Edward Pechter says, the play is "unpleasant,"[2] perhaps
because of its treatment of gender (Desdemona, Emilia, and Bianca),

---

[1]  Alan Somerset, in his 1991 catalogue index to the Festival's archives, lists only four
productions of the play at Stratford, for example, between 1953 and 1990, as opposed to seven of *Hamlet*, eight of *Lear*, and seven of *Macbeth*, among the so-
called "major tragedies." The most popular comedies, *Twelfth Night* (9), *A Midsummer Night's Dream* (8), *As You Like It* (10), *Much Ado About Nothing* (8), *The
Taming of the Shrew* (8), and even *Love's Labour's Lost* (7), even more significantly outstrip *Othello* in numbers of productions at Stratford, where even such
problematic plays as *The Merry Wives of Windsor* (5), *Julius Caesar* (5), and
*Measure for Measure* (5) have been produced more often than a play with a significantly higher canonical reputation. None of the four productions, and no other Canadian productions with which I am familiar, received unequivocally favorable reviews. Pettigrew and Portman describe the 1959 production as "something of a
shambles" by the end of the run (1985, vol. 1: 141), the 1973 production as that
season's "major disaster" (1985, vol. 2: 35), and the 1979 production as a mixed
success let down by Alan Scarfe's Othello, which one reviewer felt was less a character than a "loud, tedious vacancy" (1985, vol. 2: 163). The fourth production
Somerset lists, in 1987, with an unhealthy Howard Rollins in the title role, was even
less successful. Even before Rollins took ill, however, opening night reviews were
less than favorable, and more than one critic, found it, as Bob Pennington did, "a
major disappointment." Since Somerset's book appeared there has been one more
production at the Festival, in 1994, which again received mixed reviews, though
H. J. Kirchhoff, in the *Globe and Mail*, found it "a superb piece of theatre."
[2]  In a plenary address to the Association for Canadian College and University
Teachers of English, and the Association for Canadian Theatre Research, at the
Congress of the Humanities and Social Sciences Federation of Canada in Ottawa,
June 1998. See also his recent book, *The Endless Controversy of* Othello: *A Per-
formance History of Shakespeare's Most Disturbing Play.*

race (Othello and everyone else), and class (Othello, Brabantio, Iago and Cassio, Desdemona and Emilia, among others) in ways that cannot readily or comfortably be subsumed under the general wash of universalist humanism that dominates the review discourse and the discourses of most major Canadian theatre companies to this day. Its central role, moreover, has proven to be difficult to cast, a difficulty that perhaps uncomfortably exposes systemic racism in a mainstream Canadian theatre industry that in at least some respects lags behind Britain and the United States in dealing with the representation (and casting) of race and difference.

In each of the last three decades, however, there *has* been one significant and widely successful Canadian dramatic *adaptation* of the play that has presented itself as revisionist, in one way or another: the regionalist and populist *Cruel Tears*, by Ken Mitchell and Humphrey and the Dumptrucks, first produced at Persephone Theatre in Saskatchewan in 1975, which subsequently toured the country to some acclaim; the feminist *Goodnight Desdemona (Good Morning Juliet)*, by Ann-Marie MacDonald, first produced by Nightwood Theatre in Toronto in 1988, which also toured the country in a revised version (in 1989-90) and won the Governor General's Award for Drama in 1990; and the interventionist *Harlem Duet*, by Djanet Sears, first produced by Nightwood Theatre in 1997, which was subsequently remounted by Canadian Stage Company and won the Governor General's Award for Drama in 1997. An examination of each of these adaptations, each very much a product of its time, suggests a shifting relationship over three decades between "Shakespeare" and the construction of gender, race, ethnicity, and class in Canada. Such an analysis may serve to elucidate the different ways in which, and degrees to which, adapting Shakespeare has served as cultural intervention (resisting the gender, classed, and raced construction of dominant and normative subjectivities), or as cultural affirmation (at once renewing "Shakespeare," validating by association the adaptation itself and the cultural position from which it emerges, and consolidating dominant, if somewhat more elastic, social norms).

## I. *Cruel Tears*: Populism, Regionalism, and Ethnicity

*[T]here was Stratford. But I'm talking about Canadian theatre.*

(Ken Mitchell, "Ken Mitchell:" 153)

*Cruel Tears*, billed as a "country opera," is very much a product of its mid-1970s moment in Canadian and Canadian-theatre history, a time when counter-hegemonic (as opposed to anti-hegemonic) nationalism and anti-centric regionalisms were the alternative movements of

choice, often leaving little room for other kinds of resistance. Canadian
cultural nationalism was at its peak in theatres across the country when
*Cruel Tears* was first produced in 1975, spurred by the larger cultural
and artistic climate, the residue of celebrations of the Canadian centennial in 1967, and the founding of *Canadian Theatre Review* the previous year, as it launched its crusade against the appointment of the
British Robin Phillips as artistic director of the Stratford Festival. The
top drama prize for new Canadian play at the time, the Chalmers
Award, was won in 1977, the same year that *Cruel Tears* was runner
up, by the stereotypically "Canadian" hockey play, *Les Canadiens*, by
Rick Salutin (with an "assist" from hockey legend Ken Dryden).
Militant regionalism was also everywhere manifest, not only in various
small- "c" folk or populist cultural revivals in Newfoundland, Acadie,
the Maritime and Prairie provinces, "Souwesto'" (Southwestern Ontario), and elsewhere, but in a proliferation of separatist rhetoric in
reaction to the Trudeau government's strong centralist federalism:
there was, with varying degrees of seriousness, disgruntled talk of
nationalist movements forming in Newfoundland, Cape Breton, and
British Columbia, among other places, as well as in Québec. And in
theatres across the country regional subject matter became a selling
point, while in theatre criticism it emerged as a resistant and anti-
centrist analytical tool, as the Massey Commission's post-war model of
taking "Culture" from the centre to the uncivilized regions[3] was replaced by theorizings of cultural production as a home-grown, ground-
up activity less interested in civilizing the masses and more closely tied
to cultural and physical geography and to other forms of work and
social activity.[4] In 1985, in an survey article on "Writing the Land
Alive: The Playwrights' Vision in English Canada," Robert Wallace
grouped *Cruel Tears* with a variety of populist "regional plays that [...]
successfully toured the country"(77) in the mid-seventies, bringing
"culture" *from* the regions *to* the urban centres. Most of these, not

---

[3]   The Massey Commission was a Royal Commission initiated by Prime Minister
      Louis St. Laurent in 1949 and chaired by Vincent Massey, which issued its report in
      1951. See Rubin, 153-55 and 176-83, for a reprinting of the commission and the
      sections of the report directly related to theatre. The report led directly to the found-
      ing of the Canada Council for the Arts.

[4]   The key piece in the regionalist theorizing of Canadian drama and theatre, Diane
      Bessai's "The Regionalism of Canadian Drama," was not published until 1980, but
      it cites many of the major playwrights and theatre companies across the country in
      the 1970s development of Canadian regionalist drama and theatre. Bessai defends
      "regional" (as opposed to "provincial") as a theoretical term that "in its positive
      sense [...] means rooted, indigenous, shaped by a specific social, cultural and physi-
      cal milieu. It reflects the past as well as the present and at its best absorbs innumer-
      able influences from beyond its borders, particularly as these have bearing on the
      informing regional perspective" (1980: 7).

surprisingly, were folk-, country-, or rock-musicals, including *Paper Wheat* (Saskatchewan), *Rock and Roll* (Nova Scotia), *They Club Seals, Don't They?* (Newfoundland), as well as, oddly located in the company of these rural musicals, Michel Tremblay's gay urban fantasia, *Hosanna* (from Montreal, by way of Toronto).

Novelist, playwright, poet, and polemicist Ken Mitchell, editor of *The Prairie Anthology*, was seen at the time to be a leader among the regionalists, so much so that the section devoted to him in a 1981 book of interviews with Canadian writers is called, simply, "Prairies," and his bio there lists him as, among other things, a "former pig farmer" (163). The interview itself stresses "the so-called search for identity:" "I believe prairie people know their identity," claims Mitchell. "[T]here's a strong sense of regional involvement," he argues, and "the ethnic thing is part of it." Moreover, he says, "I believe a natural writer or poet is really somebody who is only a voice for a people or region" (165), and "[h]istory is slowly realizing that the art which originates in the prairies is stronger, on a per capita basis let's say, than art which originates elsewhere" (166). And indeed *Cruel Tears* establishes its regionalist credentials early on. The play opens with stage directions calling for a "bright prairie sun," the trilling of a meadowlark, and "a mime suggest[ing] a prairie environment." It's first line, introducing a choral song, is "Well we got a song about the West" (Mitchell and HD, 1977: 13), and the play builds on this through the careful use of localist detail ranging from prairie slang ("Holy Hannah" 94), to pan-national rural customs (such as the drinking of "Five-Star" Canadian rye whisky, 109). The play ends as it began, with a song about "a lady of the prairie" (144-45).

As a regionalist revisioning of a canonical play, taking "Shakespeare" down a peg or two, *Cruel Tears* is wittily effective, it's very co-authorship with a country-and-western band named Humphrey and the Dumptrucks making clear its resistant populist appeal. A "country opera" (Littler, 1985: 281) set in a prairie truckers' culture, the play makes loose use of the *Othello* plot, most notably its melodrama: a Ukrainian-Canadian truck driver in Saskatoon, Johnny Roychuk (Othello) falls in love with and marries the boss's daughter, Kathy (Desdemona) and after much weeping and country-music wailing is promoted to a supervisory position by her father, Earl (a conflation of Branbantio, the Duke, and the Senators). A worker's representative, union-buster, and covert company stooge, Jack Deal (Iago), whose wife Flora (Emilia) has befriended Kathy, turns against Johnny and plots to make him jealous of a fellow "hippy" trucker, Ricky (Cassio). In the end Johnny strangles Kathy with the embroidered scarf given to her by his Ukrainian mother, which she has in turn given to Flora, and when he learns from Flora of his mistake he kills Earl. As Johnny himself says, it's a play about "the big bohunk and the boss's daughter" (Mitchell and HD, 1977: 38), and as such it sets itself up as a resistant populist revisioning of Shakespeare's play, well positioned to undertake a site-specific, localist interrogation not only of imperialist and centrist notions of High Culture, but also, given the source and subject matter, of gender, race, and class on the 1970s prairie. But counterhegemonic nationalist or regionalist movements have not always been sensitive or friendly to other forms of difference – as Amanda Hale asked of the alternative theatre movement in Canada of the 1970s, "after the renaissance: where are the women?" (83) – and it is worth taking a closer look at the play's construction of gender, raced, and classed subjectivities.

Ken Mitchell claims in a number of interviews that "I'm trying to jab at some sore spots of sexual politics" in *Cruel Tears* (1978: 40; see also 1982:149), but for the most part the play seems more to reinscribe and reinforce rather than undermine or challenge traditional gender relationships in society, in *Othello*, and in country music itself. The play includes a very odd (and very politically soft) song called "Liberated Lady" by the "waitress" character, Debbie Lou, "heavily made up, still looking for her man" (20), who slings beer and sexist banter with the truckers at the Blacktop Bar – a song more about wanting "a dude/That isn't rude/To spread butter on my bread" (92) than about independent subjectivity. And in fact the play's representations of gender roles are depressingly familiar: "the men drive trucks and the girls keep house" (17), and social change is figured more-or-less exclusively as upward mobility *within* the dominant sex-gender system.

Johnny's a foreman, climbin' real fast.

He wears a tie and his pants get pressed.

Kathy's in the kitchen cookin' up a storm

Sewin' all the curtain for their cozy little home. (59)

Meanwhile, in the bar and in the workplace, the talk is all of women as "used goods" (46) and of "coppin' feels for free" (109). Jokes about "shaggin'" and penis size (18), moreover, seem to be endorsed and naturalized by the play. Even the published script's list of characters identifies Kathy only as "his [Johnny's] sweetheart and wife" (12). What gestures the play does make toward heightened consciousness, interestingly, are classed: when Flora says to Kathy "I just didden think you'd be the type to take up cookin' and cleaning and all that," Kathy replies, conscious that she has "married down" but *un*consious of insulting her new friend, "neither did I. Just no *way* Kathy Jenson was going to be trapped into a traditional housewife role." But it doesn't matter, because "[A]nyway, I *do* like cooking. Isn't that weird?" (65).

The play seems, then, to update and relocate rather than interrogate the gender hierarchies inscribed within *Othello*: Debbie Lou in her miniskirt, titillating the truckers, is a fair approximation of Shakespeare's Bianca; Flora, abused by her brutish husband and deflating Kathy's idealism, stands in naturally for her model Emilia; and Kathy, if anything, is less adventuresome than Desdemona, who at least "goes on the road" with *her* partner. Kathy's last words before joining Johnny in a romantic death song (hers), as she passes, with Desdemona-like passivity, into representation, are: "I'm so scared when you're not here. I need you – to put me to bed... Promise me you'll always be here to put me to bed, Johnny" (136-37).

Oddly for an adaptation of *Othello* the only things "black" in *Cruel Tears* are "the stage" (13) and the setting at "the Blacktop bar" (17). Although all of the characters are white, however, the racism that drives *Othello* is reproduced in *Cruel Tears* as "prejudice" on the bases of ethnicity and class. Jack/Iago's jealousy of Johnny, and Earl/Brabantio's resistance to Kathy's marriage with his Ukrainian-Canadian employee, are rooted in racist revulsion to what is constructed as ethnic miscegenation. Jack tortures Earl, Iago-like ("an old black ram/Is tupping your white ewe," I.i.89-90), with images of "a sweet little girl from the suburbs involved in some pretty funny business on the other side of town – ... you know – animal acts – like the kinda stuff you were tellin' us *you* saw down in Vegas" (42): "I know you don't get to that part of town much, Mr. Jensen – lotta DP's, yuh know, Indians. But there's this big dumb bohunk over there... and this sweet little chick from the suburbs gets the blocks put to her by the bohunk – every night..." (42). Elsewhere, too, ethnic slurs and stereotypes – "I know his kind" (50); "Just like a Uke" (66); "Kin smell the garlic from here!" (57), and "Tell her how the bohunks beat their women" (50) – are used to motivate the characters and the action against "the big Yewkerainian" (101) in a way that is clearly condemned by the play.

At the same time, however, the play's attempt to portray the Ukrainian community in Saskatchewan in a positive way is somewhat uncomfortably aligned with the Trudeau brand of liberalism that produced official multiculturalism in Canada in the 1970s, positioning French and English as the country's founding, institutionalized, and evolving "cultures" against a variety of static and exoticised "ethnicities" to be encouraged and preserved through folk practices and community-centre cultural activities (see Gomez, 1995: 29; Hawkins, 1988: 11). In *Cruel Tears,* Johnny is himself indistinguishable in terms of lived experience and material practice from the rest of the play's truckers – a fact that seems to be used to represent the prejudice against him as being particularly heinous – while his family appears as ethnic "DANCERS," with no individual identities or even familial roles (mother, father, etc.), dressed in "traditional Ukrainian costumes" (57) and unrepresented, in person or in other textual references, except at the wedding. And finally there's the scarf, which retains many of the exoticizing and therefore othering overtones of its source in *Othello*'s famous handkerchief, overtones that will resurface and claim focus in very different ways over two decades later in Djanet Sears's more extended treatment of "magic in the web" of the handkerchief in *Harlem Duet*. Here the scarf is made of expensive silk, colorfully embroidered (in presumably ethnic Ukrainian patterns) and given to Kathy at her wedding reception by Johnny's mother (61, 86). In *Cruel Tears* the scarf is presumably a kerchief, or embroidered towel, the traditional Ukrainian symbol of a woman's married status that is placed over icons in the home and taken down during the wedding ceremony to literally bind the young couple's hands together. It serves in *Cruel Tears* to reinforce Mitchell's reinscription of traditional gender roles – particularly in its resurfacing as "evidence" of Kathy's infidelity and, in a significant deviation from the source, as the weapon used to strangle her.[5]

But ethnicity (or "race") is only partly the issue here. Another, and perhaps more significant deviation from the source sees the problematics of class elevated from one root cause of Iago's envy of Cassio to a central factor in the main plot and, perhaps more significantly, in the play's overall culturally revisionist intervention. Part of the central conflict here, clearly, is that Johnny (from "across the tracks)" and Kathy ("the boss's daughter," "the sweet little girl from the suburbs") are from different social classes, a fact that his Ukrainian origins seem to naturalize, hierarchically conflating ethnic difference and class difference: *all* Ukrainians, Indians, and others, it seems, are, "naturally," from across the tracks and the class divide. In fact much of the action has the feel of a cross-class Romeo-and-Juliet story, as the young lovers fight to overcome, in this case, *her* family's (30), or her father's, problems with *his* class status:

You listen to me, you worthless bum,

It cost me a fortune to bring her up.

She's used to having everything –

Brand spanking new! (51)

---

[5]   I am grateful to Irena Makaryk for my reading of the role of the kerchief in the Ukrainian tradition.

Meanwhile, once the father is won over and Johnny is promoted, Johnny's fellow workers resent his elevation in rank, together with what they see as his class disloyalty and his related, and clearly feminized, desertion of the bar for the boudoir (75-78) and a "stuck-up bitch" (103) who "isn't going to lower herself to take in a truck driver party!" (85) – a familiar pop-culture allegory. And Kathy has trouble reconciling herself to the tastes, world view, and resignation of her new friend Flora and her world of "Korman's Cut-Rate House of Bargains" (63). The young lovers are left, *West-Side-Story*-style ("there's a place for us") to dream of how "together we'll find a way" (31).

But class plays itself out in *Cruel Tears* in ways that are perhaps more significant than simply as an object of representation or an engine of the plot. The play itself makes a conscious assault on class in Canada, on the construction of Canadian theatre audiences, and on the construction of theatre itself as high-culture artifact. In interviews Mitchell indicates a conscious intention "to open theatre up, to bring an audience into the theatre that's normally not attracted at all" (1982: 147). "I'm a populist by nature," he says (1982: 148), and in his use of popular culture from C&W to K-Tel (thinly disguised as "Kar-Tel" [Mitchell and HD, 1977: 94]),[6] together with his replacement of "Venice's noble senators and patricians" with "Knights of the Road" (Redfern, 1977: 28), he actively attempts to validate the popular. Mitchell also articulates his use of the country-opera genre and of Shakespearean source material explicitly as an attack on elitist high culture, an attempted reclamation of Shakespeare and opera as popular forms (see 1981: 40; 1982: 149-50), and "an attempt to return to the original conception of theatre" (1981: 40):

> I wanted to write a political play. It's political in the sense that I wanted to break down some of the barriers between art and politics; I wanted to reach a different kind of audience. We haven't broken through yet to this audience, a different audience than the university-educated, regular, theatre-going audience – the "elite," if you want to call it that. (1981: 40)

*Cruel Tears,* then, is a complex blend of interventionist critique on several fronts, high-cultural aspiration for popular, regional and national forms, and reification of traditional gender, class, and ethnic positionings. And among its most interesting and unusual features is its ambivalent treatment of its Shakespearean source. Mitchell and the Dumptrucks seem to want to have their cultural authority and eat it too: the play seems clearly and deliberately to *avoid* explicit citations of

---

[6]    K-Tel is a mail-order company producing cut-rate compilations of pop-music hits from earlier decades and marketing them on television through the use of short clips from long lists of songs.

Shakespeare or *Othello* that might alienate the populist "crowd" – to the degree that at least one review doesn't even mention the canonical source of the action (McIlroy); but at the same time the play thereby allows the silent and hegemonic operation of unconscious influence and provides even greater self-congratulatory rewards for the cognoscenti who recognize plot parallels and revisions. These include such moments as Kathy's remarkably faithful (to the lyrics) country version of the Willow song (133) and Othello's otherwise inexplicable lyric, "Now snuff out the candles" (137). Mitchell talks in his interview with Robert Wallace about "evoking and parodying it [*Othello*] in a contemporary setting" (1982: 150), but in many ways his attempt to recuperate the play for populism can also be seen as a project of at once reifying, renewing, and revitalizing Shakespeare while making high-culture claims for *Cruel Tears* itself. It is telling, I think, that two of the three dedicatees in the published script (the third is Brian Sklar, presumably for the playwright's personal reasons) are "Geraldi Cinthio" (Shakespeare's own primary source) and "William Shakespear" [*sic*], positioning Shakespeare himself as a revisionist, and Mitchell and the Dumptrucks as inheritors of a noble, high-cultural tradition of revising, and renewing, classic texts.

## II.  *Goodnight Desdemona (Good Morning Juliet)*: Gender and Genre

*It's like opening up a trunk that used to be full of instruments of torture and now everything has turned into toys.*
(Ann-Marie MacDonald, "Ann-Marie MacDonald:" 142)

If *Cruel Tears* filters its revisionism through a peculiarly mid-1970s variety of regionalism, ethnicity, and class, Ann-Marie MacDonald's *Goodnight Desdemona (Good Morning Juliet)* – which also draws directly on popular culture, and much more explicitly brings together *Othello* and *Romeo and Juliet* – works through a second-wave feminist focus on gender and genre that is very much of its 1980s context at Toronto's Nightwood Theatre near the end of its second mandate.[7] In

---

[7]  Nightwood's early, first mandate, in 1979, was not, in fact, feminist – or was feminist only in the sense that Nightwood was a company of women creating work for themselves. It focused on the creation of theatre based on the visual arts. What I am calling the second mandate, which seems to have begun informally in the early 1980s, concentrated on the creation of women-centered work and shifted from a period of feminist collective creations such as *Smoke Damage* (1983), *This is for You, Anna* (1983), and *Pope Joan* (1984) early in the mandate, to individually authored plays by the late 1980s. In 1989, between the first production of *Goodnight Desdemona* and its remount, the company's third mandate, the focus on women of color, came into effect.

fact according to its director, Bañuta Rubess, the original idea for *Goodnight Desdemona (Good Morning Juliet)* emerged in a revisionist reading of the death of Desdemona performed as a joke on a tour of England in 1985 of Nightwood's earlier play, *This is for You, Anna*: "Ann-Marie MacDonald crammed a pillow on my face and with great hilarity pronounced: 'Goodnight, Desdemona!'" (Rubess 1990: 7). There is no sign of regionalism in the play, except insofar as references to Queen's University mark it as Ontario-based. Nor is there much sign of nationalism of the 1970s variety, though as Joanne Tompkins argues (1996: 15-16, 20-21) the play *does* operate as what Helen Tiffin calls "canonical counter-discourse" (1987: 22), and it does assert, as Ann Wilson notes, a postcolonialist resistance to the imported cultural authority of what she calls "British cultural achievement" as represented by the canonical "Shakespeare" and the despicable Claude Night (1992: 3). (The latter is a British-born male academic with a job in the colonies, "dignified and irritated" [MacDonald, 1990a: 70], "perfectly groomed and brogued," who "speaks with an Oxford accent" [22] in a "cultivated voice" [71], "oozes confidence" [22], and exploits his female graduate students.[8]) As Mark Fortier notes, moreover, "there is little in this play about class" (1989: 51) beyond light-hearted "pok[ing] fun at the Bard" (Crew) and some acute commentary on the hierarchically classed and gender system of graduate student labor, tenure, and promotion in the academy (see Dvorak, 1994: 132). Fortier also notes, finally, that the play "completely elides the issue of race" (1989: 51); in fact, when its central character, Constance Ledbelly, first sees Othello the whole issue of race is sidestepped in a characteristic throwaway pun: "he's not a Moor!" Constance marvels in an aside, in response to which Iago, unconventionally hearing the aside, remarks "Amour? Ah-ha! C'est ça! Et pourquoi pas?"

What *Goodnight Desdemona does* provide is a lively and acute dramatic interrogation of the gender politics of genre that is characteristic of 1980s feminist critical work, and a theoretically sophisticated representation and enactment of resistant reading in a play in which, unlike in *Cruel Tears*, the metadramatic context and the overt revisioning of Shakespeare provides the opportunity, as Tompkins argues, "for a hybrid form" and the possibility "of *performatively* altering the power structures embedded in the original text" (1996: 16). "What if a Fool were to enter the worlds of both 'Othello' and 'Romeo and Juliet'?" the play asks, noting the "flimsy mistakes" on which their

---

[8]    In its original version, as performed at the Annex Theatre in 1988, there was more focus on the character of Claude Night, who returned at the end of the play to attempt further exploitations, and perhaps to begin his own quest for self-knowledge.

tragic actions turn. "[W]ould our fool defuse the tragedies by assuming centre stage as comic hero?" (21). MacDonald proceeds from this to stage the literal entry of Constance into the worlds of *Othello* and *Romeo and Juliet* as part of her investigation for her doctoral dissertation, in an attempt to prove that the plays as we have them consist of Shakespeare's own plundering and colonizing of his source texts. The original plays, she determines, were comedies, turned tragic through Shakespeare's appropriative expurgation of their interventionist wise fools. Transported into the action of the plays at their crucial moments, Constance summarily intervenes, instantly deflects their ersatz tragic inevitability, and proceeds to search through clues in her alchemical source text, the "Gustav Manuscript" (written, as is her own dissertation, on "foolscap"), for evidence of the (original) Author, and the Fool that is the agent of the plot. Not surprisingly, she discovers that the "fo-o-ol's cap" (73) is her own red toque, and that "the Fool and the Author are one and the same" – "a lass" (86). "You're it," as the ghost (imported from *Hamlet*) tells her (73-74, 86). Along the way, Constance of course encounters revisionist versions of most of the major characters in *Othello* and *Romeo and Juliet*. Much has been made of the play's representation of Desdemona and Juliet as strong and independent women, its appropriation of the male characters' best lines by strong women who are agents of the action rather than objects of the gaze, its (muted) representation of polymorphous sexuality and lesbian eroticism, and its deployment of a resistant feminist comedy (Hentgen). All of this is true and, with typical Ann-Marie MacDonald excess, then some. But perhaps the single most important contribution made by the play is its representation and enactment of female readerly agency in the production of meaning: "it's not a man you seek," the ghost also tells her, but "the Manuscript" (the man you script, yourself, as agent). The entry of Constance into the play worlds of Desdemona and Juliet, then, like the trope of ongoing rehearsal of meaning discussed by Tompkins, "creates a site for the negotiation and re-negotiation of the Shakespearean text's cultural centrality rather than a definitive negation or rejection" (Tompkins, 1996: 16). It renders Shakespearean meaning negotiable, and reconstructs the texts, in Roland Barthes' terms, as writerly rather than readerly (Barthes *passim*), or in Catherine Belsey's terms, interrogative rather than declarative (Belsey, 1980: 91).

Like *Cruel Tears*, however, *Goodnight Desdemona (Good Morning Juliet)* remains a curious blend of intervention and complicity, and like Mitchell (though perhaps with more wit) MacDonald positions herself *with* Shakespeare as revisionist: "I was being mischievous by using Shakespeare as a source in the same way he used everyone else as a source," she remarked to Rita Much in an interview (MacDonald,

1990b: 141). In any case, depending as it does on the audience's *recognition* of its revisionism, *Goodnight Desdemona* can easily be read as popular-cultural slumming for what Marta Dvorak calls an "educated audience" (1994: 131): "a farce for 'highbrows'" (Dvorak, 1994: 130), the play is, in Denis Johnston's phrase, "delightfully literate and engagingly lowbrow" (1993: 86). As such, it can even be read less as cultural intervention than mainstream literary interpretation, as when Dvorak sees its representations of Desdemona as less a feminist reappraisal than "quite a sensitive reading" of "what we actually find in Shakespeare's text" (1994: 131).[9] Like *Cruel Tears*, moreover, the play rewards the cognoscenti with the pleasures of recognition, as when Constance deciphers in the crypt the words inscribed on Shakespeare's grave (82), when the play's revisionist point rests as it often does upon the audience's recognition of lines taken out of context or given to another character, or indeed when the audience is able to decipher the difference between Shakespeare's blank verse and that of MacDonald.[10]

MacDonald has made explicit her intention to reach as wide an audience as possible with her work, and has resisted a feminist label for *Goodnight Desdemona*. As Fortier says, "she prefers to think of it as humanism through a woman's point of view" (1989: 50), a rewriting of *Othello* and *Romeo and Juliet* "as they would be if Shakespeare were a woman, with a woman's experience" (51). Indeed the play crucially circulates around, in addition to its enactment of resistant reading, a Jungian version of essentialist, unitary humanism that sees Constance's search for identity fulfilled in a coming together of three archetypes: Desdemona (as Courage), Juliet (as Passion), and Constance (as Intellect). The play ends on the birthday of all three characters, when "two plus one adds up to one, not three" (86), and represents the *re*birth of a central character who subsumes all three, but who at the play's outset had reached "*the nadir of her passage on this earth*" (26). It is this aspect of *Goodnight Desdemona* that has made it, however powerful in its original context as feminist intervention, subject to some degree of mainstream cultural appropriation in its afterlife, when it has transferred or toured to more mainstream venues (see Knowles, 1993-94: 276-83). It is this universalizing aspect, too, that has made it possible for one reviewer to call the play "a natural for production at Stratford" (Kerslake, 1994: 139).

---

[9]    Dvorak makes a similar argument about the play's reading of *Romeo and Juliet* (1994: 132).

[10]   In the published script all direct appropriations of Shakespeare are signaled by the use of italics, though the original sources of or contexts for these lines or scenes are never given. In performance the quotations are of course unmarked.

But the Jung isn't just Jung, it's an explicitly feminist Jung (see MacDonald, 1990: 142); the deference to Shakespeare is more a recognition of what (according to Fortier) MacDonald cherishes about his "multivalency and ability to challenge a heterogenous audience" (1989: 51); and the flip side of the play's openness to appropriation is a refusal to settle into unitary meanings, an acknowledgment of multiple discursive, cultural, and theatrical contexts together with the shifting meanings that attend them (see Knowles, 1993-94: 283-86), and an invitation, as Dvorak says, "to dip into competing discourses" (1994: 133). Ultimately, perhaps, what *Goodnight Desdemona* performs in Toronto in 1989 is the feminist work of what Susan Bennett calls "marginalizing the mainstream," a "strategy for replacing a theatre which celebrates the objectifying gaze with a theatre which seeks out the political and the popular in terms of performance/audience relationship" that is (inter)active (Bennett, 1989: 13). It is not incidental that Bennett's article, "The Politics of the Gaze," was published in the Summer of 1989 in a special issue of *Canadian Theatre Review* on "Sexuality, Gender and Theatre."

## III. *Harlem Duet*: Race, Sex, Gender and (Black) History

*Canada, where did you get these ideas of Harlem from?*

(Djanet Sears, *Harlem Duet:* 79)

Also in 1989, between its 1988 first production of *Goodnight Desdemona* and the national tour in 1990, Nightwood Theatre adopted a new, explicitly anti-racist mandate and turned its attention directly to women of color. Within or beyond the context of Nightwood, however, by the time Djanet Sears's *Harlem Duet* premiered at the Tarragon Extra Space in Toronto in April 1997, an adaptation of *Othello* that did not place race at centre stage would be unthinkable. Not only had Djanet Sears herself written and performed *Afrika Solo* in the intervening years, the script of which in 1990 became the first play published by a Canadian of African descent; not only had Black directors, playwrights, and actors such as Colin Thomas, Andrew Moodie, Alison Sealy-Smith and others emerged to play prominent roles in the cultural life of the city; and not only had *Canadian Theatre Review* published a special issue in 1995 on *Black Theatre in Canada/African Canadian Theatre*; but Toronto had experienced well-publicized incidents of racism in the police department, together with a significant if smaller-scale incidence of rioting and looting on Yonge Street (the subject of Andrew Moodie's first play, *Riot)* in the wake the Rodney King verdict in Los Angeles.[11] It was no longer possible to pretend that Black people were not a presence nor race an issue in Canada. So as Vit Wagner wrote in a *Toronto Star* review of the production that noticed the connection with *Goodnight Desdemona* and the irony that "*Othello* is beginning to look like a charm for Nightwood Theatre," "this time, *Othello* is glimpsed through the prism of race rather than gender." In fact, unlike the other plays under consideration here, *Harlem Duet* is *all* about race: race and nation, race and class, (especially) race and (Black) history, and (above all) race and gender.

Unlike the other plays under consideration, however, *Harlem Duet* is less an adaptation of *Othello* than a prequel, at several temporal (and anachronistic) removes from its source. Neither populist comic opera nor revisionist comedy, the play presents itself as a "rhapsodic blues tragedy" (Sears, 1996: 14), a self-consciously hybrid form that links tragedy with jazz, high-Western with Black culture even as its musical bridges perform blues on orchestral strings (see Sears and Sealy-Smith, 1998: 29).[12] It tells the story, set in 1860, 1928, and most substantially the present, of Billie (aka Sybil), Othello's Black first wife, before he met Desdemona. According to Sears's introduction to the published text (also printed in program for the Canadian Stage production) the play explicitly takes on Shakespeare's *Othello* as the habitus of "the first African portrayed in the annals of western dramatic literature" in "an effort to exorcize this ghost" (1996: 14). The 1860s action focuses on "Him" and "Her," Othello and Billie as slaves planning an escape up the underground railroad, a plan that is aborted when he announces his love for the (white) woman who owns him. The 1928 action focuses on "He" and "She," Othello as a Black, blackface minstrel with aspirations to play the classics, who is in love with a white woman; and Billie, his jealous wife, who is in possession of a razor. The present-tense action, set in Harlem, concerns Billie's deteriorating mental state in the wake of Othello's betrayal of her dream for a better future, his packing and preparations for his wedding to "Mona," and his plans to head his Columbia University department's courses in Cypress. It is punctuated by flashbacks to the better, earlier days of their arrival in

[11] Four white members of the Los Angles Police Department were notoriously found not guilty in 1992 on state charges of beating a Black man, Rodney King, after he was arrested for speeding on March 3rd 1991, in spite of an amateur videotape of the incident having been widely broadcast. The acquittal prompted riots in Los Angles, and widespread protests across North America, and two of the officers were subsequently found guilty on federal charges.

[12] Sears says "I asked Allan [Booth] to create blues music for cello and double bass. But double bass and cello says chamber music. So the blues creates that tension [between European culture and African American culture], it's beautiful and it has that drama implicit in it" (Sears and Sealy-Smith, 1998: 29).

Harlem, and by visits from Billie's landlady, Magi, her sister-in-law, Amah, and her father, Canada.

But *Harlem Duet* is not concerned with Canada or Canadian cultural nationalism as such, although the play does take pains, in spite of its setting in Harlem, to insist on there being a Black history in this country. Canada (the character), in fact, arrives on the scene unexpectedly from Dartmouth, Nova Scotia, to which the family had fled after Billie's mother died, and Sears seems compelled to include a line in which Amah says, somewhat awkwardly in the context, "I love that Nova Scotia was a haven for slaves way before the underground railroad. I love that..." (45). And of course the 1860s scenes cite Canada as the ultimate destination of the underground railroad, "a white house on an emerald hill" (35): "Canada freedom come" (35, 63). But if Canada is romanticized by some of the characters – "What's that them old slaves used to say? 'I can't take it no more, I moving to Nova Scotia'" (82) – it's no Harlem: Billie and her brother have relocated, and the one who stayed in Canada – "a sot... My Dad, the drunk of Dartmouth" (45) – seems to have found little haven there. He remains in Harlem, recovering, at the end of the play.

Neither does class seem to be a significant issue in *Harlem Duet*, though the play does make clear the middle-class status of its central characters, avoiding the type of elision caused by the merging of class and ethnicity in *Cruel Tears*, and allowing for a focus on the specifically racial quality of what George Lamming (1960: 33) has called "specific punishments" for which Black Americans, rich or poor, are the targets.[13] Othello teaches at Columbia – Magi calls it "Harlumbia, those ten square blocks of Whitedom, owned by Columbia University, set smack dab in the middle of Harlem" (67). He and Billie drink cognac (50), read Shakespeare, dream (in a flashback to their early days in Harlem) of the day when there will be "Black boutiques./Black bookstores./Black groceries./Filled with Black doctors and dentists. Black banks" (106), and aspire to "buy a place on 'strivers row', that's where all the rich Black folks live" (106). There are moments, in fact, fed by what reviewer Kate Taylor calls a "sit-com" quality to some of the writing, when this insistence on the characters' (upper-middle-) class status seems to lend the action a "Cosby-show" combination of privilege and flippancy that threatens to undermine the seriousness of its concerns. What redeems the choice, in addition to the fact that it

---

[13] Lamming writes that "To be black, in the West Indies, is to be poor; whereas to be black (rich or poor) in an American context is to be a traditional target for specific punishments" (1960: 33). I am indebted to Diana Brydon for bringing this passage to my attention.

avoids stereotypes and enables a focus on race, *tout court* – on the "specific punishments" that Lamming says are reserved for Black Americans – is the clarity it brings to the conflict, particularly around one of the play's central issues – that of African-American identity, history, and culture. At one point Othello says, "I am a middle class educated man. I mean, what does Africa have to do with me?" (72).

> I mean my culture is not my mother's culture – the culture of my ancestors. My culture is Wordsworth, Shaw, *Leave it to Beaver*, *Dirty Harry*. I drink the same water, read the same books. You're the problem if you don't see beyond my skin. If you don't hear my educated English. [...] We struttin' around professing some imaginary connection for a land we don't know. Never seen. Never gonna see. We lie to ourselves saying, ah yeh, mother Africa, middle passage, suffering, the Whites did it to me, it's the White's fault. Strut around in African cloth pretending we human now. We human now. Some of us are beyond that now. Spiritually beyond this race bullshit now. I am an American. (73-74)

This debate permeates the action, which is framed by voice-overs from Black history in America that introduce each scene, and by the literal intersection (of views) at which the action is set in Harlem. According to reviewers Jim Lingerfelt and Roger Kershaw,

> Sears describes Harlem as "both a place and a symbol. [...] It represents the best and the worst of everything about people of African descent [...]. There is an actual intersection that serves as the theoretical axis of the arguments in the play." Billie and Othello's apartment is set here, at the corner of Martin Luther King and Malcolm X boulevards. Omnipresent are the themes of self-esteem and race in concert with the contrasting black/white schism advocated by Malcolm X and the integration of Martin Luther King's "dream."

In some senses, it is the very thickness of the play's sense of "the baggage of contemporary North American black experience" (Lingerfelt and Kershaw) and of African-America history – from the 1860s action and the legacy of slavery (33-36, 62-63, 74) through the play's evocation of minstrelsy (99-100, 113), the resonance of its references to the historic Apollo theatre (57), Paul Robeson's *Othello* (113), Langston Hughes and the Harlem Renaissance (114), and Jesse Jackson's oratory (72), to the Clarence Thomas/Anita Hill hearings,[14]

---

[14] Clarence Thomas is a conservative Black Republican lawyer nominated to the Supreme Court by then-President George Bush in July 1991, in spite of a record of opposing women's rights. The appointment was challenged when Thomas was charged by Anita Hill, a Black law professor at the University of Oklahoma, with sexual harassment, after which hearings before the U.S. Senate Judiciary Committee were widely publicized. In spite of significant evidence, the Judiciary Commit-

the Rodney King riots, and O. J. Simpson trial (92) – that undermines Othello's argument that "Things change, Billie. I am not my skin" (74). As Billie says, convincingly, "A history is trapped in me" (101): "did you ever consider what hundreds of years of slavery did to the African American psyche?" (103).

The play's present tense consists of a world in which that psyche, when damaged, is treated even in Harlem itself by white psychiatric doctors and nurses who can only see their patients' questions through "flashing blue eyes" (114-15); a world in which cosmeticians' certificates, even in Harlem, are awarded for courses on "how to do White people's hair and make-up" but not how to do dreadlocks (26); a world in which "if you spend too much time among white people, you start believing what they think of you" (97). Staging debates about affirmative action (53), ethnocentrism (52), assimilation and segregation, equality and difference, the play is nevertheless deeply resistant to an inherited world in which Laurence Olivier in blackface can serve even for Black people as a cultural marker (14), and where, as Billie says to Othello, "White people are always the line for you, aren't they? The rule... the margin... the variable of control" (55). Othello argues, that "liberation has no colour" (55), and Billie teaches her young niece that "colour's only skin deep" (44), but both Billie and the play know that

> progress is going to White schools... proving we're as good as Whites... like some holy grail... all that we're taught in those White schools. All that is in us. Our success is Whiteness. We religiously seek to have what they have. Access to the White man's world. The White man's job.

"That's economics," argues Othello. "White economics," Billie replies (55).

Othello's only recourse – an exasperated "God! Black women always – " (at which point Billie cuts him off: "No. Don't even go there...") (56) – brings us to the play's central concern: the intersection of race and gender, the area where, in Sears's view, the *most* damage has been done to the African-American psyche. In each of its actions, characters, and relationships, both depicted and recounted (and framed by, among other things, voice-overs from the O. J. Simpson trial, a trial focusing on the murder by a black man of his white wife, and one around which *Othello*, not surprisingly, was frequently invoked), *Harlem Duet* is permeated by stories of Black men in relationships with white women – the central fact of Shakespeare's *Othello* that seems to have been ignored as an issue *in* itself in almost all previous

---

tee approved his appointment, and he subsequently aligned himself with the most reactionary, anti-woman, anti-civil rights wing of the court.

adaptations of the play. Here not only does the present-day, main-plot action concern itself with Othello's leaving his Black partner, Billie for a white colleague, Mona, but the 1860 story is of the Black slave Othello's betrayal of *his* Billie's plans to flee to Canada because of his perverse love – fascinating, in its construction of gender roles – for the white woman who is his master ("She respects me... When I'm with her I feel like... a man" [63]), and the 1928 story is of the actor/ minstrel Othello, "of Ira Aldrigde [*sic*] stock" (99), and his longing for the "Skin as smooth as monumental alabaster" (Shakespeare, 1984: 5.2.5; Sears, 1996: 99) of *his* Mona, the very woman who casts him only in Black Shakespearean, and Black minstrel roles. We learn from Billie, moreover, in the present-tense main plot, that her father had also for a time dated a white woman, "Debbie" – "[t]hat hairdresser you used to go with... The one with the mini skirts" – after her mother had died: "She was boasting about knowing how to do our kind of hair. And she took that hot comb to my head... Sounded like she was frying chicken... Burnt my ears and half the hair on my head. I hated her stubby little beige legs and those false eyelashes" (82). Finally, in a reversal of the general pattern, we also hear that Magi's great grand-mother had given birth to two children, one of them Magi's mother, by the white man she worked for as a maid (95), and we hear snippets from the Michael Jackson/Lisa Marie Presley television interview on ABC's *Dateline* (79).[15]

The historical relationships, of course, turn out badly, but they serve to illuminate the main-plot action. The 1928 plot, which opens the play, ends with Billie cutting her Othello's throat as he removes his minstrel's blackface (99-100, 73). The 1860s plot ends in 1862, with a pietà of Othello lying motionless in Billie's arms with a noose around his neck, while *"a presidential voice reads from the Emancipation Proclamation."* Billie speaks:

> Once upon a time, there was a man who wanted to find a magic spell in order to become White. After much research and investigation, he came across an ancient ritual from the caverns of knowledge of a psychic. "The only way to become White," the psychic said, "was to enter the White-ness." And when he found his ice queen, his alabaster goddess, he fucked

---

[15]  The interview, with ABC's Diane Sawyer, was broadcast live around the world on 14 June, 1995. It may not be stretching things to argue that the world's fascination with the troubled relationship between Jackson and Presley had less to do with the simple intersection of celebrity musical families than with the complex intersections of race and sexuality that it raised, as Jackson, a Black man with an effeminate manner, a reputed affinity for boys, and a history of plastic surgery that seemed in-creasingly to diminish stereotypically racialized characteristics, married the (white) daughter ("tupped the white ewe," in Iago's terms) of the man most directly respon-sible for the appropriation of American Black music by the (white) music industry.

her. Her on his dick. He one with her, for a single shivering moment became... her. Her and her Whiteness. (91)

The allegory underscores the main plot action. Billie's "dream," articulated in a scene that is framed by a voice-over of Martin Luther King (47), in which parts of King's famous "I have a dream" speech is shared between Billie and Othello (54), is that "one day a Black man and a Black woman might find –" (56) but the sentence is never completed. Billie is reduced early on to having...

> [...] nothing to say to him. What could I say? Othello, how is the fairer sexed one you love to dangle from your arm the one you love for herself and preferred to the deeper sexed one is she softer does she smell of tea roses and baby powder does she sweat white musk from between her toes do her thighs touch I am not curious just want to know do her breasts fill the cup of your hand the lips of your tongue not too dark you like a little milk with your nipple don't you no I'm not curious just want to know. (43)

But she determines that it's not about sex or sensuality for Othello, who ends up in bed and still in love with Billie even as he returns with Mona to pack his things. Billie and Magi postulate in one uproarious scene that Othello simply wants to "White wash his life." "Corporeal malediction," Billie calls it. "A black man afflicted with Negrophobia," "A crumbled racial epidermal schema... [...] ... causing predilections to coitus denegrification:" "Booker T. Uppermiddleclass III. He can be found in predominantly White neighborhoods. He refers to other Blacks as 'them'. His greatest accomplishment was being invited to the White House by George Bush to discuss the 'Negro problem'" (66). But the real reason for Othello's desertion of Billie for Mona seems to be that "Now he won't have to worry that a White woman will emotionally mistake him for the father that abandoned her" (though Magi wonders if "she might mistake him for the butler" [67]). Othello himself, in a lengthy and revealing speech, seems to concur with this view:

> Yes, I prefer White women. They are easier – before and after sex. They wanted me and I wanted them. They weren't filled with hostility about the unequal treatment they were getting at their jobs. We'd make love and I'd fall asleep not having to beware being mistaken for someone's inattentive father. I'd explain that I wasn't interested in a committed relationship right now, and not be confused with every lousy lover, or husband that had ever left them lying in a gutter of unresolved emotions. It's the truth. To a Black woman, I represent every Black lover she has ever been with and with whom there was still so much to work out. The White women I loved just saw me – could see me. Look, I'm not a junkie. I don't need more than one lover to prove my manhood. I have no children. I did not leave you, your mother, or your aunt, with six babies and a whole lotta love. I am a very single, very intelligent, very employed Black man. And with White women

it's good. It's nice. Anyhow, we're all equal in the eyes of God, aren't we? Aren't we? (71)

Unlike its 1860s and 1928 counterparts, we don't hear how the contemporary Othello-Mona relationship works out, but we do here a warning: "You young-uns don't know the sweetness of molasses," Canada tells Othello:

Rather have granulated sugar, 'stead of a deep clover honey, or cane sugar juice from way into the Demerara. Better watch out for that refined shit. It'll kill ya. A slow kinda killin'. 'Cause it kills your mind first. So you think you living the life, when you been dead a long time'. (111)

So what *is* the cultural work performed by this "brittle exploration of race and gender," as reviewer Geoff Chapman called it (1997)? And how does it function as an adaptation, or exorcism, of *Othello*? To begin, it does seem to take full part in a 1990s attempt to redress the imbalances of a feminist movement that to many in the period seemed problematically to elide race – as does *Goodnight Desdemona* – within a gender-based universalist solidarity among women, of which *Harlem Duet* will have no part. When Othello tells Billie of his plans to marry Mona – "I wanted to tell you... [...] Mona wanted me to tell you" – they enter an exchange that is central to the cultural work performed by the play, and is worth quoting at length:

BILLIE. Yes. Yes. Being a feminist and everything – a woman's right to know – since we're all in the struggle... I thought you hated feminists.

OTHELLO. Well... I didn't mean that. I mean... the White women's movement is different.

BILLIE. Just Black feminists.

OTHELLO. No, no... White men have maintained a firm grasp of the pants. I mean, White men have economic and political pants that White women have been demanding to share.

BILLIE. White wisdom from the mouth of the mythical Negro.

OTHELLO. Don't you see! That's exactly my point! You... The Black feminist position as I experience it in this relationship, leaves me feeling unrecognized as a man. The message is, Black men are poor fathers, poor partners, or both. Black women wear the pants that Black men were prevented from wearing... I believe in tradition. You don't support me. Black women are more concerned with their careers than their husbands. There was a time when women felt satisfied, no, honoured being a balance to their spouse, at home, supporting the family, playing her role –

BILLIE. Which women? I mean, which women are you referring to? Your mother worked all her life. My mother worked, her mother worked... Most Black women have been working like mules since we arrived on this continent. Like mules. When White women were burning their bras, we were hired to hold their tits up. (70-71)

Like *Cruel Tears* and *Goodnight Desdemona*, then, *Harlem Duet*, has its own areas of effective revisionist intervention, partaking in and helping to produce shifts in the construction of Canadian subjectivities that will not preclude Black women's experience. Like those plays, too, *Harlem Duet* has its blind spots, notably in the narrowness of its recuperative focus on middle-class and heterosexual Black life. And also like *Cruel Tears* and *Goodnight Desdemona*, Sears's play has a somewhat vexed relationship to *Othello*, to "Shakespeare," and to high Culture more generally. In her introduction and program note, "nOTES oF a cOLOURED gIRL: 32 sHORT rEASONS wHY i wRITE fOR tHe tHeatre," Sears positions her play clearly in the (counter)canonical tradition of Black women's playwriting in America, evoking in the typeface of her title and invoking in her text the work of Ntozake Shange, together with that of Lorraine Hansberry. Citing Hansberry's *A Raisin in the Sun* as a progenitor, and a production of Shange's *For Coloured Girls Who Have Considered Suicide When the Rainbow is Enuf* that she saw in New York at the age of eighteen as "the first live sage production by a writer of African descent" she had see, Sears claims in her prologue a place in that tradition and articulates her responsibility to see to it that her newly born niece will not have to wait until she is eighteen for this experience:

> She must have access to a choir of African voices, chanting a multiplicity of African experiences. One voice does not a chorus make. And I will not wait. I harbour deep within me tales that I've never seen told. I too must become an organ and add my perspective, my lens, my stories, to the ever growing body of work by and about people of African descent. (1996: 12)[16]
>
> SOMEDAY SOMBODY'LL
>
> STAND UP AND TALK ABOUT ME,
>
> AND WRITE ABOUT ME –
>
> BLACK AND BEAUTIFUL
>
> AND SING ABOUT ME,
>
> AND PUT ON PLAYS ABOUT ME!
>
> I RECKON IT'LL BE
>
> ME MYSELF!
>
> YES, IT'LL BE ME. (1996: 15)

---

[16] I have omitted from this quotation the bold-faced numberings, 7, 8, and 9 of the "32 sHORT rEASONS wHY i wRITE fOR tHE tHEATRE."

But the drive to contribute to the formation of a counter-canon also has its perils, and if the line Sears traces in her introduction places her work firmly in relation to a resistant, counterhegemonic canon of writing by African-American women, both there and in the play itself she also carves a place within perhaps more problematic canons and traditions, both African-American and white. The prominent framing device of inter-scene voice-overs used throughout the play to locate its action within Black history, for example, uses the voices of men exclusively – Martin Luther King, Malcolm X, Marcus Garvey, Langston Hughes, Paul Robeson, Jesse Jackson, Louis Farrakhan, and Christopher Darden (the Black member of the prosecution's team of lawyers at the O. J. Simpson trial). To a certain extent this makes the play's resistant point, as we hear Billie only through the filter of a Black history that tends to erase her. But the barrage of male voices also threatens to contain the play's Black feminist interventions within a normalization of the male voice as the voice of History and Culture, even as the use of Shakespeare as source and reference point, in spite of Sears's attempts to "exorcize" *Othello*, serves to reinscribe its (white, western) canonical authority.

*Harlem Duet* neither depends upon nor rewards specialized knowledge of Shakespeare to the same degree as the other plays under consideration here, but it does rely on some familiarity with the story line, and it does reward the audience's recognition of "Mona," "Chris Yago," and the planned trip to Cypress (53) as Shakespearean echoes. At one point it even inserts an awkward and seemingly gratuitous echo, in the context, when Othello confides to Canada, "I do confess the vices of my blood" (Shakespeare, 1984: I.3.123; Sears, 1996: 111).[17] And the play seems to use the artefacts of high Culture, including knowledge of Shakespeare, to claim some high-cultural authority for the play itself and for Black culture more generally – to claim a place at the table (and therefore to leave that table-as-benchmark in place rather than overturn it.) It is perhaps this evocation of Shakespeare and of a mainstream European humanist cultural tradition that makes it possible for one reviewer to read the play in universalist terms as partaking in the generic history of western tragedy and the dramatic realist tradition of individualist psychology – as one in which "the central issue [...] is self-esteem:"

---

[17]   Other Shakespearean citations include the 1928 Othello's quoting of the Duke's lines, "If virtue no delighted beauty lack,/ Your son-in-law is far more fair than black" (Shakespeare, 1984: I.3.285-86; Sears, 1996: 99), as well as lines from *Hamlet* and references to *Pericles* in the same scene; and his fractured rehearsal of parts of the speeches Shakespeare's Othello addresses to the Senators in I.3.79-94, 128-162 (Sears, 1996: 113).

[M]uch of the drama depends on the ability of [Alison] Sealy-Smith and [Nigel Shawn] Williams [playing Billie and Othello respectively] to find the tragic flaws in their characters. Through their performances, Sealy-Smith and Williams reveal that Billie and Othello are victims, not merely of culture and history, but to a certain extent by choice. (V. Wagner, 1997)

But the echoes of Shakespeare and invocations of Western high Culture are, perhaps, evoked with (critical) difference.[18] If for example, the play's reference to *"The Great Chain of Being"* is, as I suspect, a veiled citation of the influence within and beyond Shakespearean studies of E. M. W. Tillyard's reliance on that concept in *The Elizabethan World Picture*, it does not pass without criticism, grouped as it is with *African Mythology* and *Black Psychology* as "the scientific foundation for why we're not human" – and why "an African can't really be a woman" (51).[19] Perhaps audiences need to recognize Sears's reclamatory voice in Billie's apparently throwaway line, "the Shakespeare's mine, but you can have it" (52).

The play's invocations of what seem to be explicitly African and female popular histories, traditions, and cultures are themselves not without their problematic aspects. Among the plays under consideration here, *Harlem Duet* makes the most extensive use of the handkerchief motif from the Shakespearean source, which both *Goodnight Desdemona* and the main line of Shakespearean criticism take as a (too) simple plot device.[20] Sears, in fact, prints as an epigraph to her play source lines from Shakespeare's play that are echoed throughout *Harlem Duet* and explicitly trace the handkerchief to an African and female source:

... That handkerchief
Did an Egyptian to my mother give
She was a charmer...

---

[18] See Hutcheon, 1985, 5-16, and *passim* for her first formulation of parody as what she calls repetition with a critical difference, "a method of inscribing continuity while permitting critical distance" (1985: 20).

[19] Interestingly, in this context, when Amah tries to evoke sympathy for Othello from the institutionalized Billie at the end of the play, Billie replies, "I'm not that evolved" (115).

[20] Thomas Rymer, of course, initiated this tradition when he (in)famously dismissed the play by determining its morals to be: "First, this may be a caution to all Maidens of Quality how, without their parents consent, they run away with Blackamoors," and "Secondly, This may be a warning to all good Wives, that they look well to their linen" (1693/1971: 89). In the last two decades feminist criticism, in particular, has productively revisited the role of the handkerchief in the play.

There's magic in the web of it

A sybil... in her prophetic fury sewed the work. (Shakespeare, 1984: 3.4.51-68; Sears, 1996: 19)[21]

The exoticism of the story is not shirked by Sears. On the contrary, it is emphasized, reinforced, and contextualized, both historically and culturally, to an unusual degree, invoking an alternative, non-Western, and non-patriarchal African tradition of spirituality (that resonates, interestingly enough, with the Weird Sisters of Shakespeare's *Macbeth*). Throughout the action of the play Billie is busy preparing for Othello's wedding "A potion... A plague of sorts" (102) – "Saracen's Compound... Woad... Hart's tongue... Prunella vulgaris" (40) – in which she has soaked the handkerchief: "Anyone who touches it – the handkerchief, will come to harm" (102). It is eventually revealed that Billie's real name is in fact Sybil, which explicitly means "prophetess. Sorceress. Seer of the future" (81). Sears frames her story of Billie's revenge both within popular women's folk superstitions, which have their own resistant valences, and a more serious evocation of Black history. On the one hand, Billie's enchantments are grouped with a series of comic, tabloid-style women's charms – if you want to keep a man "rub his backside with margarine" (28), "boil down some greens in panty stock" (29), or "bury his socks under the blackberry bush by the front door" (29). On the other hand they are linked to the solemn marriage ritual vow of jumping over a broom, practiced by slaves who had no access to official rituals (56, 107) – a vow broken by Billie's Othello, to his eternal disgrace. Finally, the handkerchief itself and Billie's practices upon it are linked in the play with history, and most explicitly, Black women's history:

> Othello? I am preparing something special for you... Othe... Othello. A gift for you, and your new bride. Once you gave me a handkerchief. An heirloom. This handkerchief, your mother's... given by your father. From his mother before that. So far back... And now... then... to me. It is fixed in the emotions of all your ancestors. The one who laid the foundation for the road in Herndon, Virginia, and was lashed for laziness as he stopped to wipe the sweat from his brow with this kerchief. Or your great, great grandmother, who covered her face with it, and then covered it with her hands as she rocked and silently wailed, when told that her girl child, barely thirteen, would be sent 'cross the state for breeding purposes. Or the one who leapt for joy on hearing of the Emancipation Proclamation, fifteen years late mind you, only to watch it fall in slow motion from his hand and onto the ground when told that the only job he could now get, was the

---

[21]   I have quoted Sears's prologue as she punctuates and excerpts it (the ellipses are hers), but have cited the Shakespearean source as listed in my Works Cited. The edition I am using punctuates the passages slightly differently.

same one he'd done for free all those years, and now he's forced to take it, for not enough money to buy the food to fill even one man's belly. And more... so much, much more. (75-6)

In this treatment of the handkerchief – which also permeates the 1860s and 1929 plots – Sears boldly risks exoticising, and therefore further Othering, Black culture and history in ways that might be complicit with standard western orientalizing practices. But she also uses the device to question western rationalisms through African (-American) spiritualism, and perhaps to exorcize the original and canonical Othello and *Othello* through her own hybrid magic – even as her character exorcizes *her* Othello and his failures and betrayals through *her* exotic blending of ingredients.

The most significant cultural intervention made by *Harlem Duet*, as for *Cruel Tears* and *Goodnight Desdemona*, may, in fact, be generic. Where Mitchell's play recuperates the popular as art, and MacDonald's recuperates feminist comedy from the dead hand of the masculinist tragic tradition, however, Sears consciously invents a new, hybrid genre that incorporates the comic and tragic within what she calls a "rhapsodic blues tragedy" (14). In a conversation with Alison Sealy-Smith published in *Canadian Theatre Review* Sears speculates at some length on the possibility of forging a "black aesthetic" out of blues, jazz, and improvisation in ways that resonate with regionalist efforts to develop dramaturgical forms out of local landscapes and histories, and feminist efforts to forge women's forms of expression (Sears and Sealy-Smith, 1998: 28-29). *Harlem Duet* frames its action, not only within excerpts from recorded Black history, but also within forms of (live) Black musical expression that play against their Western orchestral instrumentation in much the same way as the action of the play resonates against Shakespearean tragedy. Thus scenes are introduced by "heaving melancholic blues" (21), "blues/jazz riff[s]" (32) "blues from deep in the Mississippi delta" (33), "melodious urban blues jazz" (39), "a polyrhythmic chorus of strings" (47) and so on throughout a play that makes a virtue of its hybridity, but resists any confident settling in to generic, racial, or ideological purities. This, together with the placing of the intersection of contemporary and historical Black experience, the intersection of Malcolm X and Martin Luther King (Boulevards), and the intersection of gender and race at centre stage in Toronto theatre in the late 1990s may constitute the most significant, and most visible, cultural intervention made by the play.

## Conclusion

In an article on "Re-Citing Shakespeare in Post-Colonial Drama," Joanne Tompkins argues that "Post-colonial revisions of Shakespeare's plays displace an inherited tradition in order to accommodate other cultural traditions that, while perhaps originating in a Shakespearean model, have developed in quite different social, literary, and political directions" (1996: 21). Each of the revisionings that she examines – which include Derek Walcott's *A Branch of the Blue Nile*, Louis Nowra's *The Golden Age*, Michael Gow's *Away*, Dorothy Hewett's *The Man from Mukinupin*, and Murray Carlin's *Not Now, Sweet Desdemona*, as well as Ann-Marie MacDonald's *Goodnight Desdemona (Good Morning Juliet)* – "counter-discursively resituates the cultural weight of Shakespeare to establish cultural specificities that destabilize important, unquestioned reiterations of imperial paradigms that are no longer relevant" (1996: 21). Tompkins is focusing on the cultural specificities of different *national* sites of revisioning and resistance, but her argument also applies in complex ways *intra*-nationally within Canada. An examination of adaptations and re(-)citations over time and region of a play such as *Othello*, with its different potential valences of Otherness, is suggestive *within* Canada of a cultural negotiation, over the corpus of Shakespeare, not only with "imperial paradigms that are no longer relevant" – the *colonizing* Other – but also with internal negotiations of power and cultural colonization over time. Each of *Cruel Tears*, *Goodnight Desdemona (Good Morning Juliet)*, and *Harlem Duet* is both very much a product of its historical place and moment and at the same time *productive* of its moment and of subsequent moments as a marker of, and site for the negotiation of social change around specific issues. Each in its way and to its own degree invokes "Shakespeare," "Culture," and universalist discourse to make its particular claims, and each elides other issues – sexual preference in *Cruel Tears* and *Harlem Duet*, race in *Goodnight Desdemona*, class in *Goodnight Desdemona* and *Harlem Duet*, and so on – in ways that can be read as politically problematic or retrogressive. But each also in its important way represents real cultural intervention, shifting the cultural ground in ways that permanently change the ways in which it is possible to think about Canadian subjectivities as produced through the interrelationships among (counter-)discourses of nation, region, gender, class, race, and ethnicity.

It would have been unthinkable and ineffective in the Saskatchewan of 1975 to have set *Cruel Tears*, or any adaptation of *Othello*, outside of Canada, as Sears set *Harlem Duet* in the American heart of North American Black culture. In the Toronto of 1997, however, that play's relevance to African and other Canadians could be more or less assumed, and the play's status as "Canadian," in spite of its setting and subject matter, was not an issue. Indeed, in 1975 to set *Cruel Tears* in Saskatoon was for Mitchell and the Dumptrucks an act of regionalist postcolonial resistance, a claim that historical and cultural events of significance do *not* just happen to Canadians elsewhere. Similarly, the model of resistant reading employed and enacted by *Goodnight Desdemona*, for whom the reproductive economy of recycling the Shakespearean story, as in *Cruel Tears*, was no longer felt to *be* sufficiently resistant, was not available to Mitchell and the Dumptrucks, who in any case felt the need to *claim* rather than debunk the cultural authority of "Shakespeare." And such an enactment was unnecessary for Sears as an explicit gesture in a play that was free to cite its Shakespeare less directly, or less directly confrontationally, in part because by the late 1990s, at least within a Toronto theatre community that had witnessed a great many resistant revisionings over the previous decade, "Shakespeare" was legible as a site for the *negotiation* of values rather than simply as a marker of imperialist high Culture.

Perhaps the major contribution of the three plays under consideration here to the ongoing reinvention of Canadian subjectivities, however, derives from a modeling of ongoing generic in(ter)vention and a recurrent trope of self-rebirth. Mitchell and company's "country opera" is an invented form that asserts through its hybridity the existence and value of a rural, regional, and populist high culture; Ann-Marie MacDonald's feminist comedy actively asserts its productive generic revisioning ("I've had it with all the tragic tunnel vision around here" [85]")[22]; and Djanet Sears's "rhapsodic blues tragedy" inscribes a kind of high-cultural hybridity that at once asserts, reclaims, and undermines canonical cultural authority, staging raids and making claims on Shakespeare, on African American history, on Black women's culture, and on whatever intersection works at its particular historical cultural moment, to stake claims for itself and the place of its subject(ivity) on Canadian (centre)Stage(s).

Sears talks in her nOTES oF a cOLOURED gIRL about "giving birth to myself" in *Harlem Duet* (1996: 15) in ways that echo Ann-Marie MacDonald's staging of a social/communal (re)birthday of the feminist, Jungian Self in *Goodnight Desdemona* (and, less explicitly, Mitchell's staging of the regional, populist self in *Cruel Tears*), and it

---

[22]  MacDonald here echoes a view of tragedy articulated by Annie Leclerc in an essay published in English in a collection, *New French Feminisms*, which was extremely influential in the 1980s: "I pity the masquerades of the hero. And I laugh at him, with his important airs, his tragic antics. He may count on me no longer to help him in the way he asks, in the way he demands, to establish his rule. The rule of human greatness. Because I don't give a damn" (1981: 86).

is perhaps this continual and ongoing auto-rebirthing of the national, regional, gender (and genre-ed), racial, ethnic, sexual and social self, through the inevitable and mixed blessing of Shakespeare and, in this case, *Othello*, that characterizes the reinscriptions under consideration here. It may be that adapting Shakespeare risks reinscribing His cultural Author-ity, but that authority permeates Canadian culture Willy-nilly. It may also be that "taking on" – challenging, appropriating, and disarticulating – that authority, with all the complex negotiations and elisions that doing so entails at any given cultural and historical moment – has been important as a way in which, always provisionally, Canadian cultural values and Canadian gendered, racial, ethnic and classed subjectivities have been productively renegotiated in cultural productions such as *Cruel Tears, Goodnight Desdemona (Good Morning Juliet)*, and *Harlem Duet* in the last three decades of the 20th century.

# Epilogue

In "The Task of the Translator" Walter Benjamin argues that the least important work that a translator performs is to communicate the meaning of the original work. He argues that good translation of literary work functions most importantly to transform what he calls "the mother tongue of the translator." "[N]o translation would be possible," he writes, "if in its ultimate essence it strove for likeness to the original. For in its afterlife – which could not be called that if it were not a transformation and a renewal of something living – the original undergoes a change" (73).

Although it has dealt with the topic directly only in one chapter, this has been a book about translation, broadly understood, and about the transformations that it can perform, not so much within a "mother tongue," but within a postcolonial, settler-colony culture. For in a very real sense all of the topics I have dealt with in the book's three sections – theatrical production and direction, translation, and adaptation – involve producing and transforming both "Shakespeare" and "Canada" through acts of translation between cultures and across centuries.

One kind of translation, traditionally called "faithful," "intends to perform a transmitting function" and is concerned with fixing languages and meanings. "This is the hallmark of bad translation," according to Benjamin (63). Within settler-invader cultures such as Canada, this type of "translation" can emerge from deep-seated anxieties about the preservation of the mother tongue and the culture of the motherland (including its cultural icons such as Shakespeare), fixing meanings and values over space and time in a combination of postcolonial mimicry and museum-like acts of preservation, display, and homage. It is this type of translation/transmission that I have argued in Part I has most often been performed at the Stratford Festival. At that post-war monument to British culture, productions of Shakespeare have often had to do with (re)producing a national bard as a way of producing a Canadian nation in the model of a preserved conflation of 19th century and wartime Britain, which may explain the difficulty the Festival has in reflecting contemporary Canadian cultural diversity (or even producing contemporary Canadian plays). But the Festival's productions of Shakespeare can nevertheless operate as even the most "faithful" translation always does, to mark a remove from the original even as it attempts to reproduce it, and therefore always to some small extent to mark difference, to mark lack rather than identity. The most common expression of this lack within settler/invader cultures, however, tends toward nostalgia, which in its most common operation is fundamentally culturally affirmative.

Another, more productive kind of translation within a postcolonial culture attempts to function not as transmission or reproduction of an original that is wrongly understood to be stable, but as something closer, along the production/translation/adaptation continuum, to acknowledged adaptation, transforming both the original and the culture into which it inserts itself "with a difference." Many of the works I have examined in Parts II and III attempt this sort of transformative function, and some of them achieve a degree of success. Some of these successes derive overtly from "talking back" to "Shakespeare" as originary source, authority, and representative of a dominant colonial, patriarchal, or capitalist culture. Martine Beaulne's *La Mégère Apprivoisée,* as discussed in Chapter Three, transforms in its translation the sexual politics of the source text in order to speak back to the patriarchal culture of which the original play has been in part productive. More commonly, works of translation, adaptation, and tradaptation in Canada have made use of Shakespeare's scripts as source texts to be used in quite complex ways in the renegotiation of cultural values, coat-tailing on their cultural capital while simultaneously disarticulating them, as many of the works examined in Part III demonstrate. Cumulatively, however, this book attempts to demonstrate the ways in which the theatrical production and direction, as well as the translation and adaptation of Shakespeare in Canada can play a transformative role culturally simply through inserting him into contemporary discourse as, in Benjamin's terms, an entirely "translatable" other (81), allowing him less as a Lacanian ego ideal than as a foreign language to reshape, powerfully and continually, the ways in which Canadians think, speak, and sit in their chairs.

But the critic also functions as a translator, translating the work into the frame of another discourse. Traditionally, criticism has claimed to function as translation of the faithful variety, transmitting what is "really in" the work, transmitting its meaning to an audience less proficient in the work's original "language," and performing the acknowledged service function of the translator while at the same time claiming authority over the work, which it purports to treat with detached objectivity of the scientific observer. Like the translator who claims a command of both languages, the critic has conventionally mediated the experience of readers (including audience members) while him- or herself remaining neutral and unimplicated.

In a postcolonial context, this type of criticism has proven to be problematic, as Tejaswini Niranjana has demonstrated of the role of translation in postcolonial societies, insofar as it constructs docile postcolonial subjects content to defer to the superior culture of Empire. By constructing the cultures and cultural productions of postcolonial societies as "objects of study" to be known, understood, explained, and displayed by a critic-translator whose discourses and methodologies derive from elsewhere and whose own cultural positioning remains uninterrogated, such criticism has participated in the colonial project.

One reconsideration of the role of the postcolonial critic, again, has been a writing back to the imperial centre, as the title of Ashcroft, Griffiths, and Tiffin's foundational book, *The Empire Writes Back*, would suggest. Like Québécoise feminist translation theorist Suzanne de Lotbinière-Harwood, such critics see the critic/translator not as faithful servant, but as subversive, "re-belle et infidèle." Much of this work has been highly productive and effective in challenging traditional colonialist critical assumptions. There is, however, a danger here, too, in that such work can function to reinscribe and reify the very binaries upon which the colonial project rests. Resistance depends upon and can serve to naturalize or essentialize a monolithic dominant to which it is opposed. Considerable work has been done in recent years in postcolonial and globalization studies to address this problem, most notably and most recently in a new collection of essays, *Is Canada Postcolonial: Unsettling Canadian Literature*, written by leading postcolonial critics working within Canada, most of them writing out of settler/invader cultures (Moss). I would like, as I have suggested in the introduction to this volume, to participate in this work by positing a role for the settler/invader critic in helping to construct a more mediative, multiple, and dialogic critical middle position for the settler/ invader subject, one that might perhaps be modeled on that of Benjamin's transformative translator, and one that might at its best materialize the theoretical hybridities and third positions of postcolonial critique through the actual practice of collaboration and facilitation across Canada's many differences. But that is, perhaps, a project of the future.

# Works Cited

Ackerman, Marianne. "L'Événement Shakespeare." *Canadian Theatre Review* 57 (1988): 81-85.

Althusser, Louis. "Ideology and Ideological State Apparatuses (Notes Towards an Investigation)." *Lenin and Philosophy and Other Essays*. Trans. Ben Brewster. New York: Monthly Review, 1971. 127-86.

*Antony and Cleopatra* (program). Dir. Richard Monette. Prod. Stratford Festival, Stratford, Ontario. 1993. N. pag.

"*Antony and Cleopatra.*" *The Beacon Herald* 1993, Stratford Festival ed.

Appiah, Kwame Anthony. *In My Father's House: Africa in the Philosophy of Culture*. New York: Oxford UP, 1992.

Arcand, Denys. "Jesus of Montreal." Trans. Matt Cohen. *Best Canadian Screenplays*. Ed. Douglas Bowie and Tom Shoebridge. Kingston: Quarry, 1992. 339-429.

Arnott, Brian. "The Passe Muraille Alternative." *The Human Elements*. Ed. David Helwig. Toronto: Oberon, 1978. 97-111.

Ashcroft, Bill, Gareth Griffiths and Helen Tiffin. *The Empire Writes Back: Theory and Practice in Post-Colonial Cultures*. London: Routledge, 1989.

Auslander, Philip. *Presence and Resistance: Postmodernism and Cultural Politics in Contemporary American Performance*. Ann Arbor: U of Michigan P, 1994.

Barber, Frances. "Ophelia in *Hamlet.*" *Players of Shakespeare*. Ed. Russell Jackson and Robert Smallwood. Vol. 2. New York: Cambridge UP, 1988. 137-49.

Barthes, Roland. *S/Z*. Trans. Richard Miller. London: Jonathan Cape, 1974.

Bassnett, Susan, and André Lefevere. *Translation, History and Culture*. London: Pinter, 1990.

Bassnett-McGuire, Susan. *Translation Studies*. London: Methuen, 1980.

Benjamin, Walter. "The Task of the Translator: An Introduction to the Translation of Baudelaire's *Tableaux Parisiens.*" *Illuminations: Essays and Reflections*. Trans. Harry Zohn. New York: Schocken, 1968.

Beauchamp, Hélène. "Of Desire, Freedom, Commitment and *Mise en scène* as a Very Fine Art: The Work of the Theatre Director." *Australasian Drama Studies* 29 (1996): 155-67.

Beaunoyer, Jean. "La Mégère Apprivoisée: Remarquablement Joué." *La Presse* (Montréal) 22 mars 1995.

Bélisle, Jean-François. "Mais puisqu'on vous dit qu'elle tourne!" *L'Express d'Outremont* 24 mars 1995.

Belsey, Catherine. *Critical Practice*. London: Routledge, 1980.

Bennett, Susan. "Politics of the Gaze: Challenges in Canadian Women's Theatre." *Canadian Theatre Review* 59 (1989): 11-14.

Benson, Eugene and L. W. Conolly, ed. *The Oxford Companion to Canadian Theatre*. Toronto: Oxford, 1989.

Bentley, Eric. "Stark Young." Afterword. *The Theatre*. By Stark Young. New York: Limelight, 1986. 125-46.

Berton, Pierre. *The National Dream*. 2 vols. Toronto: McClelland and Stewart, 1970-71.

Bessai, Diane. *Playwrights of Collective Creation*. Toronto: Simon & Pierre, 1992.

——. "The Regionalism of Canadian Theatre." *Canadian Literature 85* (Summer 1980): 7-20.

Bhabha, Homi K. *The Location of Culture*: London: Routledge, 1994.

Bharucha, Rustum. *Theatre and the World*. London: Routledge, 1993.

Blodgett, E. D. "Heresy and Other Arts: A Measure of Mavis Gallant's Fiction." *Essays on Canadian Writing* 42 (1990): 1-8.

——. "Is a History of the Literatures of Canada Possible?" *Essays on Canadian Writing* 50 (1993): 1-18.

Boulanger, Luc. "La Mégère Apprivoisée: Détournement Majeur." *Voir* (Montréal) 23-29 mars 1995.

Bradbury, Malcolm and James McFarlane, ed. *Modernism, 1890-1930*. Harmondsworth: Penguin, 1976.

Brassard, Marie and Robert Lepage. *Polygraph. Modern Canadian Plays*. Ed. Jerry Wasserman. 3$^{rd}$ ed. Vol. 2. Vancouver: Talonbooks, 1994. 293-315.

——. *Polygraph. The CTR Anthology*. Ed. Alan Filewod. Toronto: U of Toronto P, 1993. 647-83.

Brisset, Annie. *Sociocritique de la traduction*. Toronto: U of Toronto P, 1996.

Bristol, Michael. *Big Time Shakespeare*. London: Routledge, 1996.

Brook, Peter. *The Empty Space*. Harmondsworth: Pelican, 1972.

——. *The Shifting Point*. New York: Harper & Row, 1989.

Brydon, Diana. "Re-writing *The Tempest*." *World Literature Written in English* 23.1 (1984): 75-88.

——. "Sister Letters: Miranda's *Tempest* in Canada." *Cross-Cultural Performances: Differences in Women's Re-Visions of Shakespeare*. Ed. Marianne Novy. Urbana and Chicago: U of Illinois P, 1993. 165-84.

Brydon, Diana and Irena R. Makaryk, ed. *Shakespeare in Canada: A World Elsewhere?* Toronto: U of Toronto P, 2002.

Bulman, James C., ed. *Shakespeare, Theory, and Performance*. London: Routledge, 1996.

Burnett, Linda. "Margaret Clarke's *Gertrude and Ophelia*: 'Writing Revisionist Culture,' Writing a New Poetics." *Essays in Theatre/Études théâtrales* 16 (1997): 15-32.

Burns, Elizabeth. "Ophelia." *Ophelia and other Poems*. Edinburgh: Polygon, 1991. 40-43.

Bush, Stephen and Richard McKenna. *Richard Thirdtime*. Toronto: Playwrights Canada, 1983

Campbell, Patrick, ed. *Analysing Performance: A Critical Reader*. Manchester: Manchester UP, 1996.

*Canadian Literature* 117 (1989).

*Canadian Theatre Review* 30 (1981).

Catron, Louis E. *The Director's Vision: Play Direction from Analysis to Production*. Mountain View, CA: Mayfield, 1989.

Certeau, Michel de. *The Practice of Everyday Life*. Trans. Steven Rendall. Berkeley: U of California P, 1984.

Chambers, Colin. *Other Spaces: New Theatre and the RSC*. London: Eyre Methuen, 1980.

Chapman, Geoff. "A Brittle Exploration of Race and Gender." Rev. of Djanet Sears, *Harlem Duet*. Prod. Nightwood Theatre and Canadian Stage at Canadian Stage Berkeley Street Theatre. *The Toronto Star* 2 Nov. 1997.

Charest, Rémy. *Robert Lepage: Quelques zones de liberté*. Québec: L'instant même, 1995.

Charlebois, Gaëtan. "A Box Office Battle." *Mirror* (Montreal) 23-30 Mar. 1995.

Chaudhuri, Una. "The Future of the Hyphen: Interculturalism, Textuality, and the Difference Within." *Interculturalism and Performance: Writings from PAJ*. Ed. Bonnie Marranca and Gautam Dasgupta. New York: PAJ Publications, 1991. 192-207.

Chinoy, Helen Krich. "The Emergence of the Director." Cole and Chinoy 1-77.

Clarke, Margaret. *Gertrude and Ophelia*. *Theatrum* 33 (1993): S1-S15.

Cohen, Leonard. "Anthem." *Stranger Music: Selected Poems and Songs*. Toronto: McClelland & Stewart, 1993. 373.

Cohen, Nathan. "Stratford After Fifteen Years." *Queen's Quarterly* 75 (1968): 35-61.

Cole, Toby, and Helen Krich Chinoy, ed. *Directors on Directing: A Source Book of the Modern Theatre*. New York: Macmillan, 1963.

Conlogue, Ray. "Measure for Measure Astonishing." *The Globe and Mail*. 31 May 1985.

Connor, Steven. "Postmodern Performance." Campbell 107-24.

Cook, Michael. "In the Beginning..." *Canadian Theatre Review* 30 (1991): 12-13.

Corbeil, Carole. *In the Wings*. Toronto: Stoddart, 1997.

——. "'It's very strange to be back.'" Interview with Michael Langham. *The Globe and Mail* 24 July 1982.

Coveny, Michael. "An Island Free from Arnie's Grip." *Observer Review* 8 Jan. 1995: 10.

Crew, Robert. "Desdemona Delicious Fun." Rev. of *Goodnight Desdemona (Good Morning Juliet)*, by Ann-Marie MacDonald. Canadian Stage, Berkeley Street, Toronto. *The Toronto Star* 29 Mar. 1990.

"Critics Pan Lepage's One-Man 'Hamlet.'" *The Globe and Mail*. 13 Jan. 1997.

Cushman, Robert. "Shades of Hamlet." Rev. of *Elsinore* by Robert Lepage. *The Globe and Mail* 22 Apr. 1996.

Dasgupta, Gautam. "*The Mahabharata*: Peter Brook's 'Orientalism.'" *Performing Arts Journal* 10 (1987): 9-16.

David, Gilbert. "Célébration du couple sur fond de métissage." *Le Devoir* (Montréal) 11-12 Mars 1995.

Davies, Robertson, Tyrone Guthrie, and Grant MacDonald. *Renown at Stratford*. Toronto: Clarke, Irwin, 1953. Rpt. as special memorial ed., 1971.

——. *Twice Have the Trumpets Sounded* Toronto: Clarke, Irwin, 1954.

Davies, Robertson *et al*. *Thrice the Brinded Cat Hath Mew'd*. Toronto: Clarke, Irwin, 1955.

Delgado, Maria M., and Paul Heritage, ed. *In Contact with the Gods? Directors Talk Theatre*. Manchester: Manchester UP, 1996.

Deleuze, Gilles and Felix Guattari. *Anti-Oedipus: Capitalism and Schizophrenia*. Trans. Helen R. Lane, Robert Hurley, and Mark Seem. Minneapolis: U of Minnesota P, 1983.

Diamond. Elin. "Brechtian Theory/Feminist Theory: Towards a Gestic Feminist Criticism." *TDR (The Drama Review)* 32 (1988): 82-94.

Doane, Melanie, perf., and Ted Dykstra, writ. "Never Doubt I Love." *Shakespearean Fish*. Sony Music Canada, 1996.

Donnelly, Pat. "Playing it Shrewdly." *The Gazette* (Montreal) 22 Mar. 1995.

Dvorak, Marta. "Goodnight William Shakespeare (Good Morning Ann-Marie MacDonald)." *Canadian Theatre Review* 79/80 (1994): 128-33.

Eagleton, Terry. *William Shakespeare*. Oxford: Blackwell, 1986.

Ebert, Teresa. "The 'Difference' of Postmodern Feminism." *College English* 53 (1991): 886-904.

Edinborough, Arnold. "A New Stratford Festival." *Shakespeare Quarterly* 5 (1954): 47-50.

Edmonstone, Wayne E. *Nathan Cohen: The Making of a Critic*. Toronto: Lester & Orpen, 1977.

Eliot, T.S. *Elizabethan Dramatists*. London: Faber & Faber, 1963.

——. *Elizabethan Essays*. New York: Haskell House, 1964.

——. *The Sacred Wood*. London: Methuen, 1960.

——. "The Wasteland." *The Complete Poems and Plays, 1909-1950*. New York: Harcourt, Brace & World, 1971. 37-55.

Eysteinsson, Astrudur. *The Concept of Modernism*. Ithaca: Cornell UP, 1990.

Fanon, Frantz. *Black Skin, White Masks*. Trans. Charles Lam Markmann. New York: Grove, 1967.

Filewod, Alan. "Alternate Theatre." Benson and Conolly 16-20.

——. *Collective Encounters: Documentary Theatre in English Canada.* Toronto: U of Toronto P, 1987.

——. "The Life and Death of the Mummers Troupe." *Theatre in Atlantic Canada.* Ed. Richard Paul Knowles. Sackville, NB: Mount Allison University, 1988. 127-42.

——. "National Theatre/National Obsession." *Canadian Theatre Review* 62 (1990): 5-10.

Findlay, L. M. "Frye's Shakespeare, Frye's Canada." Brydon and Makaryk 292-308.

Findley, Timothy. *Famous Last Words.* Toronto: Clarke, Irwin, 1981.

Fischlin, Daniel and Ric Knowles, ed. *Canadian Theatre Review* 111 (Summer 2002).

Fisher-Lichte, Erika. "Staging the Foreign as Cultural Transformation." *The Dramatic Touch of Difference.* Ed. Fisher-Lichte *et al.* Tübingen: Günter Narr Verlag, 1990. 221-35.

Fortier, Mark. "Undead and Unsafe: Adapting Shakespeare (in Canada)." Brydon and Makaryk 339-52.

——. "Shakespeare with a Difference: Genderbending and Genrebending in *Goodnight Desdemona.*" *Canadian Theatre Review* 59 (1989): 47-51.

Frye, Northrop. "Conclusion." *Literary History of Canada: Canadian Literature in English.* Ed. Alfred G. Bailey, Claude Bissell, Roy Daniells, Northrop Frye, and Desmond Pacey. 1st ed. Toronto: U of Toronto P, 1965. 821-49.

——. *Divisions on a Ground: Essays on Canadian Culture.* Toronto: Anansi, 1992.

——. Introduction. *The Tempest.* Pelican Edition. Ed. Frye. Baltimore: Penguin, 1959.

——. *The Myth of Deliverance: Reflections on Shakespeare's Problem Comedies.* Toronto: U of Toronto P, 1983

——. *A Natural Perspective: The Development of Shakespearean Comedy and Romance.* New York: Harcourt, Brace & World, 1965.

Gass, Ken. *Claudius.* Toronto: Playwrights Canada, 1995.

Gilbert, Sandra M. and Susan Gubar. *The Madwoman in the Attic: The Woman Writer and the Nineteenth-Century Literary Imagination.* New Haven: Yale UP, 1979.

Glassco, Bill *et al.* "To the Stratford Board." Letter. *Canadian Theatre Review* 3 (1974): 34-35.

Godard, Barbara. "Translating (as) Woman." *Essays in Canadian Writing* 55 (1995): 71-82.

Godfrey, Stephen. "Disillusioned designers quit Stratford." *The Globe and Mail* 16 Nov. 1984.

Gomez, Mayte. "Healing the Border Wound: *Fronteras Americanas* and the Future of Canadian Multiculturalism." *Theatre Research in Canada/Recherches théâtrales au Canada* 16 (1995): 26-39.

——. "Shifting Borders: A Project of Interculturalism in Canadian Theatre" Diss. U of Guelph, 1993.

Gould, Allan and Tom Patterson. *First Stage: The Making of the Stratford Festival*. Toronto: McClelland and Stewart, 1987.

Graham. Joseph F., ed. *Difference in Translation*. Ithaca: Cornell UP, 1985.

Greenblatt, Stephen. "Culture." *Critical Terms for Literary Study*. Ed. Frank Lentricchia and Thomas McLaughlin. Chicago: U of Chicago P, 1990. 225-32.

Gurik, Robert. *Hamlet, Prince du Québec*. Montreal: Leméac, 1977.

Guthrie, Tyrone. Letter to Alec Guinness. 11 Sept. 1952. Stratford Festival Archives, Stratford, Ontario, File A1.2.9.

Hale, Amanda. "A Dialectical Drama of Facts and Fictions on the Feminist Fringe." *Work in Progress: Building Feminist Culture*. Ed. Rhea Trebegov. Toronto: The Women's Press, 1987. 77-100.

Halpern, Richard. *Shakespeare Among the Moderns*. Ithaca: Cornell UP, 1997.

Harvie, Jennifer and Richard Paul Knowles. "Reporting from the Front: Herbert Whittaker at the *Montreal Gazette* 1937-1949 and the *Globe and Mail* 1949-1975." A. Wagner, 1999, 215-33.

Hawkins, Freda. "Canadian Multiculturalism: The Policy Explained." *Canadian Mosaic: Essays on Multiculturalism*. Ed. A. J. Fry and C. Forceville. Canada Cahiers, no. 3. Amsterdam: Free UP, 1988. 9-24.

Hengen, Shannon. "Towards a Feminist Comedy." *Canadian Literature* 146 (1995): 97-109.

Hermans, Theo, ed. *The Manipulation of Literature: Studies in Literary Translation*. London: Croom Helm, 1985.

Hodgdon, Barbara. "Looking for Mr. Shakespeare After the Revolution: Robert Lepage's Intercultural *Dream* Machine." Bulman 68-91.

Hollingsworth, Margaret. "Poppycock." *Endangered Species: Four Plays*. Toronto: Act One, 1988. 47-74.

Homel, David, and Sherry Simon, ed. *Mapping Literature: The Art and Politics of Translation*. Montreal: Véhicule, 1988.

Hutcheon, Linda. *A Theory of Parody: The Teachings of Twentieth-Century Art Forms*. London: Methuen, 1985.

——. *Irony's Edge: The Theory and Politics of Irony*. London: Routledge, 1994.

——. *Narcissistic Fiction: The Metafictional Paradox*. New York: Methuen, 1980.

——. *Splitting Images: Contemporary Canadian Ironies*. Toronto: Oxford UP, 1991.

Jameson, Frederic. *Fables of Aggression: Wyndham Lewis, the Modernist as Fascist*. Berkeley: U of California P, 1979.

Johnson, Barbara. *The Critical Difference: Essays in the Contemporary Rhetoric of Reading*. Baltimore: Johns Hopkins UP, 1980.

——. "Taking Fidelity Philosophically." Graham 142-48.

Johnston, Denis. Rev. of Allan Stratton, *Bag Babies*, Ann-Marie MacDonald, *Goodnight Desdemona (Good Morning Juliet)*, and John Krizanc, *The Half of It*. *Canadian Theatre Review* 74 (1993): 85-86.

——. *Up the Mainstream: The Rise of Toronto's Alternative Theatres*. Toronto: U of Toronto P, 1987.

Juliani, John. "On Being Invited: A Comment." *Canadian Theatre Review* 1 (Winter 1974): 65-67.

Kaplan, E. Ann. "Feminism(s)/postmodernism(s): MTV and Alternate Women's Videos and Performance Art." Campbell 82-103.

Kennedy, Dennis. *Foreign Shakespeare: Contemporary Performances*. Cambridge: Cambridge UP, 1993.

Kennedy, Lorne. Interview. *The Beacon Herald* 1993, Stratford Festival ed.

Kermode, Frank. *The Sense of an Ending*. London: Oxford UP, 1967.

Kershaw, Baz. "The Politics of Performance in a Postmodern Age." Campbell 133-52.

Kerslake, Barbara. "Three Keepers." Rev. of Ann-Marie MacDonald, *Goodnight Desdemona (Good Morning Juliet)*, Morris Panych, *7 Stories*, and Maryse Pelletier, *Duo for Obstinate Voices*. *Canadian Literature* 140 (1994): 138-39.

Kirchhoff, H.J. "Tapping into the primal." Rev. of *Othello*, The Stratford Festival's Avon Theatre, Stratford, Ontario. *The Globe and Mail* 29 June 1994.

Knelman, Martin. *A Stratford Tempest*. Toronto: McClelland and Stewart, 1982.

Knowles, Richard Paul. "Making Strange." *Books in Canada* (1990): 9-10.

——. "Reading Material: Transfers, Remounts, and the Production of Meaning in Contemporary Toronto Drama and Theatre." *Essays on Canadian Writing* 51-52 (1993-94): 258-95.

——. "Representing Canada: Teaching Canadian Studies in the United States." *The American Review of Canadian Studies* 25 (1995): 9-26.

——. "Shakespeare, Voice, and Ideology: Interrogating the Natural Voice." Bulman 92-112.

Kristeva, Julia. *Powers of Horror: An Essay on Abjection*. Trans. Leon S. Roudiez. New York: Columbia UP, 1982.

——. "The Semiotic Chora Ordering the Drives." *The Kristeva Reader*. Ed. Toril Moi. New York: Columbia UP, 1986. 93-98.

Krizanc, John. *Tamara*. Toronto: Stoddart, 1989.

Kruger, Loren. *The National Stage: Theatre and Cultural Legitimation in England, France, and America*. Chicago: U of Chicago P, 1992.

Kulyk Keefer, Janice. "Mavis Gallant and the Angel of History." *University of Toronto Quarterly* 55 (1986): 282-301.

Labrecque, Marie. "L'Adaptation des classiques: Passé (re)composé." *Voir* (Montréal) 30 mars-5 avril 1995.

Lacan, Jacques. "The Mirror Stage as Formative of the Function of the I as Revealed in Psychoanalytic Experience." *Écrits: Selection*. Trans. Alan Sheridan. New York: Norton, 1977. 1-7.

Laing, R.D. *The Divided Self*. Harmondsworth: Penguin, 1965.

"La Mégère apprivoisée." *Le Devoir* (Montréal) 26 mars 1995.

Lamming, George. *The Pleasures of Exile*. London: M. Joseph, 1960.

Leonard, Paul. "The Tempest x2 in Toronto." *Canadian Theatre Review* 54 (Spring 1988): 7-12.

Leclerc, Annie. "Woman's Word." *New French Feminisms: An Anthology*. Ed. Elaine Marks and Isabelle de Courtivron. New York: Schocken, 1981. 79-86.

Lefevere, André. *Translation, Rewriting, and the Manipulation of Literary Fame*. London: Routledge, 1992.

Lepage, Robert. *Elsinore*. Dir. Lepage. Perf. Peter Darling. National Arts Centre, Ottawa. 13 Sept. 1997.

——. "Lepage tourne la page." *Le Devoir* 16 Nov. 1995.

——. "Robert Lepage in Discussion with Richard Eyre." *The Twentieth Century Performance Reader*. Ed. Michael Huxley and Noel Witts. London: Routledge, 1996. 237-47.

Lessard, Annie. "La Mégère apprivoisée de Shakespeare/mise en scène: Martine Beaulne." CITÉ radio, 17 mars 1995.

Lévesque, Robert. "La gentille Mégère de monsieur Micone." *Le Devoir* (Montréal) 21 mars 1995.

Levine, Ira. "The Critic as Cultural Nationalist: Don Rubin at the *Toronto Star* 1968-1975 and the *Canadian Theatre Review* 1974-1983." A. Wagner, 1999, 304-18.

Lieblein, Leanore. "'Le Remaking' of le Grand Will: Shakespeare in Francophone Quebec." Brydon and Makaryk 174-91.

Lingerfelt, Jim and Roger Kershaw. "Harlem's Two Solitudes." Rev. of Djanet Sears, *Harlem Duet*. Prod. Nightwood Theatre at Tarragon Theatre Extra Space 20 Apr.-18 May 1997. *Stage Door*. 1997. 4 Mar. 2003. <http://www.stage-door.org/reviews>.

Littler, William. "Developing Opera and Musical Theatre." A. Wagner, 1985, 274-82.

Lotbinière-Harwood, Susanne de. *Re-belle et Infidèle: La Traduction comme pratique de réécriture au féminin: The Body Bilingual: Translation as Rewriting in the Feminine*. Montréal/Toronto: Les éditions du remueménage/Women's Press, 1991.

MacDonald, Ann-Marie. *Goodnight Desdemona (Good Morning Juliet)*. Toronto: Coach House, 1990a.

——. "Ann-Marie MacDonald." Interview with Rita Much. *Fair Play: 12 Women Speak: Conversations with Canadian Playwrights*. By Judith Rudakoff and Rita Much. Toronto: Simon & Pierre, 1990b. 128-43.

MacDougall, Jill. "Le Festival de Théâtre des Amériques," *TDR (The Drama Review)* 117 (Spring 1988): 9-19.

——. Translator's note to Micone, 1995a. Back cover.

Mannoni, Octave. *Prospero and Caliban: The Psychology of Colonization.* Trans, Pamela Powesland. 2$^{nd}$ ed. New York: Praeger, 1964.

McIlroy, Randal. "Truckers' Tale Delivers Light Load." *Winnipeg Free Press* (16 February 1990): 34.

McCullough, Christopher J. "The Cambridge Connection: Towards a Materialist Theatre." *The Shakespeare Myth.* Ed. Graham Holderness. Manchester: Manchester UP, 1988. 112-21.

Micone, Marco. *Beyond the Ruins.* Trans. Jill MacDougall. Montreal: Guernica, 1995a.

——. "La critique folliculaire," *Le Devoir* (Montréal) 21 mars 1995b.

——. *La Mégère de Padova* (d'après La Mégère Apprivoisée de William Shakespear). Unpublished script for *La Mégère apprivoisée* at Le Théâtre du Nouveau Monde, Montréal, 14 March-8 April 1995, directed by Martine Beaulne.

"*A Midsummer Night's Dream.*" *The Beacon Herald* 1993, Stratford Festival ed.

Mitchell, Ken. "Ken Mitchell's Progress as a Writer, from *Cruel Tears* to Thoughts on Booze." Interview with M. T. Kelly. *Books in Canada* 7 (May 1978): 40.

——. "Prairies." Interview with Alan Twigg. *For Openers: Conversations with 24 Canadian Writers.* By Alan Twigg. Madeira Park, BC: Harbour Publishing, 1981. 163-73.

——. "Ken Mitchell." Interview with Robert Wallace. *The Work: Conversations with English-Canadian Playwrights.* By Robert Wallace and Cynthia Zimmerman. Toronto: Coach House, 1982. 141-55.

Mitchell, Ken and Humphrey and the Dumptrucks [HD]. *Cruel Tears.* Vancouver: Talonbooks, 1977.

Mitter, Shomit. *Systems of Rehearsal: Stanislavsky, Brecht, Grotowski and Brook.* London: Routledge, 1992.

Monette, Richard. Interview. *The Beacon Herald* 1993, Stratford Festival ed.

Montessuit, Carmen. "La Mégère apprivoisée: superb." *Le Journal de Montréal* 20 mars 1995.

Morrison, Thelma and Barbara Reid. *A Star Danced: The Story of How Stratford Started the Stratford Festival.* Toronto: Robert Reid, 1994.

Morrow, Martin. "A Viking free-for-all." Afterword. Michael O'Brien 152-54.

Moss, Laura, ed. *Is Canada Postcolonial? Unsettling Canadian Literature.* Waterloo, ON: Wilfrid Laurier UP, 2003.

Mulvey, Laura. "Visual Pleasure and Narrative Cinema." *Visual and Other Pleasures.* Bloomington: Indiana UP, 1989. 14-26.

Niranjana, Tejaswini. *Siting Translation: History, Post-structuralism, and the Colonial Context.* Berkeley: U of California P, 1992.

O'Brien, Lucy. "'Sexing the Cherry': High or Low Art? Distinctions in Performance." Campbell 234-43.

O'Brien, Michael. *Mad Boy Chronicle.* Toronto: Playwrights Canada, 1995.

Ostriker, Alicia. "The Thieves of Language: Women Poets and Revisionist Mythmaking." *Signs* 8 (1982): 68-90.

Ouzounian, Richard. "Lepage's Struggle to Stay Free." *The Globe and Mail* 12 Aug. 1997: C1.

Pavis, Patrice. *Languages of the Stage*. New York: PAJ Publications, 1982.

——. *Theatre at the Crossroads of Culture*. Trans. Loren Kruger. London: Routledge, 1992.

——, ed. *The Intercultural Performance Reader*. London: Routledge, 1996.

Pechter, Edward. *The Endless Controversy of* Othello: *A Performance History of Shakespeare's Most Disturbing Play*. Iowa City: U of Iowa P, 1999.

Pennington, Bob. "Rollins' Othello falters." Rev. of *Othello*. The Stratford Festival, Festival Theatre. *The Toronto Star* 3 August 1987.

Peters, Helen. "Towards Canadian Postmodernism." *Canadian Theatre Review* 76 (1993): 13-17.

Pettigrew, John and Jamie Portman. *Stratford: The First Thirty Years*. 2 Vols. Toronto: Macmillan, 1985.

Phelan, Peggy. *Unmarked: The Politics of Performance*. London: Routledge, 1993.

Phillips, Robin. "On Being Invited to Canada." Interview. *Canadian Theatre Review* 1 [1974]: 60-64.

Program. *La Mégère apprivoisée*. Le Théâtre du Nouveau Monde, 14 mars au 18 avril 1995.

Reaney, James. "To the Avon River above Stratford, Canada." *Selected Shorter Poems*. Erin, Ontario: Press Porcepic, 1975. 79-80.

Redfern, Jon. "Tribal Brecht and a wail of an Othello." Rev. of Herschel Hardin *The Great Wave of Civilization*, Ken Mitchell and Humphrey and the Dumptrucks, *Cruel Tears*, and Julius Hay, *Have*. *Books in Canada* 6 (1977): 27-28.

Rice, Phillip, and Patricia Waugh, ed. *Modern Literary Theory: A Reader*. London: Arnold, 1989.

Richardson, Alan and Don Rubin. "From the Colonial Twilight." *Canadian Theatre Review* 30 (1981): 34-40.

Ripley, John. "Art in Quest of Craft?" Rev. of Cam Hubert, "Rites of Passage;" Herschel Hardin, *The Great Wave of Civilization*; Ken Mitchell and Humphrey and the Dumptrucks, *Cruel Tears*; and Julius Hay, *Have*. *Canadian Literature* 82 (1979): 110-13.

Robichaud, François. "La Mégère apprivoisée au TNM: Partie de plaisir sur fond amer." *Le Quartier libre* (Montréal) 28 mars 1995.

Robinson, Douglas. *The Translator's Turn*. Baltimore: Johns Hopkins UP, 1991.

Rose, Jacqueline. "Sexuality in the Reading of Shakespeare." *Alternative Shakespeares*. Ed. John Drakakis. London: Methuen, 1985. 95-118.

Rubess, Baņuta. Introduction to MacDonald, 1990a. 7-9.

Rubin, Don, ed. *Canadian Theatre History: Selected Readings*. Toronto: Copp Clark, 1996.

——. "Creeping Toward a Culture: The Theatre in English Canada Since 1945." *Canadian Theatre Review* 1 (Winter 1974): 6-21.

——, Stephen Mezei, and Ross Stuart. "An Editorial Viewpoint." *Canadian Theatre Review* 1 (Winter 1974): 4-5.

Rudakoff, Judith. "Theatre Passe Muraille." Benson and Conolly 543-44.

Rutter, Carol Chillington. "Shadowing Cleopatra: Making Whiteness Strange." *Enter the Body: Women and Representation on Shakespeare's Stage*. London: Routledge, 2001. 57-103.

Rymer, Thomas. *A Short View of Tragedy: It's Original, Excellency, and Corruption*. Facsimile of original 1693 edition. London: Frank Cass, 1971.

Said, Edward. *Orientalism*. New York: Random House/Vintage, 1979.

Salter, Denis. "Between Wor(l)ds: Lepage's Shakespeare Cycle." *Theater* 24 (1993): 61-70.

——. "Body Politics: English-Canadian Acting at NTS." *Canadian Theatre Review* 71 (1992): 4-14.

——. "The Idea of a National Theatre." *Canadian Canons: Essays in Literary Value*. Ed. Robert Lecker. Toronto: U of Toronto P, 1991. 71-90.

Salutin, Rick and Theatre Passe Muraille. *1837: The Farmers' Revolt*. Toronto: Lorimer, 1976.

Schechner, Richard. *Environmental Theater: A New and Expanded Edition Including 'Six Axioms for Environmental Theater.'* New York: Applause, 1994.

——. "Race Free, Gender Free, Body-Type Free, Age Free Casting." *TDR (The Drama Review)* 121 (1989): 4-12.

Scolnicov, Hannah. *The Play Out of Context: Transferring Plays from Culture to Culture*. Cambridge: Cambridge UP, 1989.

Sears, Djanet. *Harlem Duet*. [Winnipeg]: Scirocco, 1996.

– and Alison Sealy-Smith. "The Nike Method." *Canadian Theatre Review* 97 (1998): 24-30.

Selbourne, David. *Culture and Agitation*. London: Action Books, 1972.

Shain, Merle. "Pursuing the Need for a Guerrilla Theatre." Interview with Jim Garrard. *The Toronto Telegraph* 1 Mar. 1969.

Shakespeare, William. *Othello*. New Cambridge Shakespeare. Ed. Norman Sanders. Cambridge: Cambridge UP, 1984.

Shand, G. B. "Realizing Gertrude: The Suicide Option." *Elizabethan Theatre 13*. Ed. A.L. Magnusson and C.E. McGee. Toronto: P. D. Meany, 1994. 95-118.

——. "Two Toronto *Hamlets.*" *Hamlet Studies* 13 (1991): 98-107.

Shaw, Grace Lydiatt. *Stratford Under Cover: Memories on Tape*. Toronto: New Canadian Publications, 1977.

Shevstova, Maria. "Interculturalism, Aestheticism, Orientalism: Starting from Peter Brook's *Mahabharata.*" *Theatre Research International* 22 (1997): 89-101.

Showalter, Elaine. "Representing Ophelia: Women, Madness, and the Responsibilities of Feminist Criticism." *Shakespeare and the Question of Theory.* Ed. Patricia Parker and Geoffrey Hartman. New York: Methuen, 1985. 77-94.

Sinfield, Alan. "Royal Shakespeare: Theatre and the Making of Ideology." *Political Shakespeare: New Essays in Cultural Materialism.* Ithaca: Cornell UP, 1985. 158-81.

Singleton, Brian. "The Pursuit of Otherness for the Investigation of Self." *Theatre Research International* 22 (1997): 93-97.

Smith, Iris L. "The 'Intercultural' Work of Lee Breuer." *Theatre Topics* 7 (1997): 37-58.

Somerset, J. Alan B. *The Stratford Festival Story: A Catalogue Index to the Stratford Ontario Festival.* New York: Greenwood, 1991.

Spivak, Gayatri Chakravorty, and Sneja Gunew. "Questions of Multiculturalism." *The Cultural Studies Reader.* Ed. Simon During. London: Routledge, 1993. 193-202.

Stanislavski, Constantin. *Building a Character.* Trans. Elizabeth Reynolds Hapgood. New York: Routledge, 1989.

——. *Creating a Role.* Trans. Elizabeth Reynolds Hapgood. New York: Routledge. 1989.

Steen, Shannon and Margaret Werry. "Bodies, Technologies, and Subjectivities: The Production of Authority in Robert Lepage's *Elsinore*." *Essays in Theatre/Études théâtrales* 16 (1998): 139-51.

Stone-Blackburn, Susan. "Recent Plays on Women's Playwrighting." *Essays in Theatre/Études théâtrales* 14 (1995): 37-48.

Stoppard, Tom. *Cahoot's Macbeth. Tom Stoppard: Plays.* Vol. 1. London: Faber and Faber, 1996. 175-211.

*Stratford Festival 1993 Season Brochure.* Stratford Festival publication. N.pag.

*Stratford Festival 1993 Souvenir Program.* Stratford Festival publication. N.pag.

Stuart, Euan Ross. "The Stratford Festival and the Canadian Theatre." *Theatrical Touring and Founding in North America.* Ed. L. W. Conolly. Westport, CT: Greenwood Press, 1982. 173-91.

Styan, J. L. *The Shakespeare Revolution: Criticism and Performance in the Twentieth Century.* Cambridge: Cambridge UP, 1977.

Suleri, Sarah. *Meatless Days.* Chicago: U of Chicago P, 1989.

Taylor, Kate. "Characters Lost in Political Lessons." Rev. of Djanet Sears, *Harlem Duet.* Prod. Nightwood Theatre at Tarragon Theatre Extra Space, Toronto. *The Globe and Mail* 28 Apr. 1997.

——. "Dancing Exuberantly on Hamlet's Grave." Rev. of *Elsinore* by Robert Lepage. *The Globe and Mail* 15 Nov. 1995.

*The Stratford Story.* Stratford Festival publication. N.pag.

Thompson, Ann, ed. *The Taming of the Shrew.* By William Shakespeare. New Cambridge Shakespeare. Cambridge: Cambridge UP, 1984.

Thompson, Judith. *Lion in the Streets*. Toronto: Coach House, 1992.

Thompson, Paul. "An Interview with Paul Thompson." Interview by Ted Johns. *Performing Arts in Canada* 10 (1973): 30-32.

Tiffin, Helen. "Post-Colonial Literatures and Counter-Discourse." *Kunapipi* 9 (1987): 17-34.

Tillyard, E. M. W. *The Elizabethan World Picture*. London: Chatto & Windus, 1943.

Tompkins, Joanne. "Re-Citing Shakespeare in Post-Colonial Drama." *Essays in Theatre/Études théâtrales* 15 (1996): 15-22.

Tragically Hip, The. "Cordelia." *Road Apples*. MCA Records, 1991.

Ure, Joan. "Something in it for Ophelia." *Joan Ure: Five Short Plays*. Glasgow: Scottish Society of Playwrights, 1979. 31-57.

Usmiani, Renate. *Second Stage: The Alternative Theatre Movement in Canada*. Vancouver: U of British Columbia P, 1983.

Vitez, Antoine. *Le théâtre des idées*. Paris: Gallimard. 1991.

Wagner, Anton, ed. *Contemporary Canadian Theatre: New World Visions*. Toronto: Simon & Pierre, 1985.

——. *Establishing Our Boundaries: English-Canadian Theatre Criticism*. Toronto, ON: U of Toronto P, 1999.

Wagner, Vit. "Theatre as it should be." Rev. of Djanet Sears, *Harlem Duet*. Prod. Nightwood Theatre at Tarragon Theatre Extra Space. *The Globe and Mail* 27 Apr. 1997.

Wallace, Robert. "Paul Thompson and Theatre Passe Muraille: Bits and Pieces." Interview. *Open Letter* (2nd series) 7 (1974): 49-71.

——. *Producing Marginality: Theatre and Criticism in Canada*. Saskatoon: Fifth House, 1990.

——. "Writing the Land Alive: The Playwrights' Vision in English Canada." A. Wagner, 1985, 69-81.

Wasserman, Jerry, ed. *Modern Canadian Plays*. 1st ed. Vancouver: Talonbooks, 1985.

Weimann, Robert. *Shakespeare and the Popular Tradition in the Theatre: Studies in the Social Dimension of Dramatic Form and Function*. Baltimore: Johns Hopkins UP, 1978.

West, Rebecca. *The Court and the Castle: Some Treatments of a Recurrent Theme*. New Haven: Yale UP, 1957.

Whitmore, Jon. *Directing Postmodern Theatre*. Ann Arbor: U of Michigan P, 1994.

Whittaker, Herbert. *Whittaker's Theatre*. Ed. Ronald Bryden with Boyd Neil. Greenbank, ON: The Whittaker Project, 1985.

William, David. "Welcome to the 1993 Season." *Stratford Festival 1993 Season*.

Williams, David, ed. *Peter Brook and the Mahabharata: Critical Perspectives*. London: Routledge, 1991.

Williams, Raymond. *Culture and Society*. 1958. London: Hogarth, 1990.

——. *The Politics of Modernism: Against the New Conformists.* London: Verso, 1989.

Wilson, Ann. "Critical Revisions: Ann-Marie MacDonald's *Goodnight Desdemona (Good Morning Juliet).*" *Women on the Canadian Stage: The Legacy of Hrotsvit.* Ed. Rita Much. Winnipeg: Blizzard, 1992. 1-12.

Winsor, Christopher. "Alas, poor Robert! Lepage is hoist with his own Hamlet." *eye* 25 Apr. 1996.

Woodcock, George. "More Than an Echo: Notes on the Craft of Translation." *Canadian Literature* 117 (1988): 72-79.

Worthen, W. B. *Shakespeare and the Authority of Performance.* Cambridge: Cambridge UP, 1997.

——. "Staging 'Shakespeare': Acting, Authority, and the Rhetoric of Performance." Bulman 12-28.

Zuber-Skerritt, Otrun. *From Page to Stage: Theatre as Translation.* Amsterdam: Rodopi, 1984.

# Index

# Dramaturgies
## Texts, Cultures and Performances

This series presents innovative research work in the field of twentieth-Century dramaturgy, primarily in the anglophone and francophone worlds. Its main purpose is to re-assess the complex relationship between textual studies, cultural and/or performance aspects at the dawn of this new multicultural millennium. The series offers discussions of the link between drama and multiculturalism (studies of minority playwrights – ethnic, aboriginal, gay and lesbian), reconsiderations of established playwrights in the light of contemporary critical theories, studies of the interface between theatre practice and textual analysis, studies of marginalized theatrical practices (circus, vaudeville etc.), explorations of the emerging postcolonial drama, research into new modes of dramatic expressions and comparative or theoretical drama studies.

The Series Editor, **Marc MAUFORT**, is Professor of English literature and drama at the *Université Libre de Bruxelles*.

### Series Titles

**No.12–** Malgorzata BARTULA & Stefan SCHROER, *On Improvisation. Nine Conversations with Roberto Ciulli*, 2003, ISBN 90-5201-185-0

**No.11–** Peter ECKERSALL, Naoto MORIYAMA & Tadashi UCHINO (eds.), *Alternatives. Debating Theatre Culture in the Age of Confusion* (provisional title) (forthcoming) ISBN 90-5201-175-3

**No.10–** Rob BAUM, *Female Absence. Women, Theatre, and Other Metaphors*, 2003, ISBN 90-5201-172-9

**No.9–** Marc MAUFORT, *Transgressive Itineraries. Postcolonial Hybridizations of Dramatic Realism*, 2003, ISBN 90-5201-990-8

**No.8–** Ric KNOWLES, *Shakespeare and Canada: Essays on Production, Translation, and Adaptation*, 2004, ISBN 90-5201-989-4

**No.7–** Barbara OZIEBLO & Miriam LÓPEZ-RODRIGUEZ, *Staging a Cultural Paradigm. The Political and the Personal in American Drama*, 2002, ISBN 90-5201-990-8

**No.6–** Michael MANHEIM, *Vital Contradictions. Characterization in the Plays of Ibsen, Strindberg, Chekhov and O'Neill*, 2002, ISBN 90-5201-991-6

**No.5**– Bruce BARTON, *Changing Frames. Medium Matters in Selected Plays and Films of David Mamet* (provisional title) (forthcoming), ISBN 90-5201-988-6

**No.4**– Marc MAUFORT & Franca BELLARSI (eds.), *Crucible of Cultures. Anglophone Drama at the Dawn of a New Millennium*, 2002 (second printing 2003), ISBN 90-5201-982-7

**No.3**– Rupendra GUHA MAJUMDAR, *Central Man. The Paradox of Heroism in Modern American Drama*, 2003, ISBN 90-5201-978-9

**No.2**– Helena GREHAN, *Mapping Cultural Identity in Contemporary Australian Performance*, 2001, ISBN 90-5201-947-9

**No.1**– Marc MAUFORT & Franca BELLARSI (eds.), *Siting the Other. Re-visions of Marginality in Australian and English-Canadian Drama*, 2001, ISBN 90-5201-934-7